INTERPERSONAL COMMUNICATION

BUILDING YOUR FOUNDATIONS FOR SUCCESS

MICHELLE BURCH

KENDALL/HUNT PUBLISHING COMPANY
4050 Westmark Drive   Dubuque, Iowa 52002

Book Team

Chairman and Chief Executive Officer *Mark C. Falb*
Senior Vice President *Thomas W. Gantz*
Director of National Book Program *Paul B. Carty*
Editorial Development Manager *Georgia Botsford*
Developmental Editor *Angela Willenbring*
Vice President, Production and Manufacturing *Alfred C. Grisanti*
Assistant Vice President, Production Services *Christine E. O'Brien*
Prepress Project Coordinator *Angela Puls*
Permissions Editor *Renae Heacock*
Designer *Suzanne Millius*

Illustrations created by Steve Varble
Author photo courtesy Bruce Dunbar Photography

Cover Images © Photos.com and Comstock

11

Dedications

For my Heavenly Father—Who taught me to be open to my gifts and we will find each other. Thank You for continuing to bless my life even when I am not looking.

For my son, Calvin Michael Burch—Who once said, "It's tough having a Communication Professor for a mom." May we remain friends, as we walk through the changing times.

For my students—You have told me you want a textbook that is easy to read, practical, enjoyable, and useful. I believe this is what you asked for, and if not, look for your suggestions in the second edition. I appreciate all that I learn from you.

Greatness cannot be achieved, unless one knows what greatness is.

Acknowledgments

My blessed family, without you I wouldn't have so many great examples in this book and in the classroom. I love you, and I appreciate you. To my sisters—Monica Burch and Melissa Burch—thank you for reading my book and offering your insight. I love you two more than you will ever know.

My massage therapists, Linda Vanarsdall and Sonja Bond-Clark—you connect my mind, body, and spirit. Thank you for sharing your healing gifts. This book would not have been completed, and I would not function as well without you! Thank you.

My professors at the University of Illinois at Springfield—you welcomed me in to the world of Communication, then challenged me throughout the journey. Thank you.

My colleagues—you are an amazing family. I enjoy coming to work because of you. Thank you for welcoming me into your family and appreciating my idiosyncrasies. A special thank you to my colleague and friend, Melissa Hunter, thank you for reading my book and challenging me to look at it from a different perceptive.

"The real winners in life are the people who look at every situation with an expectation that they can make it work, or make it better."
—Barbara Pletcher

CONTENTS

List of Tables and Figures vii

List of Articles ix

List of Activities xi

Preface xii

**UNIT I   LAYING A FOUNDATION FOR EFFECTIVE
COMMUNICATION** 1

Chapter 1 – The Communication Process 3

Chapter 2 – Making Listening Work 45

Chapter 3 – Your Perception Is Your Reality 85

UNIT II   UNDERSTANDING HOW YOU COMMUNICATE 125

Chapter 4 – Verbal vs. Nonverbal Communication 127

Chapter 5 – Understanding the Self 167

Chapter 6 – All About Emotions 201

**UNIT III   BEING SUCCESSFUL—COMMUNICATING IN
RELATIONSHIPS** 243

Chapter 7 – Developing Decision Making Skills and Values 245

Chapter 8 – Developing Healthy Relationships 279

Chapter 9 – Conflict and Power 317

APPENDICES 359

Appendix A – Service Learning Project 361

Appendix B – Intrapersonal Portfolio Project 363

Appendix C – Team Research Project 367

Appendix D – Debate Project 371

WRAP UP

Answers Key for Chapter Quizzes 375

References and Suggested Readings 377

Index 381

Author Biography 389

Suggestion Form for Future Editions 391

LIST OF TABLES AND FIGURES

UNIT I **LAYING A FOUNDATION FOR EFFECTIVE COMMUNICATION** 1

Figure 1.1 – The Communication Process 10

Table 1.1 – The Communication Process Defined 11

Table 2.1 – Listening Patterns—Examples 53

Figure 2.1 – The Listening Process 57

Figure 3.1 – The Perception Process 89

Figure 3.2 – Perception Process—Example #1 91

Figure 3.3 – Perception Process—Example #2 92

Figure 3.4 – Shared Perception 94

Figure 3.5 – Perception Checking 96

UNIT II **STRENGTHENING THE FOUNDATION—HOW YOU COMMUNICATE** 125

Figure 4.1 – The Triangle of Meaning 130

Figure 5.1 – Understanding the Roles We Play 170

Figure 5.2 – Maslow's Hierarchy of Needs 173

Figure 5.3 – Your Real Self, Your Ideal Self 178

Table 6.1 – Increase Your Emotion Vocabulary 206

Figure 6.1 – Plutchik's Emotion Wheel 207

UNIT III **BEING SUCCESSFUL—COMMUNICATING IN RELATIONSHIPS** 243

Table 7.1 – Terminal & Instrumental Values 248

Figure 7.1 – The Ripple Effect Values Model .249

Figure 8.1 – Johari Window 281

Table 8.1 – Relationship Maintenance 283

Table 9.1 – Conflict Styles—The Good and the Bad 329

Table 9.2 – Conflict Styles 330

Table 9.3 – Collaborator Terms 332

LIST OF ARTICLES

UNIT I   LAYING A FOUNDATION FOR EFFECTIVE COMMUNICATION .1

Breaking Off the Conversation, by Ira J. Hadnot 17

Communication Skills Crucial for Law Enforcement, by Roberto Ceniceros 23

Privacy Is Overrated, by David Plotz .25

Listening to Your Body, by Gail Raborn 65

Listening, by Heather Antonissen 69

When to Shut Up, by Peter D. Kramer, Oprah Magazine 103

We Can't Stop Fighting Over Money, by Margery O. Rosen 107

UNIT II   STRENGTHENING THE FOUNDATION—HOW YOU COMMUNICATE .125

Please Touch! How to Combat Skin Hunger in Our Schools, by Sidney B. Simon 141

"What Are You Telling the World?" by Kare Anderson 147

Gender Differences in Nonverbal Communication, by M.A. Griffin 151

What Kids (Really) Need, by Nancy Gibbs .181

Self-Esteem: A Two-Edged Sword, by Lou Marano 185

When a Best Friend Breaks Your Heart, by Deborah Gregory 217

After Great Pain, by Andrew Solomon 223

UNIT III BEING SUCCESSFUL—COMMUNICATING IN RELATIONSHIPS .243

My World Now: Life in a Nursing Home, from the Inside, by Anna Mae Halgrim Seaver 257

No Wedding? No Ring? No Problem, by Jay Tolson 261

Married Again . . . With Children, by Wendy Swallow 295

Bring Me Home a Black Girl, by Audrey Edwards 299

From Conflict to Collaboration, by Greg Giesen 335

Tips for Solving Family Communication Problems, by Sean Brotherson 339

Adoption by Lesbian Couples, by Susan Golombok 343

LIST OF ACTIVITIES

UNIT I   **LAYING A FOUNDATION FOR EFFECTIVE COMMUNICATION** 1

Creating Goals for Your Success in the Classroom 33

Getting to Know Each Other 35

Barriers to Effective Communication 37

Creating a Communication Scenario 39

Develop Your Intrapersonal Listening Skills 73

Working through the Listening Process 75

Develop Your Interpersonal Listening Skills 77

How Would You Respond? 79

Create a Perception Box 113

Checking Your Perception 115

Try Walking in My Shoes 117

What Do You Perceive? 119

UNIT II   **STRENGTHENING THE FOUNDATION—HOW YOU COMMUNICATE** 125

Nonverbal Observations 155

Taking Responsibility for What You Say—Even on the Internet 157

What Are They Communicating? 159

Semantic Reactions 161

Analyzing the Roles You Play—Finding Your True Self 189

Fulfilling Your Hierarchy of Needs 191

Understanding the Many Selves That Create You 193

What if You Just Opened Up? 195

Emotions on the Internet 229

Exploring Your Emotions 231

Emotions from Other Perspectives 235

Working through the Emotional Liberation Process 237

UNIT III BEING SUCCESSFUL—COMMUNICATING IN RELATIONSHIPS 243

Assessing Your Values 265

Decision Making in Action through Observation .269

Lost in a Lifeboat 271

What Affects Our Values 273

Finding Out What Your Friends Think about the Relationship 305

Creating Johari Windows 307

Exploring How Relationships Develop & Deteriorate 309

Relationships in the Movies 311

Understanding and Applying Intrapersonal Conflict 347

Reflecting on How Your Perception of Conflict Has Changed 349

Understanding & Applying Interpersonal Conflict 351

Becoming More Collaborative 353

PREFACE

DON'T EVEN TRY IT! Do not read any further. I'm serious. The journey of Interpersonal Communication is serious business. It is one of the few courses you will ever take which focuses completely on YOU! You cannot read any further unless you are prepared for the journey. Here are the tools you need for our journey through this textbook/workbook:

- An open mind
- A positive attitude
- A willingness to get out of and redefine your comfort zone
- A willingness to reevaluate your current communication techniques
- A willingness to listen to someone else's perspective

Are you ready now? Interpersonal communication can be one of the most rewarding classes that you will ever take. Some of you may feel that you know how to communicate effectively already. I hope so. However, we can always learn a few things. For example, why do we communicate the way we do? How can we express our emotions with clarity and control? Why do men (or women) do some of the things that they do? Ok, you get the picture. Now, some of you are feeling a little excited; however, some of you may be a little nervous at what you could learn about yourself. You are not alone. Consider this—you may even be in the majority.

This is the first edition of *Interpersonal Communication: Building Your Foundations for Success.* You will finish this textbook/workbook with a better understanding of who you are, how you communicate, what you need in your relationships, and how to have the most fulfilling experiences possible in your lifetime. In addition, you will understand how others communicate, and you will find out that you cannot change the way someone else communicates, and that you can only be an example of an effective communicator. This textbook does not simply tell you how communication should work. I will interpersonally communicate with you throughout the textbook, by sharing my own life stories and asking you questions to make you think about your communication habits.

The use of gender pronouns is a common discussion ("He said this . . . " or "She did this . . . "). Many will try to interpret or make assumptions about which the author is referring to based on the author's use of gender terms. I have tried to avoid those two words since they can create discussions about issues other than the topic at hand. In an effort to keep you and the discussions on topic, I have tried to use other pronouns (for example I, we, and you). If a gender-specific pronoun is necessary, I will alternate between the pronouns "he" and "she." The use of other pronouns (I, we, and us) can personalize the dialogue that I would like us to have in this text, and I know you will appreciate it.

UNIQUE FEATURES WITHIN EACH CHAPTER

Student Quotes. Throughout each chapter you will find quotes from previous Interpersonal Communication students. They share what they have learned from the course; they share the struggles they still face in their relationships; and they share what they appreciate about communication. If you would like to submit a quote for future editions, please fill out the suggestion form in the back of this textbook. If we can use your quote, and/or your name, please include a statement that gives us permission.

Key Terms. The key terms are presented at the beginning of each chapter. It is important to understand not only how the term is defined, but also how to apply that term. Therefore, you will see many examples throughout each chapter. Keep in mind that your instructor will ask you to put the definition in your own words and come up with your own example. Consider what I have provided for you as a starting point; it will be up to you to continue the dialogue. Developing your own ideas is important for your learning process; however, sometimes it may take you some time. It will happen—be patient. When it doesn't, make sure you ask questions!

Articles. Each chapter contains articles that discuss diverse and current issues which affect interpersonal communication and our society. At the end of each article there are discussion questions. You will find the questions helpful in understanding the purpose of the article, analyzing, and interpreting the article. Your instructor may use the questions as a discussion tool in the classroom or as assignments.

Individual/Group Activities. Located toward the end of each chapter are both individual and group activities. In an Interpersonal Communication class, it is extremely important to practice interpersonally communicating. Your instructor will guide you through the exploration of the concepts and theories, and then you need to try out some of the activities for application. If there are activities you are particularly fond of, let your instructor know that you would like to discuss or try out that activity. It is possible that you may have seen or heard of some of the activities. Some of them are revised versions of activities I have seen, participated in, or learned from my own students. If I am aware of the original author, s/he is given credit. I have tried to give credit whenever possible.

Chapter Review. Reviewing terms can be challenging and sometimes monotonous. In this textbook I have attempted to "spice up" a very important element in your review process. Understanding the terms will help you in the classroom, it will help you in future communication courses, and most importantly, learning the terms will expand the limits of your current vocabulary. You will also find chapter quizzes at the end of each chapter. Keep in mind that simply reviewing the terms and answering the questions on the quizzes will not completely prepare you for exams that your instructor may give you.

APPENDICES—INDIVIDUAL AND GROUP PROJECTS

Toward the end of this textbook/workbook, you will find four interesting projects. Each project is designed to guide you through the practice of effective interpersonal communication. The following is a brief explanation of each project.

The Service Learning Project gives you an opportunity to go into the community and explore how others interpersonally communicate, while doing a service project to improve your community. This can be an individual or group project.

The Intrapersonal Portfolio Project gives you an opportunity to explore, in depth, who you are, what you want out of life, and what you need to overcome, and finally, to create goals for your future. The activity is very enlightening and will challenge your ability to verbalize your wants and your needs. This is an individual project.

The Team Research Project gives you an opportunity to unobtrusively or obtrusively observe, survey, or interview people about a specific topic in interpersonal communication. You will research a topic, develop a hypothesis, observe, survey, or interview people, analyze the research data, and finally, draw conclusions. Your instructor may have the teams give a presentation about the research project; this alternative is outlined in the project description. This is a project that is best spread out over the entire term. This is designed to be a group project; however, it can easily be turned into an individual project.

The Debate Project provides you with an opportunity to challenge your interpersonal communication skills. You will be expected to research either an area of interpersonal communication or a social issue, and then develop arguments and rebuttals. Your instructor will decide (or will have the class decide) the details of this project. It may be done individually, in small teams, or in larger teams. Your instructor may choose the side you will argue or you may have the opportunity to choose your side.

In summary, this textbook/workbook is centered on the idea of active learning. You will find it to be an amazing journey, if you are willing to open yourself up to the process of learning. If you have any questions, concerns, or comments, there is a form in the back of the book for you to fill out and submit to the author. I am more than happy to customize this textbook/workbook for you; therefore, I look forward to hearing your ideas. This is your book—enjoy it.

> "Far away there in the sunshine are my highest aspirations.
> I may not reach them, but I can look up and see their beauty,
> believe in them, and try to follow where they lead."
> —Louise May Alcott

U N I T 1

LAYING A FOUNDATION FOR EFFECTIVE COMMUNICATION

Chapter 1—The Communication Process

Chapter 2—Making Listening Work

Chapter 3—Your Perception Is Your Reality

THE COMMUNICATION PROCESS

KEY TERMS

Channel

Competent
  communicator

Encoding

Extrapersonal
  communication

Fidelity

Interpersonal
  communication

Message

Privacy

Self-disclosure

Communication
  environment

Decoding

External noise

Feedback

Internal noise

Intrapersonal
  communication

Metacommunication

Receiver

Source

CHAPTER OBJECTIVES

1. Explain and understand various types of communication, including interpersonal communication, intrapersonal communication, and extrapersonal communication.

2. Understand the role of self-disclosure in communication.

3. Explain metacommunication, and understand the value of practicing it.

4. Determine the factors that influence our ability to communicate.

5. Describe the importance of privacy and trust.

6. Understand how a communication process works, including the following elements: sender, receiver, encoding, decoding, message, feedback, noise, channel, and fidelity.

7. Explain communication competence, and identify key characteristics of a competent communicator.

It's been coming for weeks. You know it will be here any minute. You are frightened. Why does it have to happen now? Things have been moving along smoothly. Your heart begins to beat rapidly. Your palms feel clammy. You hear the car pull in the driveway. The front door begins to squeak— somebody was supposed to use WD-40 on that door last week! Your mouth is dry— where is the water when you need it? Your mind begins to think about all of the other things that you could be, should be, and definitely want to be doing right this very minute. Why? Why today? Why now? Why here? Why do we have to have a CONVERSATION!

TYPES OF COMMUNICATION

Many people feel this way about communication. We are not talking about everyday, saying hello to someone on the street, communication. We are talking about **interpersonal communication**—communicating and interacting with others, while self-disclosing. You interpersonally communicate with your significant other, your family, close friends, and even with complete strangers. Interpersonal communication develops and changes a relationship. It takes a relationship to another level—one that is more private or personal. A specific example of interpersonal communication is in a literature class you may be asked to give your interpretation of an author's work. When you share your feelings, your interpretations, you are self-disclosing. You are putting yourself out there, in front of a classroom full of people, who may disagree with you. You are taking a risk. Those are all qualities of interpersonal communication.

What should you know about interpersonal communication?

- Interpersonal communication begins, changes, maintains, and improves relationships.
- Interpersonal communication is a skill that requires ongoing training to maintain effectiveness.
- Interpersonal communication is irreversible and unrepeatable. This is probably the scariest part of communication: knowing that what you say can never be "taken back." You can apologize for something you said and you can try to re-word what you said for more clarity; however, the words have already been spoken. Also you cannot repeat something you said, because once the message is out there the experience is different, if you try to repeat it. For example, you can tell a child to clean her room. If she "ignores" you or asks you what you said, then while you are preparing and repeating the message she is able to consider her new response.
- Interpersonal communication affects others; therefore, it is your responsibility to assess what you are going to say before you say it, and try to determine what the implications will be from what you say.
- We learn how to interpersonally communicate from others and from the world around us. We learn from our family, friends, strangers, enemies, bullies, the media, and our environment.
- Interpersonal communication is a unique or special interaction between people; the interaction may last for a few seconds with a stranger or a few hours with your best friend.
- Interpersonal communication is vital to our survival. Can you recall the movie, *Castaway*, starring Tom Hanks? In that movie Tom Hanks' character was stranded on a desert island. In order to survive, he found solace in communicating with "Wilson." Wilson, to you and me, was a volleyball with dried blood on it in the shape of a face. To Tom Hanks' character, Wilson was his best friend, someone he cared for very deeply, and his source of survival.
- Interpersonal communication is not limited to close family members and friends. Believe it or not, you interpersonally communicate more often than you think that you do.

In this textbook/workbook, you will be challenged to take many of the risks that come with interpersonally communicating. Since this textbook is completely based on understanding interpersonal communication, it only makes sense that we practice those skills. The very thought of interpersonally communicating may make some of you cringe. I challenge you, right now, to approach this textbook with a willingness to not only explore how communication works, but to also explore *how* you currently communicate, and how you *want* to communicate with yourself and with others.

Self-disclosure refers to sharing your thoughts, needs, wants, and/or desires. The more you self-disclose to someone, the more depth you will have in your relationship. The more you self-disclose the easier it becomes. *Yeah—right!* It doesn't always get easier. Sometimes self-disclosure gets harder—maybe you got hurt because of what you said, or a parent disciplined you, or you lost a friend, or maybe you were fired from a job because you expressed your needs. These are valid reasons to say, "Well, I tried, and I tried again. I am not successful, so I am not going to try again!" Challenge number two: don't let the past give you a reason to quit! Effective ways of self-disclosing will be discussed in greater detail in chapter 5.

Self-disclosure has to begin with you. You must first learn to communicate with yourself, called **intrapersonal communication,** before you can be successful when communicating with others. Have you ever heard someone say, "You should think before you speak"? That is a type of intrapersonal communication. However, it can go (and should go) much deeper. *Intrapersonal communication is the single most important type of communication.* You cannot effectively communicate with others until you can communicate with yourself.

What should you know about intrapersonal communication?

- You are not crazy, nor do you belong in a mental institution, if you talk to yourself. Talking to yourself, even when you are talking aloud, is very healthy.
- You can figure out your goals or what you want, need, and desire from talking to yourself.
- It is best to communicate with yourself before you communicate with others.
- Every day, for the rest of your life, you only have one person to look at in the mirror, and you need to like what you see. You must begin learning how to communicate with yourself, even if you do not like your physical attributes. Remember that you are much more than a physical body; communicating with yourself will help you appreciate this notion.

Another form of communication is **extrapersonal communication,** or communicating with nonliving or nonhuman things. Have you ever yelled at your computer for not doing what you asked it to do? Ever whispered encouraging words to your car, when it's -20° F outside, to encourage it to start just one more time? Have you ever noticed your plants looking

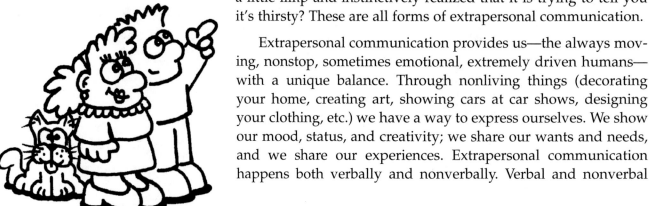

a little limp and instinctively realized that it is trying to tell you it's thirsty? These are all forms of extrapersonal communication.

Extrapersonal communication provides us—the always moving, nonstop, sometimes emotional, extremely driven humans—with a unique balance. Through nonliving things (decorating your home, creating art, showing cars at car shows, designing your clothing, etc.) we have a way to express ourselves. We show our mood, status, and creativity; we share our wants and needs, and we share our experiences. Extrapersonal communication happens both verbally and nonverbally. Verbal and nonverbal communication is discussed in chapter 4. Through communicating with the nonhuman (plants, animals, gardens, etc.) we figure out ourselves, and we grow to understand ourselves; or maybe we simply stop moving so fast and appreciate things. The nonliving and nonhuman lack judgment. They can teach us about love, forgiveness, peace, joy, happiness, and so much more, without the judgment that humans are so willing to express. Extrapersonal communication is truly *extra*personal. We need to cherish it. With that in mind, excuse me for a few minutes while I go water my plants, hug my dogs, and massage my cat's belly.

METACOMMUNICATION AND RELATIONSHIPS

Metacommunication is communicating how you should communicate, how you expect to communicate, and how you want to communicate. Sounds simple enough, right? It's not. It is something we don't do often enough and need to do more of, if we want healthy, successful relationships. Metacommunication is one of the most challenging activities you can ever do in a relationship. It means talking about things like:

- How will we handle our communication with each other in an argument? Will we take time to cool off and think about why we feel the way we do before we express it? Will we have "code words" to indicate that we need a break, if the argument turns into a fight? Will we allow 30 minutes to pass before we talk about our feelings, or 2 days?
- How will we communicate with our children when we are disciplining them? Will we consult each other on all decisions prior to disciplining them? Will we both do the disciplining?
- Will we ever argue in front of the children or in front of anyone?
- Will we talk about our expectations when it comes to moving our relationship to the next level? When and how will we discuss our individual needs and goals for the relationship?

Those are some tough questions—the toughest questions in life for some of you. Effective metacommunication is a sign of a healthy relationship. It allows people to assert their goals, wants, needs, and desires. Metacommunication is something that we do not always see examples of while growing up or in relationships throughout our lives.

What should you remember about metacommunication?

- It is a way to discuss your emotions before you are consumed by them. Especially if you are passionate about a topic in a debate or emotionally involved in a relationship, metacommunication assists you with planning what you will say before you say it.
- It may feel uncomfortable at first. Metacommunication may feel corny because it may not feel normal to you or it may not come naturally to you. It is another skill that has to be developed and nurtured for successful relationships.
- It enables a relationship to grow and change in a healthy way. Both people in the relationship feel like their needs are important and valid through metacommunication.
- It teaches people how to assert themselves in a relationship; it teaches us how to express our wants and our needs.

> "I have discovered that I have some un-dealt with emotions.
> This class has helped me to deal with them one step at a time
> and I have come out feeling great."
>
> – Cathy Harris

FACTORS THAT INFLUENCE COMMUNICATION

The positive factors:	*The negative factors:*
Emotions	Emotions
Family	Family
Friends	Friends
Self-Concept	Self-Concept
Listening	Listening
Relationships	Relationships
Perception	Perception
Culture	Culture
Gender	Gender
Power	Power
Conflict	Conflict

Do you notice the pattern? This is not a complete list because everything influences your ability to communicate effectively. It can, it may have, or it will influence you either positively or negatively. Understanding what influences your ability to communicate lays an important foundation for what we are exploring throughout this entire textbook, and we will tackle those factors, along with others, throughout each chapter.

 It is time to pause and reflect on what you have read. You will notice that I will ask you to pause and reflect in the middle and at the end of every chapter. This allows you to think about what you have read in preparation for a class discussion. Now that we have looked at the types of communication (interpersonal, intrapersonal, extrapersonal, and metacommunication) and the factors that influence communication, consider the following questions, and write down some notes in the space provided:

1. What didn't you know about the things you have read so far?

2. What surprised you the most about what you have read so far?

3. With what you've read so far, what don't you understand?

4. Is there anything you don't agree with, or is there anything you need more information about?

PRIVACY AND TRUST

Part of learning how to interpersonally communicate is determining what, how, and when it is appropriate to communicate. Have you ever met someone who will tell you his/her life story in the first five minutes of meeting him/her? Then there is the other extreme—the person who will never open up to you. Somewhere in the middle lies effective interpersonal communication.

It can be challenging to learn when it is appropriate to interpersonally communicate and how much to communicate. Some things you may simply want to *intra*personally communicate about, in other words, you want to and should be able to just keep some things to yourself. Privacy is a fundamental right, one of the liberties that you and I enjoy as American citizens. **Privacy** is to keep something to your self and to not communicate it with anyone else. In relationships, some may consider this need for privacy a way of being secretive; which in turn, can become a thorn in the relationship, if metacommunication is not regularly practiced.

With privacy there must come trust. Trust must be established in a relationship before one can feel comfortable self-disclosing. When you self-disclose to another person, you expect the receiver to use discretion before sharing your private information. However, in a society where adults play political games more than they played four-square as a child, discretion can be limited to the "what is in it for me" syndrome. Don't get me wrong—this is not about cynicism. This is about reality. For example, sharing with others how you feel about Ohio State's football team is one thing (Go Buckeyes!); sharing with others how feel about your boss is another thing. In case you aren't sure, the latter should be shared very cautiously if you like your job. In corporate America, or even on your college campus, the lines between someone's personal and professional lives are often blurred. You spend so much time with the people you work with that you want to self-disclose, you want to interpersonally communicate, and you want to make a few friends. However, you don't want to be skipped over when promotion time rolls around because of something you have said in the past.

As a student of interpersonal communication, you must learn when, where, and how much is appropriate to communicate to others. Having a genuine trust for humankind is important to your happiness and to your sanity. Trust gives you the freedom to take chances and make mistakes; both are important to the fulfillment and growth in your life.

What should you remember about privacy and trust?

- Privacy is a fundamental right that is consistently being challenged in courtrooms across this country, according to Ellen Alderman and Caroline Kennedy in *The Right to Privacy.*
- Trusting people enough to practice self-disclosure and having that trust betrayed is a part of life. You will experience it and you will need to move past it. Don't let it consume you. Simply ask yourself, "What can I learn from this?" Your answer will allow you to learn, move forward, and improve as a communicator.

THE COMMUNICATION PROCESS

The communication process is a very important part of laying the foundation for effective communication. If you understand how the process works, you will be able to identify specific areas that you want to improve in your own communication. Figure 1.1 provides a visual representation of the communication process. There are many ways to present this visual representation, you might ask your professor for other visual interpretations or design one yourself. Table 1.1 provides you with a summary of the terms, and definitions, and a sample scenario to assist you seeing the process in action.

Every form of communication begins with a source. The **source** is the one who initiates and delivers the initial message. The mental or written preparation that the source goes through prior to sending a message is **encoding.** This may be a rough draft of an English paper or simply thinking through the most appropriate way to say something before you say

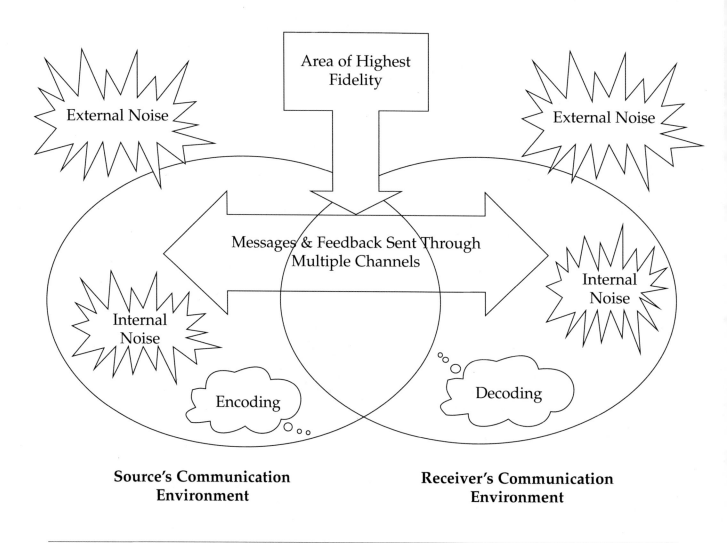

FIGURE 1.1
The Communication Process

The Communication Process Defined

Term	Definition	Sample Scenario
Source	The initiator of the message(s)	Georgia is waiting to be interviewed for a job; her prospective employer, Gary, is late. Georgia is informed that Gary will be there shortly and she is asked to wait in Gary's office. Gary walks in and greets Georgia: "I apologize for being late, let's get started."
Receiver	The recipient of the message(s)	Georgia replies, "I understand; I'm ready whenever you are!"
Nonverbal Messages	The process of consciously and unconsciously sending various messages, using anything except language. Ex.—nodding of the head, gestures, posture, etc	Georgia adjusts her body position, in the squeaky chair, in anticipation of the interview.
External Noise	Environmental interference. Ex.—cars passing, other people talking, etc	Gary begins asking Georgia his standard questions as his intercom buzzer goes off; it's his secretary announcing the next interview has arrived early.
Internal Noise	Psychological or physiological interference from within either person. Ex.–other thoughts, headache, etc	Georgia thinks to herself that she will never get a fair interview, with Gary being late and the next prospective employee already waiting. Gary continues explaining the mission of the company, but Georgia is confused by the company jargon.
Feedback	The receiver sending verbal and/or nonverbal responses to the message sent by the source	Georgia decides she would rather ask and look foolish, than not know what she is getting herself into: "Gary, I apologize but I do not understand all the terms you have been using. Do you think you could put it in lay terms?"
Message	The information that is developed, processed, and sent	Gary responds, "I appreciate your honesty, Georgia; I actually have put together a definition of terms here that we can go over together."

(continued)

TABLE 1.1
Continued

Term	Definition	Sample Scenario
Channel	The medium for sending the message. Ex.—visual channel, auditory channel, olfactory channel, and tactile channel	"Go ahead and look over the information, while I step out to let them know we need a little more time. Please don't hesitate to ask if you have any questions."
Encoding	The internal process of preparing the message(s)	Georgia looks through the material and asks many questions when Gary returns. As she asks the questions, Gary is thinking about examples that will help Georgia understand the answers to her questions.
Decoding	The internal process of understanding the messages that are being sent	After some time of working together, and getting her questions answered, Georgia gains a better understanding of what the company and Gary expects from her.
Fidelity	The attempt at accuracy during the communication process	Gary is impressed with Georgia's commitment to understanding the job before knowing if she would accept it, and offers her the job that day. Georgia accepts the job, knowing everything that is expected of her in her new position.

it. As you know, once someone initiates a conversation, the dialogue can take many turns; and many times the way the conversation begins has nothing to do with where it ends up. To that end, a source can easily become the receiver. The receiver is described in a few minutes.

Before we go any further, I must applaud anyone who practices encoding. One lesson that I learned very young is to "think before I speak." This is something that still challenges me today as there become more media (or channels) for sending messages, especially, for example, when it comes to email. It is so easy to simply type an email and send it off, without doing the following: (1) checking your spelling and grammar, (2) considering how the message could be interpreted, and (3) saving a draft. Then send the email after you have had a chance to consider what you have written. What you should know right now is if you practice encoding, it will improve the way others interpret you.

The person whom the source sends the message to is called the **receiver.** The receiver is then responsible for decoding the message. **Decoding** is the mental process of interpreting the message. This may be a quick pause to mentally consider what type of feedback is appropriate or useful for the conversation, or it may be reading and re-reading a letter to ensure you are correctly interpreting the message. *Anyone who practices decoding also deserves applause.* When you decode a message you are not only considering what is appropriate for the conversation, but you are also considering what would reach the source, either verbally, nonverbally, or both.

It is important to mention that though encoding and decoding is an important process, there are those who encode and decode messages too much (to a point of obsession). Obsessive encoding is where you analyze what you are going to say to the point where the message is no longer relevant or you don't say anything at all because you are afraid of how it will be interpreted. Obsessive decoding is when you analyze what the person said to you to the point where you begin making assumptions about what she meant to say or what he was trying to say. Finding a balance between some encoding/decoding and becoming obsessive about encoding/decoding will only come with practice and feedback.

A **message** is the nonverbal and/or verbal information that is passed between the source and the receiver(s). Messages are coded into symbols (nonverbal) or language (verbal) that should be understood between both the source and the receiver. Symbols are only as good as the people who understand them, and they usually are culturally based. We will discuss language and symbols in later chapters. Unfortunately, when it comes to decoding the message, we make a lot of assumptions about what we think the person is trying to say. This is where feedback is essential to the communication process, as it can minimize the assumptions that we make. **Feedback** is both the verbal and nonverbal response the receiver gives to show that the message is understood. In order for feedback to be effective, listening must take place.

Channels refer to the mediums used in sending messages and feedback. Messages are sent using all of your senses. The **visual channel** picks up nonverbal communication. The **auditory channel** hears words and sounds. The **olfactory channel** uses your sense of smell to receive a message, as when restaurants communicate the quality of their food so that customers who receive the olfactory message are enticed into buying a meal. If that works, then you use your **gustatory channel** to taste the food. If the food tastes good, then we are likely to tell our friends about it. It is another reason why many restaurants will give you a sample of the food; they want to please your gustatory channel. The olfactory channel can also be used to send and receive unconscious messages, for example, if someone has bad breath or has not showered lately. Depending on a person's cultural values, the receiver may make some assumptions about the person with bad breath or body odor that could create internal noise (as discussed in the next paragraph). Finally the **tactile channel** includes touch, for example, when a source puts his hand on the receiver's arm to emphasize his verbal message. Most channels use nonverbal communication; this is why nonverbal communication represents 75 to 95 percent of our total communication.

Next let's look at two areas that interfere with the communication process. First, **internal noise** is anything psychological or physiological that interferes with the communication process. For example, a stomach-ache can be bothering you to the point where you do not watch the nonverbal part of the message, and therefore miss something that may be crucial. Another example is daydreaming. If you are thinking about something besides what the source is telling you, you may again miss an important part of the message. **External noise** is noise that is going on in the environment. For example, someone may drive by, honk, and wave hello which may interrupt your train of thought. Another example is trying to watch television and talk to someone at the same time. Unless you are discussing what is on the television, it can become something that distracts the source, receiver, or both. The examples presented for both internal and external noise can quickly become a source of distraction, either consciously or unconsciously. When it becomes a conscious act, you can then make changes to minimize the effect of the noise.

We are now nearing the completion of how the communication process works. There are two more important elements you need to understand in order to complete the process. First, we must be aware that perception plays an important role in how we understand what others are communicating. That perception is what creates our own **communication environment,** or the past experiences, assumptions, biases, and judgments that we bring to a communication situation. The communication environment is discussed in chapter 2, listening. Perception is discussed in chapter 3. The second element you should know is that the ultimate goal of effective communication is high fidelity. **Fidelity** is the accuracy of the entire communication process. Fidelity comes when you understand the person you are communicating with, that s/he understands you, and that you both understand the verbal and nonverbal messages being sent to each other.

Taadaa—the communication process—isn't it amazing! Who knew so much went into something that we do every day? Maybe if we understood all of the elements that create the communication process, and we tried to practice those elements, we could finally communicate more effectively. I love it!

> "Communication is vital to everyone's life.
> Without communication people would die."
>
> —Vickie Rockwell

A COMPETENT COMMUNICATOR IS:

Knowledgeable
Skilled
Self-motivated
Concerned for others
Concerned for themselves
Ethical
Flexible
Nonjudgmental
Unbiased
Trustworthy
An effective listener
Able to choose appropriate communication tactics
Willing to continuously learn

This is a tall order. A competent communicator embraces all of those qualities; however, a competent communicator is not perfect. A **competent communicator** is someone who has incorporated the preceding qualities, and practices them to a skilled level.

You have the ability to be a competent communicator. Are you willing to examine your own communication? Are you willing to acknowledge that you are not perfect? Are you willing to take risks and try new ways of communicating? Are you willing to practice metacommunication? Are you willing to intrapersonally communicate? Everyone has the ability to be a competent communicator. The difference between those who are competent communicators and those who are not is simple; a competent communicator answered yes to the preceding questions and took action. It is a great journey, one that you can begin right now—if you say yes!

In the second half of the chapter, we discussed privacy and trust, the communication process, and becoming a competent communicator. With that in mind, consider the following questions and write down some notes in the space provided:

1. What didn't you know about the things you have read so far?

2. What surprised you the most about what you have read so far?

3. With what you've read so far, what don't you understand?

4. Is there anything you don't agree with, or is there anything you need more information about?

This textbook will challenge you in ways that you may have never been challenged before now. You will be asked to examine your toughest critic—yourself. Some of you will blow it off or get angry. Some will say, "I'll BS my way through it." Some of you will embrace the journey from day one. Some of you will appreciate what you have learned near the end of the book, and some will appreciate it years from now. Regardless of which category you'll fall in, your communication skills will improve if you open your mind to a textbook that is 100 percent dedicated to you.

If employers truly believe that communication is the number one skill they are looking for, as several surveys have concluded, then here it is for you to learn. Only you can improve your ability to communicate. I will guide your learning process and if you want to learn, you will.

BREAKING OFF THE CONVERSATION
EXPERTS SAY INTIMACY IS LOST WHEN TECHNOLOGY LIMITS TALKING FACE-TO-FACE

Ira J. Hadnot

Social conversation is on the list of endangered human activities—along with manually changing television channels and cooking without microwaves. To deal with the fast pace of society, some of us have cut the small talk. But talk is everywhere—it's even the title of a new magazine from editor Tina Brown of VANITY FAIR and THE NEW YORKER fame. Yet there is very little intimate discussion. Face-to-face communication is declining because machines have become our surrogate communicators, experts say. E-mail, voice mail, pagers, answering machines, ATMs, beepers and faxes. Machines are mediating disputes, announcing personal events such as births and deaths and insulating us from one another. Talk shows substitute for interpersonal communication, linguists say, giving people strangers' conversations as spectator sport. The dinner hour, one of the few opportunities for families to really talk each day, has been shrinking for decades, according to various studies, from one hour throughout the '50s and '60s to about 30 minutes in the '90s.

"We are losing our personal voices," argues Dr. John L. Locke, a specialist in the science of language. "During a period in which feelings of isolation and loneliness are on the rise, too many of us are becoming emotionally and socially mute." Dr. Locke is the author of THE DE-VOICING OF SOCIETY: WHY WE DON'T TALK TO EACH OTHER ANYMORE. Computers have expanded the ability to communicate and at the same time, he writes, are cutting society's vocal chords. Others say computers are changing, in better ways, the dynamics of human communication. Every new tool—from the printing press to the telephone—is used in a different way to get meaning across, says Dr. Steve Jones, head of the communications department at the University of Illinois at Chicago.

"My quibble is the way in which we assume there is something uniquely special about oral and face-to-face communication. There are circumstances in which it is better, easier and more fruitful to use e-mail or the telephone," says Dr. Jones, who studies ways in which social relationships have been changed by the Internet.

"E-mail is a disinhibiting medium. You don't see the other person. You don't have the social pressure. What you lose in body language and voice, you gain in the more deliberate use of language with less contradictions."

BUSINESS APPROACH

A survey released in June by the Institute for Operations Research and Management Services noted that e-mail may be the "white knight for organizations reluctant to deliver bad news to employees." There are pluses and minuses to forms of communication, whether the content is written or spoken, transmitted by memo, e-mail or telephone, Dr. Jones says.

"Fifty years ago, a pink slip would have been a memo. That does not necessarily make e-mail or memo the right way to fire someone. It means the person charged with the responsibility is trying to avoid the pain of performing such a task in person."

Technology is creating a big minus in the development of human communication, according to Dr. Locke, Senior Research Fellow with the Faculty of Social and Political Sciences at the University of Cambridge. He has been watching society "lose its voice' for more than 20 years. The topic is part of a burgeoning discussion attracting a variety of scholars. Dr. Locke's work is based on volumes of language research, including the earliest kind—studies of primates. It is also based on contemporary observations of people in places such as public parks, train stations, cocktail parties and street corners. The results from the audio test for his theory of devoicing? What often passes nowadays for personal communication are clipped phrases such as: "Wait a minute, I got e-mail"; "Let me get this other call"; "Can you hold on five minutes?". Or personal communication that is "increasingly swollen with facts, info-speech and news bulletins," maintain Dr. Locke and several communications researchers and theorists.

"Our culture is full of faux communications," says Dr. Rita Kirk Whillock, an assistant professor of public relations at Southern Methodist University and co-editor of SOUND BITE CULTURE: THE DEATH OF DISCOURSE IN A WIRED WORLD.

"We give the illusion of communication when we aren't communicating. An example is those generic letters that begin with your first name and end with a machine made signature in real ink that bleeds. These people are communicating with you as though they know you, but they don't."

PERSONAL TOUCHES

"Personalized" form letters are far from early humans' use of what linguists term "social calls"—facial expressions, utterances, laughter, chattering—which began hundreds of thousands of years before language emerged. These "social calls" and spoken words give communication its meaning, Dr. Locke writes. And they are disappearing.

"Just as we need to reverse rising levels of distrust by achieving greater familiarity, we are becoming increasingly still. The underlying problem is that we don't socialize enough to know and trust each other. . . There are now fewer intimate social relationships than at any previous time in modern history." The consequences, he says, are "a rise in unfamiliarity, suspiciousness, distrust and loneliness."

A person's voice gives cues to gender, age and emotional state. The pitch can convey nervousness, excitement or fear. There are important nuances machines cannot discern. Without these details, communication is devoid of personality, style and individuality, some experts say. Tone of voice can often contradict the words being spoken, revealing true feelings. Facial expression and eye contact can show insincerity. All these attributes and expressions are lacking from electronic communication.

"Human beings like to be listened to. We need to be heard," Dr. Locke says. Intimate talk and the social gestures [hugs, embraces, hand holding] provide internal validation necessary for personal growth. Talking fulfills a biological need. Much has been written about the "evils" of the technological age and the purported loss of personal identity. Man versus machine is the parable of our age. But the computer is not the sole culprit for a decline in social talk. There are a number of factors, with the two most influential being urbanization and the advent of the printing press, Dr. Locke writes in his book. Once information was shared within small tribes made up of members that were dependent upon one another for survival. Modern man, dispersed across vast areas and living in fragmented communities, can now access information of all types with the click of a computer key.

As the printing press helped literacy spread, Dr. Locke notes, people began to experience the ability to "exchange massive amounts of information without ever seeing other human beings." Business deals once sealed by handshakes were replaced by written documents considered more orderly and efficient. As information proliferated toward the end of the 20th century, the computer became essential to managing it. People's appetite for mass media grew. And their communications habits changed. "At one time our relationships were primary and the message almost incidental," Dr. Locke writes. "Now the exchange of information is too often the reason for speech, and personal relationships are secondary."

MIXED MESSAGES

People are getting mixed messages on what machines are intended for, says David Slayden, an associate professor of journalism and mass communication at the University of Colorado in Boulder. He is co-editor of SOUND BITE CULTURE: THE DEATH OF DISCOURSE IN A WIRED WORLD. "Electronic machines are most efficient at the transfer of information, and we're trying to exchange that efficiency for human interaction," he says. "As awkward, messy and emotional as it may be at times, we benefit enormously from close contact, talking with each other." Are these new technological forms of communication displacing earlier ones or renewing appreciation for conversation? If human exchange is less frequent, will it be more meaningful when it happens?

"I don't think anything has been displaced yet," Dr. Whillock says. "We are relying on these devices more to facilitate com-

munication. But we don't feel inundated enough by it to start a rebellion."

It is a "myth that all this fascinating conversation was going on before computers came on the scene," Dr. Slayden says. " . . . I haven't seen that we had been in some golden age of conversation."

"When I think of technology and communication, I am reminded of the part of THE WIZARD OF OZ where Dorothy and friends are told to pay no attention to the man behind the curtain. They are supposed to speak to this great and powerful machine," he says.

"We are speaking to the great and powerful machines. I cannot go so far as to say they have completely consumed personal communication. The think to pay attention to is the contrast between the natural and the 'mediated' experience. Talking to someone on a computer is not a natural experience. When people leave voice-mail messages, some people believe those messages are likely to be more thorough because the person has to focus on what they are saying." Dr. Slayden says such messages are "scripted, prepared and do not have the give-and-take of talking with a person. Cell-phone conversations are public performances. Someone wants to be noticed with a phone. Our attention is more riveted to electronic means than to human exchange."

It took 40 years for the telephone to become pervasive in human life, says Dr. Jones. It has taken five years for the Internet to have such an impact, he adds. That is a faster pace but no less ominous, he says, than predictions about what televisions and telephones would do to social communication.

"We are terribly resilient as human beings. We're not at the mercy of our tools to the extent we will end up at one exaggerated extreme or another. The pendulum will swing back and forth with lots of subtle, fascinating changes taking place along the way."

Name: _____ Date: _____

QUESTIONS FOR DISCUSSION—

BREAKING OFF THE CONVERSATION

By Ira J. Hadnot

1. What are your top 3 reactions to this article?

2. Is social conversation losing its importance in the fast-pace society that we live in?

3. Is email an effective way of interpersonally communicating?

(Questions continued on back)

---

4. Can you have a personal conversation while doing one or more of the following—driving, answering your call waiting, watching television, listening to the radio, cooking supper, etc?

5. Is the world losing the personal touch with technology?

6. Other thoughts about the article?

COMMUNICATION SKILLS CRUCIAL FOR LAW ENFORCEMENT POLICE: OFFICERS' INTERPERSONAL SKILLS IMPORTANT

Randy Means

Dateline: RENO, Nev. —

The neighborly sheriff portrayed in the 1960s television series "The Andy Griffith Show" is a perfect example of how modern law enforcement officers should act, a risk management consultant says.

In the hit TV show, the easygoing lawman applied folksy wisdom and **interpersonal** skills to settle disputes and outwit criminals, the consultant explained.

Interpersonal communication skills and human relations expertise are crucial to reducing lawsuits stemming from heavy-handed police work, which can occur when law enforcement agencies try to ratchet up their crime fight efforts, said Randy means, a partner at Charlotte, N.C.-based consulting firm Thomas & Means L.L.P.

The nature of police work usually means that increased law enforcement efforts bring not only lower crime rates but also more complaints, lawsuits, injuries and deaths, he said.

Aggressive crime-fighting efforts regularly **conflict** with a public risk manager's task of reducing liability losses, Mr. Means said during a session at the Public Risk Management Assn.'s annual conference in Reno, Nev., last month.

But by training police officers to become better communicators-capable of managing their own emotions as well as other peoples' anger and hostility-public risk managers can help achieve both goals, said Mr. Means, who specializes in police operations and risk management.

Mr. Means warned that risk managers who push for improved **interpersonal** skills in police departments would encounter stiff resistance.

"Actually, there are some people in law enforcement who are remarkably good at doing this, and some people are remarkably bad at doing it, and they create a vast disproportion of our problems," he said.

Although **interpersonal** skills often are not taught as part of law enforcement protocol, many police officers understand their importance, the consultant said. When he surveyed more than 10,000 police veterans, asking them about the skills required to effectively fight crime, more than 80% ranked human relations and **interpersonal communications** as most important.

Yet most police officers won't engage those skills unless their leadership insists on it and provides mandatory training, he said.

Encouraging police to use **interpersonal** skills in their work has brought big returns, said Michael G. Fann, director of loss control for Tennessee Municipal League Risk Management Pool in Brentwood.

The self-insurance pool provides coverage for 500 Tennessee municipalities with a total of 260 police agencies employing about 6,000 police officers. Despite those numbers, over the past 10 years TML has averaged only $1 million in annual law enforcement losses, which Mr. Fann says is low.

More than 50% of the $1 million is spent on defense costs, he noted, so the pool's actual payouts to plaintiffs, including settlements, amount to less than $500,000 annually.

Advocating human relations and **interpersonal** skills at the state's police academies and among city managers, police chiefs and police trainers helps TML keep its losses to those levels, Mr. Fann said.

"Everywhere we go, we talk about it," he said.

Mr. Means advocates that law enforcement agencies start the process by hiring people who already possess strong **communications** abilities and who are inclined to apply those abilities to the job.

Agencies can design or purchase personality tests to screen job applicants for these attributes, he said.

One such test requires a job applicant to role-play in response to people and situations presented on a video. It's a very simple test, but it can provide insight into the job applicant's attitude, Mr. Means said.

Police departments also should test the abilities of officers who are already on the force, Mr. Means advises. Although they may object to an emphasis on better **inter-personal** skills, "You make it clear that this is not negotiable," he said.

Officers who score well on the tests should be made mentors, and remedial training should be provided to those who don't fare as well, he advised. And those who fail should not be fired, he emphasized, because an agency will run into more stumbling blocks, such as having to validate the test's effectiveness in employment lawsuits.

"You can't even get people fired for lying on search warrant applications in some places and here we are going to try to fire them because they are not nice enough?" he said.

Mr. Fann moderated the session.

"You can't even get people fired for lying on search warrant applications in some places and here we are going to try to fire them because they are not nice enough?"
Randy Means
Thomas & Means L.L.P.

QUESTIONS FOR DISCUSSION—

COMMUNICATION SKILLS CRUCIAL FOR LAW ENFORCEMENT
By Roberto Ceniceros

1. What are your top 3 reactions to this article?

2. Why are interpersonal communication skills so important to law enforcement?

3. What do the various law enforcement agencies do to assist their officers in improving their communication skills?

(Questions continued on back)

4. In your opinion, or in your experience with law enforcement, are they doing enough to assist their officers? What else could they be doing?

5. Other thoughts about the article?

ARTICLE FOR DISCUSSION—

PRIVACY IS OVERRATED
THEY'RE WATCHING YOUR EVERY MOVE. BIG DEAL.
By David Plotz From GQ

Let's start by invading my privacy. I own a three-bedroom house on Ontario Place in Washington D.C. I have a mortgage from National City Mortgage Co. I am married to Hanna Rosin. We have a two-year-old child. I drive a 1990 Chevy Caprice with D.C. license plates.

I have no criminal record. I have never been party to a lawsuit. I have no tax liens against me. I have never declared bankruptcy (unlike 2 of the 11 other David Plotzes in the United States). I have no ties to organized crime.

The James Mintz Group, a leading corporate investigation firm headquartered in New York City, learned all this about me in a few hours with a computer, an Internet connection, and a single phone call—and without even bending the law.

If you spent a bit more time, you would discover my Social Security number, how much I paid for my house, and where I bank. You could have my listed home telephone number in two mouse clicks and my unlisted cell phone number if you paid the right data broker.

Corporations, meanwhile, are recording my every move. I don't watch what I eat, but Safeway does, thanks to my club card. Telecoms can pinpoint where I am when I make my cell-phone calls. Clothing stores analyze my purchases in detail, recording everything from the expansion of my waist (up to 35 from 32) to my recent infatuation with three-button suits.

The credit reporting agencies know every time I have made a late payment to my Citibank MasterCard (number 6577 . . . I'm not that stupid) and every time I have applied for credit. This is all going on my permanent record.

Surveillance cameras are watching me in malls and sometimes on public streets. Even my own computer is spying on me. A scan of my hard drive turns up 141 cookies, deposited by companies that track me around the Web. I recently surfed a porn site (just because a high school friend runs it, I swear). The cookies may know about it. My employer probably does too. After all, my employment contract permits the boss to track all my on-the-job Web surfing, and read all my work e-mail too.

If my company isn't watching, perhaps the FBI is: Its Carnivore program rafts through vast rivers of e-mail flow in search of criminal activity.

They—a *they* that includes the feds, a thousand corporations, a million telemarketers, my employer, my enemies and maybe even my friends—know all this about me, and more. And unless you are a technophobe hermit who pays for everything in cash, they know all this about you too.

To which I say, "Hallelujah!"

I'm in the minority. Privacy paranoia has become a national obsession. Since last November, pundits, politicians and privacy activists have been shouting about the latest government intrusion on privacy. The Defense Department's office of Total Information Awareness plans to collect massive quantities of information about all Americans—everything from what you buy to where you travel—in gigantic databases, and then sift through the information for clues about terrorism. Total Information Awareness has been denounced as Orwellian, and there are efforts to stop the program.

You could fill a library with privacy-alarmism books (*The End of Privacy; Privacy: How to Protect What's Left of It*). Congress and the state legislatures are awash in proposals to protect privacy. Horror stories fuel the fire to anxiety. The sailor the Navy tried to boot out after he used the word *gay* in a supposedly confidential AOL profile. The stalker who bought his target's address from a Web information broker, tracked her down and murdered her. The sale of Social Security numbers by LexisNexis.

You can more or less distill the essence of the privacy-rights movement to this idea: Big Brother and Big Business observe us too often, without our consent. The most intimate details of our lives are being sold and used secretly to make judgments about us, and we have no control over it.

It sounds appalling. But, in fact, the privacy crusade is built on a foundation of hypocrisy, paranoia, economic know-nothingism and bogus nostalgia.

The first flaw of privacy: People care a great deal about their own, but not at all about anyone else's. We figure, why should anyone get to review my real-estate records or read my divorce proceedings? My life is my own business.

But I bet you want to know if your babysitter has ever been convicted of child abuse, if your business partner has a history of bankruptcy, if your boyfriend is still married. When your husband flees the state to duck child support payments, wouldn't you use his Social Security number, driving records, real estate filings and whatever else you could get your hands on to track him down?

You don't want the Total Information Awareness office to know what you bought at the hardware store or where you take vacations. But if your neighbor is stockpiling fertilizer and likes to holiday in Iraq, don't you want the government to notice? If government had been using even basic data-mining techniques before September 11, at least 11 of the hi-jackers might have been stopped, according to a report by the Markle Foundation. Wouldn't that be worth letting the feds know you bought an Xbox last month.

Hysteria is growing that companies are shadowing us constantly. They are. But here, too, privacy is a silly value, both because "protecting" it is enormously costly and because it's not really being violated.

Ignorant companies are bankrupt companies. A recent study found that restricting marketing data would raise catalog clothing prices up to 11 percent, costing shoppers $1 billion per year. By buying address lists and consumer profiles, Victoria's Secret knows to send a catalog to my house, and International Male knows not to bother. Their marketing costs plummet. We get less junk mail, lower prices and catalogs for clothing we might buy.

Your father probably shopped with a clothier who knew he wore a 44 long suit and preferred a faint pinstripe. Such friendships are extinct, murdered my megastores and armchair shopping. But today, when I log on to Amazon.com, I am pitched another book about privacy, because Amazon has learned that I am the kind of guy who buys books on privacy. They are saving me time (which is money) by delivering what I like.

Information sharing is also an engine of entrepreneurship. Thanks to cheap mailing lists, upstarts can challenge titanic businesses, lowering prices and bringing clever products to market.

Losing privacy has made it much cheaper to use a credit card or buy a house. Credit card and mortgage companies collect and share information about who pays, who doesn't, etc. Because they have an idea who will default, they offer significantly lower rates to people with good records and make credit much more available to poorer customers.

It's true that identity theft has become easier. On the other hand, credit card fraud—a much more common crime—is harder. Companies often catch a thief before a customer even notices her card is missing. (Their observant computers notice that her buying habits have suddenly changed.)

Similarly, surveillance cameras reduce shoplifting and stop ATM robberies, while cameras in police cars reduce incidents of police brutality. Lack of privacy actually tends to fight crime, not cause it.

There is one notable exception to the argument for transparency, however. If medical records are unsealed, especially to employers, people may avoid treatment, fearing they will be stigmatized or fired for their health problems.

Philosophically, many people don't like the idea that a soulless corporation records that they buy sexy underwear, subscribe to *Penthouse* and collect heavy metal CDs. Friends were freaked out to receive ads for infant formula soon after they gave birth. How did the company know? Is the hospital selling your baby already?

But this worry is an example of the egocentric fallacy: the belief that because people know something about you, they care. One wonderful, terrible thing about modern capitalism is that companies don't care. You are not a person. You are a wallet. Privacy advocates like to say, "It didn't used to be this way." They hark back to a time—it generally sounds like 19th-century rural America—when stores didn't record your every purchase and doctors didn't report your ailments to a monolithic insurance company. You could abandon a bad life in one state,

reinvent yourself 50 miles away, and no one needed to know. Nothing went down on your permanent record, because there was no permanent record.

This nostalgia imagines a past that never existed. Small-town America never guarded anyone's privacy. In small towns, as anyone who lives in one can attest, people can be nosy and punish nonconformity viciously.

The right to privacy is not mentioned in the Constitution, and was not even conceived until 1890. Censuses in the 18th and 19th centuries demanded answers to intrusive questions, such as one compelling Americans to reveal any history of insanity in the family.

Nostalgists also fail to recognize that technology is creating a golden age for what they actually care about: real privacy. This is nothing that Amazon.com cares about. Nothing that Total Information Awareness can track down. Nothing that needs to be protected by encryption.

The opposite of privacy is not invasion of privacy: It is openness. Real privacy is what allows us to share hopes, dreams, fantasies, fears, and makes us feel we can safely expose all our faults and quirks and still be loved. Privacy is the space between us and our dearest—where everything is known and does not matter.

There has never been a better time for real privacy. The Internet allows people who have peculiar interests, social awkwardness or debilitating health problems to create communities that never could have existed before. Online, they can find other folks who want to re-enact the Battle of Bull Run or sunbathe nude or whatever your bag is, baby.

By surrendering some privacy—that is, by revealing our humanity with all its peculiarity in chat rooms or on e-mail or in newsgroups—we gain a much greater privacy: an intimacy with others, a sense of belonging. To be less private sometimes is to have more privacy. To be less private is to be more ourselves.

Name: _____ Date: _____

QUESTIONS FOR DISCUSSION—

PRIVACY IS OVERRATED
by David Plotz

1. What are your top 3 reactions to this article?

2. How do you feel about your privacy, specifically?

(Questions continued on back)

3. Do you think we, as a nation, should be concerned about the privacy issue right now or can it wait? Why/why not?

4. Do you believe the Internet should give us more cause to be concerned? Explain.

5. Other thoughts about the article?

Name: _____ Date: _____

INDIVIDUAL ACTIVITY #1
Creating Goals for Your Success in the Classroom

PURPOSE—

To provide you with an opportunity to assess what you want to get out of your class. This will serve as a basis for the way you approach the class and the amount of time that you choose to put into the class.

PROCEDURE—

Rank the following 18 statements in order of how closely the statement relates to you, with 1 being "this relates to me a lot" and 18 being "this doesn't relate to me at all." There are 2 blank lines at the end for you to create your own goals.

_____ I do not like talking to people I do not know.

_____ I feel that people judge me before they get to know me.

_____ I want to improve my listening skills.

_____ I am not very good at relationships.

_____ I do not understand how nonverbal communication works.

_____ I use too much slang when I talk to others.

_____ I want to understand how the communication process works.

_____ I cannot verbalize my emotions.

_____ I am usually overwhelmed by my emotions.

_____ I want to know/learn more about myself.

_____ I want to change my beliefs.

_____ I do not handle conflict effectively.

_____ I want to make better decisions.

_____ I am afraid that people will laugh at me when I talk to them.

_____ I want to be able to assert my wants and needs to others.

_____ I want people to listen to what I have to say.

_____ I am just looking to pass this class.

_____ I am not looking to learn anything about myself.

_____

_____

GROUP ACTIVITY #1
Getting to Know Each Other

PURPOSE—

In an Interpersonal Communication course, it can be challenging when you first begin trying to self-disclose to the class. However, self-disclosure is what makes the class a success. This activity is designed to "break the ice" and give you a chance to get to know your fellow classmates—interpersonally.

PROCEDURE—

Let's pretend you are a researcher for the Harvard Research Group. Your job is to research the name of someone in your class, and information about him or her that fits one of the following descriptions. You may use a classmate's name for only one category. Use the space provided for your answers.

1. Find someone who likes fish. Why? What kinds?

2. Find someone who likes chitterlings. Why? What are they? How are they cooked?

3. Find someone who likes liver. Why? How does s/he like it cooked?

4. Find someone who collects shoes. Explain the collection.

5. Find someone who paints. Explain what, when, how, etc.

6. Find someone who meditates. Explain how, when, why, etc.

7. Find someone who gardens. Explain what, why, etc.

(Continued)

From Michelle Burch, *Interpersonal Communication: Building Your Foundations for Success.* Copyright © 2005 by Kendall/Hunt Publishing Company.

8. Find someone who cooks. Explain favorite meals, how s/he got started, etc.

9. Find someone who enjoys public speaking. Explain why, favorite speaker, etc.

10. Find someone who reads science fiction books. What are his/her favorite authors, books, etc?

11. Find someone who reads fantasy books. What are his/her favorite authors, books, etc?

12. Find someone who reads romance. What are his/her favorite authors, books, etc?

13. Find someone who practices martial arts. Explain how long, why interested, etc.

14. Find someone who plays on a college athletic team. Explain why, what motivates, etc.

15. Find someone who is active in a club/organization on campus. Explain why, what the club does, etc.

16. Find someone who collects coins. Explain why, where the interest began, etc.

17. Find someone who enjoys comic books. Explain why, where the interest began, etc.

18. Find someone who practices a religion other than Christianity. Explain what s/he enjoys about their religion, why, etc.

19. Find someone who enjoys being with children. Explain what they enjoy doing, favorite age of children, etc.

20. Find someone who is a communication major. Explain what field of communication s/he is studying, what career ideas s/he is interested in, etc.

Name: _____ Date: _____

GROUP ACTIVITY #2
Barriers to Effective Communication

PURPOSE—

To begin interpersonally communicating, by sharing various reasons you believe we do not communicate as effectively as we could in our relationships.

PROCEDURE—

Divide the class into small groups. Since this is only your second group activity, first share a little bit about yourself. We cannot interpersonally communicate unless there is a high level of trust and we feel comfortable in our environment. I would suggest sharing— (1) Why are you in this class? (2) Where are you from? (3) Describe a little about your family. (4) What is your major?

Next, answer the following question in your small group. When you are finished, the class will discuss the answers.

QUESTION TO ANALYZE—

1. Why do we choose not to interpersonally communicate? Describe as many barriers as you can. Consider why you choose not to speak up with family, friends, strangers, etc.

FOLLOW-UP—

As a class, discuss the barriers that people came up with in the small groups. Now that you have heard from other groups, any there more barriers that you can think of?

Name: _____ Date: _____

GROUP ACTIVITY #3
Creating a Communication Scenario

PURPOSE—

To ensure that you understand the terms used in the communication process.

PROCEDURE—

Divide the class into small groups. Each group should create a communication scenario using all of the components in the communication process (use table 1.1 for an example). The setting of the scenario can be in a classroom, a hospital, a bar, a living room, etc. The scenario can be between two people or among a group of people. Your scenario can demonstrate either effective or ineffective communication.

YOUR COMMUNICATION SCENARIO—

FOLLOW-UP—

Share the scenario your group created with the class. Get feedback regarding whether or not the communication in your scenario was effective or ineffective, what made it effective or ineffective, and if the terms were used correctly.

WORD SEARCH
Reviewing the Terms

```
D Z G X E A E R I Z C H A N N E L S U L C C S C
W F C N M Y R Y G E U X D K U J W M A D T S O Y
N Q Q Y I W U M E S G O X E Y P O N E G Z M U R
U O T O F D S D C X V U M D U V O Z E E M I O E
K Z I V U S O Z B M T T Y G Z S D K O U N E X V
C H P T M C L C N Q M R D P R D C C N F M U H I
O F Y S A Y C L E I R E A E T A S I U I E G E E
Q Y T U U C S I N D X P P P B U C N N Y S L X C
P U J A M W I O L N E R Q D E A K T J M S K T E
E R Z F T D D N R V E D E L T R E L O Z A V E R
U I I U N S F P U T Q E W I M R S K H Z G C R U
U R S V O D L I N M F J O G N I D O C N E V N O
Z A H U A B E I Y A M N W A A I E V N A Y C A G
N L R S A C S I V G E O L N X A B I E A R E L E
I C J T I D Y D A N C N C L W G L R K B L E N C
E M D E R I Z U V V O E X A U W F M F F Q D O S
J D W D O M J I E I G M J I T H A H L X N V I X
K O I Q Q U R Z S I N T R A P E R S O N A L S Z
D B H A E O S E E C I M R O C A M S T Y J G E J
J F L Y N O L O L X F H N A X K T Y S O Y Q B J
C Q S M R L Z U G N N E O W G C S R B E C W S M
P L E B V T S J O O K G L Z M I P L K S E S T H
U N Z X M O A B E B B P Y X I L M H K Y I W F V
T R O T A C I N U M M O C T N E T E P M O C W A
```

Definitions for the terms in the word search:

1. communicating and interacting with others while self-disclosing
2. sharing your thoughts, needs, wants, and/or desires
3. communicating with yourself
4. communicating with nonliving or nonhuman things
5. communicating about how to communicate
6. to keep something to yourself
7. one who prepares the initial message
8. mental or written preparation for sending a message

(Continued)

9. one who receives the message

10. mental process of interpreting the message

11. the nonverbal and/or verbal information passed between the source and the receiver

12. responses the receiver gives to show the message is understood

13. media used in sending the message

14. psychological and physiological noises

15. interferences from the environment

16. past experiences, assumptions, biases, and judgments that one brings to a situation

17. a skilled communicator

Name: _____ Date: _____

CHAPTER QUIZ
Reviewing the Chapter

TRUE OR FALSE

_____ 1. Intrapersonal communication is the single most important type of communication.

_____ 2. When communicating with someone, you can repeat the same message, if necessary.

_____ 3. If you talk to yourself, you are in need of therapy.

_____ 4. Privacy is an individual right.

_____ 5. Self-disclosure changes a relationship.

_____ 6. You do not need communication to survive.

_____ 7. Interpersonal communication is a natural ability.

_____ 8. Metacommunication is communicating about communication.

_____ 9. Your emotions do not influence your communication.

_____ 10. Intrapersonal communication is communicating with nonliving things.

_____ 11. Anybody can be a competent communicator.

_____ 12. Encoding is how the receiver understands the message.

_____ 13. Past experiences, assumptions, biases, and judgments make up someone's communication environment.

_____ 14. A stomach ache or thoughts about things that you need to be doing are examples of external noise.

_____ 15. Someone who examines that effectiveness of conversation is an example of a competent communicator.

CHAPTER 2

MAKING LISTENING WORK

KEY TERMS

Active listening

Advisory listening

Critical listening

Evaluative listening

External noise

Hearing

Impersonal listening

Internal noise

Interpersonal listening

Intrapersonal listening

Listener's communication
environment

Listening patterns

Passive listening

Pseudo-listening

CHAPTER OBJECTIVES

1. Understand the difference between hearing and listening.

2. Recognize the types of listening.

3. Recognize the listener's communication environment and how it relates to the communication process as a whole.

4. Describe and explain the listening process.

5. Understand the many reasons why we listen and why we do not listen.

6. Determine how to be a more effective listener.

7. Understand the physiological and psychological aspects of listening.

8. Practice skills for improving your listening habits.

UNDERSTANDING THE DIFFERENCES

Shhhh. Can you hear it? Can you hear the sounds around you? Go outside and hear the sounds of the trees, the grass, the rain, and the cars (not all at once). Try to appreciate each sound. Can you hear the whispers of people talking or the shuffling of feet by those near you? Now listen to what the trees are saying or recognize what the wind is saying to you. Some of what you are doing is the ability to hear and some of what you are doing is the ability to listen. Didn't know there was a difference or knew there was but couldn't explain what it was? Let's examine the differences. **Hearing** *is a physiological process. Unless you have an impairment (and you may have without knowing it), you can hear.* **Hearing** *is an automatic process that involves sound waves making a connection to the brain.*

I was watching the *Today* show on NBC this morning and they were talking to a man who, by the miracles of science, can see again. This man has not been able to see since he was three years old, about 45 years ago. The most impressive thing he said was that he could tell his twin boys apart when he was blind; however, now that his vision is restored it is difficult to tell them apart. When you learn to use your other senses, you can hear an entirely different language of sound. Our ability to hear can be greatly improved, if we learn how to truly listen to the world around us.

Hearing begins in the body. Listening begins at the brain. Listening is a tricky process. How many times have you listened to what you wanted to hear, only to be corrected later? Or how about this—have you ever dressed a particular way because you expected the weather to be a certain temperature simply by looking out the window or because of the season? Here's another one—have you ever expected someone to be rude or disrespectful, only to find out that s/he is very kind? Listening is tricky because of our perception and our expectations of others and the environment.

Listening is a conscious, psychological process. In simplistic terms, **listening** involves selecting information we have heard, choosing whether or not to respond to it, and finally, deciding if we want to remember the information. Some will argue that listening doesn't have to be conscious, that we can unconsciously listen to many things. For example, how many people say they can drive and talk on their cell phone at the same time successfully? How about driving, talking on the cell phone, listening to the radio, and eating? How about driving, talking on the cell phone, listening to the radio, eating, smoking a cigarette, and maybe even shifting gears? Many, many people do all of those things—at the same time—and say they are both consciously and unconsciously listening to everything. Wrong! The person trying to complete all of those tasks at the same time may be *hearing* a lot of different sounds; however, you can only effectively *listen* and process one of those sounds at a time. OK, so a lot of people drive and listen to the radio at the same time. However, I challenge you to try this exercise:

TRY IT OUT!

The next time you are alone in your vehicle, drive without the radio on, or the cell phone, and no food. At each red light, write down the sounds that you hear. Even if they are sounds that you normally hear, write them down. Write down everything that you hear. Try this for about 30 minutes, then turn the radio back on, eat something, make your phone call, or have a cigarette. However, I do not suggest that you participate in all of those activities at once! Drive for awhile and see if you can still hear those sounds. When you do turn on your radio, for example, I have a feeling that you won't remember the details of what is on the radio. If you are still trying to consciously listen to the sounds you heard earlier, anything else you try to do will become more of a challenge.

The process of listening is not complex; however, it does require effort on your part to be successful, just like healthy eating or exercising. Those are not difficult tasks, but they do take consistent effort to achieve the results you are looking for. The consistent effort is the challenge, not the actual task. In this chapter you will learn how the process of effective listening should work, reasons why we do and do not listen, and the tools you need to become an effective listener.

We are not usually taught how to listen effectively, except when people point out what we are doing wrong, by using one or more of the following phrases:

- "Look at me when I talk to you."
- "Don't walk away from me when I'm talking."
- "You can't talk to your friends and listen to me at the same time."
- "If you want to remember this, you had better write it down."
- "I know you're not listening to me, you're watching television."
- "Your listening skills need work."

This is how many people are taught to listen—pitiful isn't it? It is easy as a parent, friend, teacher, or partner to tell someone what they are doing wrong. However, it becomes more difficult to positively teach others how you expect them to listen effectively. That process gets into expressing your needs and wants (see chapter 5). As a child, you make a lot of "mistakes" as you learn how to listen. I put the word "mistakes" in quotations because that is what they really are, just *mis*-takes as we learn.

CONSIDER THIS

Do you think children see chocolate as a reward? Do you see it as a reward? We don't know that chocolate is a reward until we are taught. Amazingly enough, children listen to not only what we say but also to what we do. When we, as adults, get excited about a chocolate dessert, children learn to do so as well. Or you simply say to a child, "If you finish your homework, you can have some cookies." Ughhhh! No wonder Americans have issues with food! When my son was young, I tried to change the "reward system." For example, rather than making reading time a punishment (as some parents do), I made it a reward. Bedtime may have been 8:00 p.m.—however, he could stay up and read until 8:30 p.m. He felt rewarded; therefore he **listened**, and guess what? He enjoys reading (staying up an extra half-hour is pretty nice too). At our house, chocolate or cookies are simply foods that are in the house, and if you want some, OK. However, they are not rewards (or punishments—though that would be interesting).

Stop Here—Before we go any further, you need to recognize how you learned your listening behaviors. Write down the various ways your parents, peers, significant others, and so on taught you how to listen appropriately. This could make for an interesting in-class or online discussion, so write down at least ten of your learned behaviors.

1.

2.

3.

4.

5.

6.

7.

8.

9.

10.

> "Listening is one of the hardest things to do."
> —Stacey Hines

THE TYPES OF LISTENING

There are 3 types of listening: interpersonal listening, intrapersonal listening, and impersonal listening. Many researchers discuss various other types of listening, that is, advisory listening, defensive listening, active listening, and so on. Those are what I call our **listening patterns** or our listening tendencies when we are in one situation or another. Not all listening patterns are effective; some of the specific types of listening patterns will be discussed in the next section. For now, let's look at the types of listening.

One aspect of the communication process discussed in chapter 1 is listening. *Listening is the single most neglected skill in the communication process.* Knowing that, I have always wondered why listening, specifically, isn't taught in our public schools. We are taught how to write, read, and (in high school) even how to speak in public (maybe). Listening is just something we are expected to know how to do, since we supposedly do it all the time. OK—I will stop being critical; however, it is for those reasons there is a chapter dedicated to understanding the many facets of listening, what is effective and ineffective listening, what creates a listener's communication environment, and how the listening process works.

Intrapersonal listening is a developed awareness of your mind and body. According to Matthew Westra in his book, *Active Communication*, "Paying attention to your own thoughts and feelings may sound easy, but it usually requires some conscious development."

In Rebecca Shafir's book *The Zen of Listening*, "The lack of self-listening is often the cause of communication breakdown. If we could hear our words and comments through the ears of our listeners, we would be appalled at the overgeneralizations."

Intrapersonal listening involves being silent with your self and your thoughts. Silence is also a form of nonverbal communication in relationships; therefore, it is discussed in that context in chapter 4. In terms of intrapersonal listening, silence is a major part of the development process.

Benefits of learning to be silent:

- Silence can make you feel good, as you look in the mirror and appreciate your beauty.
- Silence can make others feel good, as you focus completely on what that person is saying.
- Silence requires patience; it requires stopping when you want to talk and shutting your mouth when you want it open; this is your challenge.
- Silence will help your relationships grow because you will hear things that you may have missed before.
- Silence will make you a better person because of the time you spend listening to the person who you are and the person you strive to become.

Intrapersonal communication is the single most important form of communication; to that end, it is essential that one develop an ability to intrapersonally listen. Learning to meditate or simply to be silent is the first step.

The next type of listening is interpersonal listening. **Interpersonal listening** is consciously listening to someone for the sake of the relationship. Have you ever wanted to ignore someone because s/he is rambling on about something that does not interest you? Have you ever pretended to listen because you were simply bored with the subject? Then what happens when the person calls you on it or questions you to see if you are really listening? Do you feel bad or guilty for not listening? Could it possibly damage the relationship? Yes! This is where interpersonal listening comes into play.

"Listening increases relationship satisfaction. When individuals fail to listen to each other, relationships usually experience problems. On the other hand, effective listening can help cement a relationship .. , " according to Gamble and Gamble in their book *Contacts: Communicating Interpersonally.*

They go on later in their book to say, "Listening is hard work. When you listen actively, your body temperature rises, your palms become moist, and your adrenaline flow increases. Your body actually prepares itself to listen. You are a catalyst in this operation—you set the listening process in motion. Making a conscious effort to listen has its benefits; refusing to listen has its cost."

Interpersonal listening is one of the most challenging activities, yet most rewarding, that you will ever encounter. There are many reasons why interpersonal listening is challenging. We will examine those reasons in the section on understanding what makes up the listener's communication environment.

Finally, there is **impersonal listening,** which is listening to someone without a relationship. It is important to acknowledge that sometimes we need to listen to a person without having a relationship with him or her. If a police officer pulls us over, you need to listen to what she tells you. If the guy behind the cash register tells you that you owe $59.22, you need to listen in order to present him with the correct dollar amount. In both cases there isn't necessarily a relationship; however, we need to listen using one of our listening patterns.

EFFECTIVE AND INEFFECTIVE LISTENING PATTERNS

Every listening pattern has a positive and a negative side, as described in various scenarios in table 2.1. Below we will look at seven listening patterns. I am confident you can come up with other listening patterns and discuss them in class or online.

Advisory listening is when you listen to someone solely to give advice. Sometimes giving advice is appropriate and even wanted; however, it is not as often as one may believe. According to Shafir, "Unsolicited advice sends the message that the receiver is not capable of solving his own problems—it's the ultimate putdown."

Some things you should keep in mind before you give advice:

- Give only when asked.
- Stick to your point.
- Minimize your emotional advice.
- Leave out your biases and your judgment.
- Know that just because you give advice doesn't mean the other person has to take your advice. You are merely providing possible solutions or ways to deal with something.
- Never begin advice with, "If I were you . . . ." Instead say, "One possible idea is . . . " or "My thought is . . . ." Your advice needs to be based on what is best for the other person.

Evaluative listening is when you listen simply to evaluate, judge, or criticize what the person is telling you. It is way too easy for many of us to evaluate, judge, and criticize someone else; however, when it is happening to you, you realize how hard it is to actually understand what that person is saying to you.

Some things you should keep in mind before you evaluate someone else:

- Evaluate or criticize only when your input is invited.
- Consider your values compared to the values of the other person.
- Consider your experiences compared to the experiences of the other person.
- Most importantly—don't judge other people. It is a waste of time and is ultimately damaging to the relationship.

Active listening is verbally and nonverbally participating in the conversation as a listener. Active listening is typically favored over other listening patterns because you are showing the speaker that you are interested in what she has to say.

Some characteristics of an active listener:

- Nodding of the head to reinforce that you are listening and understanding.
- Paraphrasing what you hear for understanding, or clarity, and to improve memory.
- Taking notes while listening.
- Leaning forward to convey interest.
- Asking questions for clarity, as long as you are only seeking clarity and not interrupting.
- Uncrossing arms and legs with an open, relaxed body posture.

Passive listening is minimizing any verbal and nonverbal communication in a conversation; for the most part it is the opposite of active listening. With this listening pattern you are actually listening; however, others may not feel like you are listening. You may not have any eye contact, you may have your body turned away, or you may not be verbally or nonverbally responding to what the person is saying to you.

"I thought listening was something you did if you wanted to; however, I found out that you have to *learn* to listen effectively."
—Felicia Jackson

Pseudo-listening is pretending to listen when you are not actually listening. This commonly happens if you are trying to do two things at once. For example, maybe you are talking on the phone while you are trying to watch television; or you are cooking dinner while your children are trying to tell you about their day at school. With this listening pattern you usually you get caught in your pseudo-listening and someone gets their feelings hurt, or you miss something important.

 **Defensive listening** is listening simply to defend yourself, your ideas, or your ego. You may listen defensively because you feel like that is how people listen to you, you feel like you are not being heard by others, or you feel like your pride is being damaged. Sometimes children listen defensively out of frustration because they feel like they are not being heard. This goes back to the philosophy of "children are to be seen and not heard." Some of you can relate to this philosophy because that is how you were raised, and it may explain why you currently have some of the listening patterns that you do.

Critical listening is listening to analyze, assess, and validate the messages being sent. You will find this can be similar to defensive listening, if you are not careful with your intentions. This type of listening most often occurs in the classroom. As you are reading your text and listening to your professor, you need to consider the messages that are being sent, and analyze and assess the authors' and professor's perceptive, intention, and so on. This will either increase or decrease the message; however, either way it will help you understand and personalize the messages.

Listening Pattern	One Perspective	Another Perspective
Advisory listening	A friend has an important decision to make and has asked you to brainstorm possible resolutions. Together you two come up with several possibilities and *your friend* chooses the one that he thinks is best.	Your sister calls you up to tell you that she is engaged to her long-term boyfriend. You do not like this guy and immediately begin telling her what a mistake she is making. She hangs up on you and doesn't return your calls.
Evaluative listening	A friend tells you about a decision that she made and immediately you know it was a bad decision. However, since she tends to be aggressive, nobody is willing to speak up and tell her the decision was bad. You decide to take the risk and tell her your opinions about the decision she made.	You call your grandfather to tell him that you have decided to drop out of college to travel around the world. Immediately he begins telling you how difficult it will be to come back to college after leaving, how you won't make enough money to live without a college degree, and how this is simply a bad decision.
Active listening	Someone you are trying to get to know wants to tell you about something that recently happened to him. As you listen to him, you ask questions and paraphrase what he said for clarification. At the same time, you use effective eye contact and nod your head to show that you understand what he is telling you.	Your wife is telling about her day; you are making a conscious effort to listen. You use effective eye contact, nod your head, and turn your body toward her to show you are interested. This is new behavior for you and your wife thinks you are making fun of her. Since you normally do not show her you are listening, she gets very upset with your new behaviors.
Passive listening	A friend has had a tough day and she wants to tell you about it. You sit and listen, while not saying a word and using little eye contact. You are not doing anything else and your friend genuinely appreciates simply being able to vent about the day's events.	A friend is having "girl trouble." He calls you up and wants you to hear about the drama going on in his love life. You have the phone to your ear, but do not say a word. You don't say "un-huh" or "wow – I can't believe that." You say nothing and your friend thinks you're not listening, even though you are listening.

(continued)

TABLE 2.1
Continued

Listening Pattern	One Perspective	Another Perspective
Pseudo-listening	Similar to passive listening, your friend needs someone to listen. He recently got into an argument with his boss, and he is very angry. You look at him, as he vents, and you nod your head while he talks. However, while you are pretending to listen you are thinking about how you like your boss. Your friend is relieved that you are there and that he was able to vent.	Similar to passive listening, and using the scenario above, your friend hears a television in the background. Initially you were listening; however, now that the commercials are over you tend to "zone out" and focus more on the TV. Your friend asks you a question about what he just said. You weren't listening and try to stumble through an answer.
Defensive listening	You missed a day of work because your two-year-old son is ill. When you return to work your boss says to you, "How is your excuse, oops, I mean your kid?" You boss begins telling you about how he enjoys the single life and how he is happy he does not have children. While listening to him, you are trying to decide how to defend yourself as a parent and how you do not like to miss work but sometimes it is necessary.	You are a soccer player and have enjoyed the sport for many years. Your friends think that it is a "sissy" game and they are consistently ridiculing you for playing the sport. Whenever the topic of soccer comes up with you and your friends, you immediately want to protect your ego and defend your sport. Therefore, you interrupt them as they make comments, you roll your eyes, and sometimes you even storm off while they are talking.
Critical listening	You get to class on time, you are happy you got enough sleep last night, you get out your paper and pen, your mind is open, and you are focused on your professor. As your professor discusses the chapter you read last night, you consider what she is telling you and you compare it with what you read. You ask some questions, as you are assessing the validity of the information being presented.	You get to class on time, but you hate this class. You think the professor is opinionated and you do not agree with her opinions (you do not want to either). You did not read the chapter last night because you think this class is a breeze; however, it would have been an enjoyable blow-off class with a different professor. The professor begins discussing a theory you know a little about, so you ask a few "analytical" questions, just to show that you know a little something about this discussion. You assess her response and quickly decide that her response is invalid.

 Now that we have looked at the differences between hearing and listening, the types of listening, and listening patterns, it is time to pause and reflect on what you have read. Consider the following questions and write down some notes in the space provided:

1. What didn't you know about the things you have read so far?

2. What surprised you the most about what you have read so far?

3. With what you've read so far, what don't you understand?

4. Is there anything you don't agree with, or is there anything you need more information about?

"It takes more than just hearing someone. When you are listening the mind and the body have to work together."
—Vickie Rockwell

> "I consider listening an art form. You can hear things, but you must
> be aware of what the person is saying, you cannot assume you
> already know what they will say, don't put something in
> to the statement that isn't there. You must be attentive,
> open-minded, willing to hear what they have to say. It is not
> easy to listen. For some, it takes a great deal of effort."
>
> —Diana Shirk

A LISTENER'S COMMUNICATION ENVIRONMENT

A **listener's communication environment** is your perception of a communication situation, which determines how you will listen in any given situation. There are four major areas of a listener's communication environment: internal and external noise, your expectations, your learned behaviors, and the development of your response. Figure 2.1 gives you a visual idea of the listener's communication environment and the listening process

Internal and external noise were defined in chapter 1; now let's look at some examples regarding how they influence our listening patterns. Some examples of internal noise (IN) are:

- Preoccupation with the self
- Negative self-talk
- Preconceived ideas about the other person or the environment
- Stereotyping
- Values, beliefs, and attitudes
- Prejudices
- Biases
- Intimidation
- Thinking about what you want to say

Your internal noise, or the thoughts in your head, can easily become external noise (EN). Let's examine how:

- Say you have a poor *attitude* (IN) about what the person is saying, so you begin *swearing* (EN). This is external noise because it disrupts the other person's thought process and it can be offensive.
- Say you are *thinking about what you want to say* (IN) because your friend has sparked your interest, so you *interrupt* (EN) him to tell him what is on your mind. The interruption can be in the form of verbal and/or nonverbal communication. Due to your interruption, your friend may forget what he was saying and in turn may become angry with you.
- Say the president of the college walks up to you and wants your opinion about a new school policy. You know it is the president of the college and immediately you are *intimidated* (IN), so you begin *fidgeting* (EN) with your hands and playing with your hair. The president sees this and thinks you are not interested or do not care about the new policy. You do not get your ideas heard.

FIGURE 2.1
The listening process.

A Listener's Communication Environment

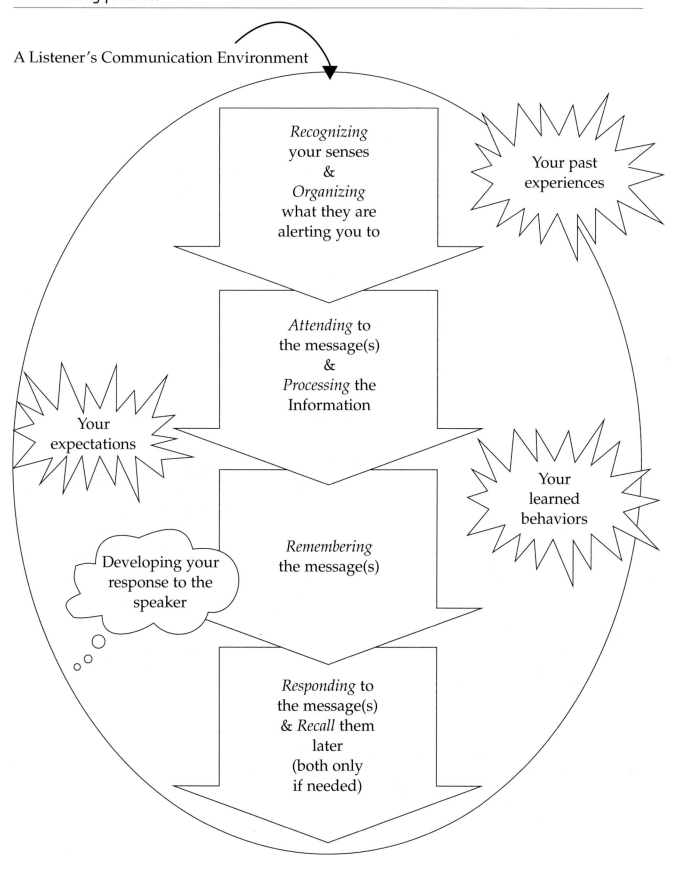

Internal noise *comes from* or *leads to* external noise. The preceding examples showed us how our internal noise led to the external noise. Now we will examine some examples where the reverse happens—our external noise will lead to internal noise.

External Noise	leads to	Internal Noise
Suit on a man or woman	you believe	business person, going to a job interview, wealthy, or a snob
Ripped shirt	you believe	slob and doesn't care about appearance or what happened and are you hurt
Nose piercing	you believe	young and disrespectful or cool and hip
Tattoo	you believe	no money and lower status or cool, hip, and eccentric

Whatever your internal noise is, either positive or negative, it is still noise. External and internal noise is just that—noise—and it will minimize the effectiveness of the listening.

Finally, and most importantly, you need to remember that in a communication scenario, the speaker usually becomes the listener and the listener will become the speaker. This is what makes the process interactive. Therefore, you have to learn (1) how to switch between being a speaker and being a listener, and (2) how to know when it is your turn to be the speaker and when it is your turn to be the listener.

> "I never understood the difference between hearing and listening before I took this class. Hearing happens without even trying; whereas, listening is more of a choice. I can hear my mom telling me to clean my room, but whether I actually listen is another story."
>
> —Samantha Stream

THE LISTENING PROCESS

Could we be more effective listeners? Absolutely! Is listening important? One hundred percent! Since there are so many mediums for communication (telephones, fax machines, cell phones, email, etc.), don't we already listen effectively? Nope, we just talk more! As with the many aspects of communication that we discuss in this text, how we listen is cultural. One of the ways we can be more effective listeners is by learning how the listening process works.

Before we discuss the listening process, you should know a few statistics about listening. Various research studies have shown that we communicate about 45 to 50 percent of our waking time. Some argue, however, that if you include all three forms of communication (interpersonal, intrapersonal, and extrapersonal) we listen about 80 percent of our waking time. Knowing that, how *effectively* do you think we listen during that time? Less than 50 percent?

You're getting there—about 25 percent of our daily listening can be considered effective. Of course, that depends on a few factors—who is involved in the communication, how many, how often, is it important to you, is it relevant to you, and so on. If you refer back to the communication process (figure 1.1) in chapter 1, you will remember that a lot goes into communication.

> "Listening helped me immensely in my own relationships,
> not only with my husband but also with my children.
> I learned how to listen more effectively."
>
> —Cathy Harris

The process of listening is more involved than one may think. Because we listen every day, many think we don't have to work very hard at it. That idea is both right and wrong. We don't have to work hard at listening if we have developed the skill and regularly use the four steps in the process. However, if we do not listen effectively (for whatever reason), then we do have to work hard at developing our new skill. The listening process must link together, similar to how creeks link to streams, which link to rivers, which finally link to our oceans. Everything is a part of a larger picture. However, in Shafir's book, she describes listening as involving a focus "on the *process* of listening versus the *payoff*." Let's examine the process and know that our payoff will come in time.

The process of listening involves four major steps. The first step in listening is *recognizing* your senses and *organizing* them to understand what they are alerting to. This may be your eyes telling you to see something, your ears telling you to hear something, and so on. When you become acutely aware of your senses, you are able to listen effectively on many levels. To understand how you use your senses, refer back to chapter 1 and the discussion on channels in the communication process.

The second step is to *attend* to the message and *process* the information. Here you are drawing your attention to the stimuli and determining what is appropriate to focus on while you listen. When you attend to the message you are able to concentrate effectively on the stimuli, and process it. For example, you decide if you should listen to the details of what someone is saying, or using another example, you decide if you should pay attention to the directions on a billboard.

The third step of the listening process is to *remember* the message. To put something into your memory requires three things: (1) decoding the message; (2) storing it in to your short-term or long-term memory, only accomplished with practice; and (3) learning how to retrieve that information when necessary.

The final step of the listening process is to *respond* to the message (only if needed). Many people believe that you can respond to a message prior to remembering the message, this is not true. When you respond to the message you have moved on to another thought, maybe even a new communication scenario. You will not be able to recall some of the important details of the original message.

LISTENING AFFECTS YOU PHYSIOLOGICALLY AND PSYCHOLOGICALLY

Psychologically (the mental barriers), it is difficult to listen when you are faced with someone who acts like a blamer, a complainer, a rambler, a gossiper, a competitor, a name dropper, and so on. There are many things that people do, when they are communicating, that makes it challenging to listen. A few things that people do:

- Use too much jargon
- Use too many details
- Overuse "um" or "uh"—filler words
- Have a lack of eye contact
- Go over the allotted speaking time in a presentation
- Use too many examples
- Overuse **"I"** statements—or just talk about himself or herself
- Speak in a monotone voice

It can also be physiologically (the biological barriers) difficult to listen if you are faced with attention deficit disorder, high blood pressure, extreme stress, extreme depression, ulcers, or a shortness of breath.

SO WHAT DO YOU DO? We all will face the situations or people described above. Now what do you do? I am sorry to say there isn't a magic pill or an instant remedy. In the following "Consider This" box I have seven questions for you to consider about listening in tough situations. Answer the questions and then discuss your answers in class.

MOVING TOWARD EFFECTIVE LISTENING

According to Shafir, "Listening isn't necessarily a technique to be learned; rather, it's about reaching inside yourself and using the resources that are already there." If you want to listen effectively in your relationships (family, friends, colleagues, or even strangers in the checkout lane), you must first create that developed awareness of your mind and body, or intrapersonally listen. Next, you should determine your answers to the following questions and decide how you can minimize your listening shortcomings.

1. Do you stop listening, or begin thinking about other things, if the conversation isn't interesting?
2. Do you stop listening, or begin thinking about other things, if you feel like the conversation doesn't apply to you?
3. Do you stop listening, or begin thinking about other things, if you think you have heard that information or story before?
4. Do you get enough rest at night, so you can listen without dozing off?
5. Do you eat right and drink enough water, so you can listen without feeling fatigue?
6. Do you exercise, so you can listen without feeling tired or feeling like you cannot concentrate?
7. Do you have relationships with only those when you genuinely care about, or are you friends with anyone, just for the sake of having a lot of friends?
8. Do you pretend to listen even if you are not really listening?
9. Do you listen for the meaning behind what the speaker is "really" saying?
10. If you do not understand something that someone said, do you ask for clarity?
11. Do you listen without bias, judgment, or criticism?
12. Do you ask the other person questions to ensure they understand what you are saying?
13. Do you take notes when you need to remember something?

Become an effective listener:

- Breathe—or to take it one step further—meditate. Take a time out to intrapersonally listen every day. You would be amazed at what your body is trying to tell you. You have the ability to prevent illness, if you would listen to your body. A disease is merely a "dis" ease of the body, according to Louise Hay, author of many self-help books. Learn to enjoy and appreciate the silence.
- Concentrate on the present activity, however small or mindless it may seem. Find something beautiful or mind-worthy in the activity and appreciate it. Do not worry about the past or the future, simply focus on what you are currently doing. We can learn from the past; however, it is gone, and we must not dwell on it. We can create goals for the future; however, it is not here yet and in order to fulfill those goals we must be mindful of our present.
- Pay attention to how you are processing information, and do not worry about the end result. This is especially true in times of conflict. When you finally learn how you process the information, you can then learn how to improve how you process it. With all of that to do, who has time to worry about the end result? The end result will come—whether you worry about it or not!
- Take a pause before you respond to what someone has said to you. Why are we always in such a rush to respond? The person is not going to leave if you take a pause, and if that person does leave, then s/he didn't care about what you had to say anyway! Focus more on the listening and less on the responding.
- Minimize your emotional involvement when it is necessary and appropriate. Develop your empathy skills. However, remember that not everything needs your emotion. That is too much to ask of any one person.
- Treat listening as a challenging mental activity. Figure out what you can learn or how this could help you become a better person, no matter how small, and appreciate that you have the ability to listen.

CONSIDER THIS FINAL IDEA

Listening to the garbage collector is the same as listening to the president. I am sure the garbage collector would appreciate it if we all believed that idea. We are all equals. Yes—some have more education, more prestige, higher self-esteem, and even more money. However, some have more heart, more forgiveness, more understanding, and more patience. The luckiest ones have found a way to balance them all and understand the payoff.

"Listening is a skill and is not something everyone can do effectively. I learned that I am a good listener."

—Myra Howard

In closing, it is time to pause and reflect on what you have read. Consider the following questions and write down some notes in the space provided:

1. What didn't you know about the things you have read so far?

2. What surprised you the most about what you have read so far?

3. With what you've read so far, what don't you understand?

4. Is there anything you don't agree with or is there anything you need more information about?

LISTENING TO YOUR BODY

By Gail Raborn

You know that familiar scratchy, achy feeling in your throat and the heavy tiredness that pervades your body? It's a cold coming on. Unfortunately, you have no time to rest and recover. You might even feel angry at your body for conking out on you. Maybe you pop an antihistamine and take an aspirin so you can go back to work; after all, you're not going to let a little cold stop you, are you? The last thing you want to do is admit that this bout of illness is your body's way of telling you your life is out of balance and that you need to make some changes in your lifestyle, your relationships, or even your job.

I learned years ago to listen to the message an illness can send when I had a problem with laryngitis. My episodes always seemed to occur just before a workshop I was scheduled to lead. So without guilt I'd cancel the workshop, lie abed with cayenne tea and my favorite novel, and keep my mouth shut until I healed. Several canceled workshops later, I began to see a pattern and recognized a darker reason for my lost voice than a simple infection. For behind laryngitis lurked the terror of failing, of inadequacy as a workshop leader! Resolution of those fears has prevented any further loss of voice. For fear, like all negative emotions, weakens the immune system.

Then there was the woman I worked with who couldn't get pregnant. Yet fertility tests showed that she and her husband were both normal. Regression work to reveal the source of this problem revealed a tragic story of grief and remorse over the accidental death of her two-year-old son several years before. Amidst sobs, she listened to her body tell her that her undeserved grief for the accident had made her sterile, and that it was time to forgive herself since she could have done nothing to prevent the accident. With forgiveness, came renewed fertility. When I saw her a year later, she was holding her newborn child in her arms.

Sickness and injury can be symbolic of feelings you just can't verbalize, like developing neck pain when you've got a boss or wife who's "a pain in the neck" or getting an ulcer when there's a situation you just can't stomach. Sometimes illness is just your body's message to stop and rest, nurture yourself, stop pushing so hard. Or your body may be telling you your life is devoid of meaning. A woman I knew healed her second bout of breast cancer when she realized she needed radical change to find the joy and meaning her life lacked. Instead of more surgery, she cut out of her life her unhappy marriage and her hated job. She then jumped with both feet into her lifelong fantasy of writing a book while living on a Greek island. Twenty years later, she's healthily and happily writing away while listening to the pounding surf.

Of course, understanding the message for change that might lie behind your illness or injury does not guarantee physical healing. But the probability is dramatically increased once you bring your life back into balance. In any case, the emotional and spiritual healing that results is its own reward.

How do you listen to your body, you ask? Guided imagery is one of my favorite techniques. Start with a relaxation exercise, then allow an image to come to mind that represents your symptom or body part. Don't worry if the image isn't totally clear. Talk with it to find the message behind your illness or injury and discover what changes in your life are necessary to speed healing. The change might be minor, like getting better walking shoes, or major, like changing your job. Later you can muse over the information you received during the imaging and decide if it seemed valid and vital to implement. If you get stuck, find a hypnotherapist, healer, or therapist who knows how to guide you through the process. An excellent book for learning guided imagery is Dr. Martin Rossman's "Healing Yourself."

So the next time you feel a cold coming on, get a headache, or injure your back, talk to your body. Bodies don't lie. Listen to yours and you'll find your life healing in amazing ways.

Name: _____ Date: _____

QUESTIONS FOR DISCUSSION—

LISTENING TO YOUR BODY
by Gail Raborn

1. What are your top 3 reactions to this article?

2. Why is it important to listen to your body? Consider psychologically and physiologically.

(Questions continued on back)

3. How can you listen to your body effectively and regularly?

4. Other thoughts about the article?

ARTICLE FOR DISCUSSION—

LISTENING

By Heather Antonissen

Looking for answers? Seeking connection? Wanting release? So many of our deepest needs are based on the ability to hear and to understand; and while this may seem simple to do, most of us struggle with this basic skill. Read this month's article to see how our yoga practice can help us develop the ability to truly listen.

Listening. Each day we experience a constant flow of sound, yet little of it is truly heard. As you read this, stop for a moment and listen. How many sounds do you hear—clocks, traffic, vents, speech?—and beneath those sounds there is still more—the breath, the pulse inside the ear, even our thoughts. There is a constant symphony of sound that plays on, largely unheard.

Of course, it is impossible to be aware of every sound we hear. Our brains have evolved to make unconscious judgments about the stimuli received from our senses to determine what is important and what is not. This ability enables us to focus and concentrate; yet this skill for most of us has been developed to such an extent, that we are able to tune out most sounds without being truly aware of them. We become desensitized to the constant flow of sound and thought. We learn to be with more and more noise both externally and internally. We become accustomed to a high level of distraction and become unable to hear or understand clearly. We are wrapped up in the rush of sound and are pulled away from the quiet center of knowing.

Listening is a fundamental part of communication and connection to one's self,

one's environs and other beings. There are two components to listening, that of hearing and that of understanding. The difficulty is that as we have become accustomed to hearing without listening, we are often not able to truly listen when it is required as thoughts, sights and other sounds often distract us. And as we are unable to truly listen, we are not able to truly understand. We are not free to let go of our perspective to understand from where the other is speaking. Our perceptive also distorts our perception of reality. We interpret our experiences through our biases and fail to comprehend other truths that may be present.

Part of our yoga practice is to re-learn how to truly listen. By quieting our minds, and really listening to our breath, we start to become aware of how much is being said both by our bodies and our minds. The breath becomes a screen over which our thoughts pass, and we are able to observe what is being thought and where those thoughts come from without judgment. As we observe our thoughts, we are also able to observe our bodies and hear quiet messages that had previously gone unnoticed. We begin to re-evaluate what is important and to listen with new awareness and clarity. We become aware of what we need as we listen to what our bodies tell us. Suddenly, it becomes easy to choose that which promotes wellness and happiness—breathing, quietness, eating and resting well, openness, compassion and love. No longer do these actions arise out of discipline or training, they are simply a following of what that inner knowing suggests to do; and as we follow what that inner voice suggests, we are able to hear more keenly, both internally and externally. We are able to listen better and be more open, more accepting and compassionate and grounded. We are no longer looking for answers or seeking release. We wait and listen and hear.

As you practice, both on and off the yoga mat, listen. Listen to the breath, flowing in and out. Let it quiet you; let it cleanse you. As you move throughout your day, try and come back to taking a moment to really listen—to be open and to connect with every sound around you. You will begin to hear things you've never heard before, answers you have been seeking. Let go of judgments, quiet the mind, and listen.

Become more quiet to hear more clearly.

Name: _____ Date: _____

QUESTIONS FOR DISCUSSION—

LISTENING
by Heather Antonissen

1. What are your top 3 reactions to this article?

2. Is yoga a practical way for you to learn how to listen? Why/why not?

(Questions continued on back)

3. Which of your senses do you think you use when you practice yoga?

4. Other thoughts about the article?

Name: _____ Date: _____

INDIVIDUAL ACTIVITY #1
Develop Your Intrapersonal Listening Skills

PURPOSE—

In order to develop your listening skills, you must first assess your abilities at the current time. This activity will give you an opportunity to practice your intrapersonal listening abilities.

PROCEDURE—

Find a quiet spot outside (on your school campus, a park, your backyard, etc.). You are to simply listen to your environment. While you are listening you are to do two things: (1) Write down everything that you hear, and (2) write down how you feel. As you participate in this activity consider all of your senses—see, hear, smell, touch, and taste. Be mindful of all of your senses. Whatever you are feeling, write all of your feelings down. Use the space below and the back of this page.

FOLLOW-UP—

Discuss the activity with a friend, with a group in class, or with the entire class. Discuss what you heard and how you felt. Finally, discuss why you think you felt the way you did; and if you had a lot of negative thoughts, discuss why you felt that way and if you can find a way to make the experience more positive, if you had to do it again.

Name: _____ Date: _____

INDIVIDUAL ACTIVITY #2
Working Through the Listening Process

PURPOSE—

To give you an opportunity to experience and focus on how the listening process works. Once we become aware of the listening process, and see how we go through the process in everyday communication, we are more likely to develop more effective communication.

PROCEDURE—

In the space provided, or on another sheet of paper (as instructed), describe at least three communication scenarios that you experienced over a two- or three-day period. Give a description of the situation, describe the people involved, and finally discuss the steps of the listening process. The focus should be a detailed description of your going through the steps in the listening process.

FOLLOW-UP—

Discuss the activity with your classmates. Analyze each other's scenarios and discuss how the listening process could have been improved, or what made it successful. Finally, discuss if the listening process was successful, what made it successful and how we can maintain a successful level of listening.

Name: _____ Date: _____

GROUP ACTIVITY #1
Develop Your Interpersonal Listening Skills

PURPOSE—

To work with another member of the class and see how effectively you can listen to one another.

PROCEDURE—

Pair up with one other person in the class, preferably someone you don't know, so you can get to know someone new today. Each of you need to have one 8 1/2" x 11" sheet of blank paper or use the back of this page. Determine who will be person 1 and who will be person 2. Next, you are to turn your chairs (or desks) so you are back to back. This activity will be done by listening only; you cannot look at your partner until the follow-up.

Person 1—You are to draw a picture, using your entire sheet of paper. Remember, your partner cannot see your drawing. This is not art class, so just have fun and draw whatever comes to mind.

Person 2—While your partner is drawing the picture, you are to simply sit and wait for your partner to finish drawing.

Next, without looking at each other, person 2 will attempt to draw the exact same picture that person 1 drew.

Person 2—you may ask as many and whatever questions you want, as you attempt to draw the exact same picture as person 1. The only rule is that you cannot look at your partner or look at your partner's drawing.

Person 1—you may only answer questions. You are not allowed to offer any more information, simply answer the specific question that was asked of you.

FOLLOW-UP—

Now it is time to see the picture that your partner drew. Compare your pictures to determine the similarities and the differences. Discuss why the pictures are either (1) so different and what happened, or (2) what you did that allowed them to look similar.

Finally, look around at the other pictures. As a class, discuss how successfully the activity went, and what could have made it more successful.

GROUP ACTIVITY #2
How Would You Respond?

PURPOSE—

To develop your vocabulary of advice and empathy. Many times we hear the statements below and we don't know what to say or what is appropriate to say. This activity will allow you to hear the perspectives of others; therefore, you will leave with a new sense of how to deal with the situations if they come up.

PROCEDURE—

With a group of your classmates, discuss how you would react to the following statements. Look at the statements from two different perspectives: (1) the person making the statement is looking for advice, and (2) the person is not looking for advice; rather s/he is looking for empathy. Write your response in the space provided:

1. "My husband is cheating on me with his secretary."

2. "My wife thinks I should quit my job."

3. "I gained 30 pounds during my pregnancy and I feel ugly."

(Questions continued on back)

4. "My significant other and I argue all the time."

5. "I love my job but I hate our boss."

6. "How do I look in this outfit?"

7. "My children are the biggest brats. They get on my last nerve."

8. "Our president doesn't have a clue what he is doing."

9. "My best friend is a liar and I do not trust her anymore."

10. {Make up your own statement here.}

Follow-Up—

Compare your answers with the answers of the other groups. Discuss how much of your reaction or advice was based on personal experience or emotion. Discuss how your responses could have been improved or better developed.

CROSSWORD PUZZLE
Reviewing the Terms

ACROSS

1. listening and trying to give advice
8. listening to without a relationship
9. protecting your ego while listening
10. listening to yourself
11. a psychological process
12. listening to analyze, assess, and validate the messages being sent

DOWN

1. verbally and nonverbally participating in the conversation
2. minimum listening participation in a conversation
3. judging what someone is saying while listening
4. a physiological process
5. how you tend to listen to someone
6. fake listening
7. listening in a relationship

Name: _____ Date: _____

CHAPTER QUIZ
Reviewing the Chapter

TRUE OR FALSE

_____ 1. Listening is a natural process.

_____ 2. Feedback is not an important element of listening.

_____ 3. We use all of our senses when listening.

_____ 4. Sometimes we have to listen because it is important for the relationship.

_____ 5. Intrapersonal listening is about being silent with your thoughts.

_____ 6. Listening to give advice is always a good thing to do.

_____ 7. Listening is a very challenging activity for many people.

_____ 8. Active listening is when you minimize your verbal and nonverbal communication.

_____ 9. Thinking about what you want to say while someone is talking to you is an example of internal noise.

_____ 10. Taking notes while someone is talking is always a good thing to do.

_____ 11. Making assumptions about what a person is "really" trying to say is not an example of internal noise.

_____ 12. In the listening process, you should remember a message before you respond to the message.

_____ 13. A stomach ache is an example of a physiological challenge when you are trying to listen.

_____ 14. An effective listener will pause to decode the message before he responds.

_____ 15. Most people listen to others best when they feel like they can relate to the story.

_____ 16. Paraphrasing is an example of feedback.

_____ 17. When you actively listen, your body temperature rises.

_____ 18. When you actively listen, your palms do not get moist.

CHAPTER 3

YOUR PERCEPTION IS YOUR REALITY

KEY TERMS

Attribution theory
Closure
Complacency
Cultural influences
Familiarity
Frame of reference
Halo effect
Horn effect
Interaction constructs

Interpretation
Organization
Perception
Perceptual awareness
Physical constructs
Physiological
    influences
Psychological
    constructs

Psychological
    influences
Role constructs
Selection
Selective attention
Selective exposure
Shared perception
Singularity
Social influences

CHAPTER OBJECTIVES

1. Understand how perception works and it's role in the communication process
2. Identify and apply the perception process
3. Identify the major aspects of perception
4. Understand perceptual limitations and how we can achieve shared perception
5. Describe and practice perception checking
6. Understand the influences on perception
7. Practice skills for improving your perception.

Several students in my Interpersonal Communication class were given this photo and asked to describe what they saw. Here are their responses:

"This is a private prep school in Britain with students and faculty engaged in a game of croquet. It is leisure time, somewhat windy, and played on the school grounds."
    — Diana Shirk

"Looks like a bunch of rich people in England playing a foreign sport. The well organized background gives a feeling of orderly nature, making it look like a posh place."
    — Chung Li Wu

"Kids at school in London or somewhere playing golf or putt-putt or some kind of game."

—Myra Howard

"This is a picture of people playing croquet. I see five people with pretty buildings in the background. The men and women look old and the place doesn't look like Ohio. It reminds me of San Francisco, at least the buildings in the back do. The picture is relaxing to look at and the game does not look competitive at all."

—Samantha Stream

"I see people playing croquet on a roof. They're in England. It's windy."

—Felicia Jackson

"It looks like a British family is playing a game of croquet. It appears to me that maybe the daughter is ahead of the father, while the mother waits."

—Vickie Rockwell

"Some elderly people are playing croquet together in a city."

—Ashley Kolp

The responses from that one picture are examples of how much our perception varies from one individual to another. We hear this all the time when witnesses to a crime are asked to recall an event and each person has a different version of the same events. We do not always recognize that perceptual differences occur all of the time, even when two people are discussing an event that is going on right before their very eyes. During this chapter we will examine what perception is, how the process works, how to achieve shared perception, how various factors influence our perception, and how we can become more perceptually aware.

PERCEPTION DEFINED

"Many of us feel exhausted, burned out, and ill from all of the demands and pressures in our lives. We think that the stress we experience comes primarily from the external world," according to Loretta LaRoche in her book, *Relax—You May Only Have a Few Minutes Left.* "However, most stress really comes from how we interpret, label, and judge the world."

Perception is primarily an intrapersonal phenomenon. However, as you read in the quotation above, most of the time we blame the external world, or we blame other people, for the way we perceive others and our environment. Perception affects all of our relationships in some way, shape, or form. Have you ever heard statements like the following?

- That is not what I said to you!
- That is not the way things happened; you don't know what you are talking about.
- Why don't you understand what I am telling you?
- He doesn't understand me.
- She expects me to read her mind.
- I know he saw what happened; he just won't admit.
- The papers are right there in front of you; do you need glasses?

Perception is a process of developing awareness through your senses to create meaningful experiences. How you process, and in turn then create, your perception is your ultimate reality. To that end, there is no one true reality. Everyone has their own image of the world and their experiences within the world. This partly explains why people have so many different responses when someone asks, "What do you think of our world today?"

"We know the world in different ways, from different stances, and each of the ways in which we know it produces different structures or representations, or, indeed, 'realities.' As we grow to adulthood (at least in Western culture), we become increasingly adept at seeing the same set of events from *multiple* perspectives or stances and at entertaining the results as, so to speak, alternative possible worlds," according to Jerome Bruner in his book *Actual Minds, Possible Worlds.*

THE PERCEPTION PROCESS

How do we create this unique reality? How do we develop such diverse perspectives of the same situation? Let's answer these questions as we explore the process of perception. See figure 3.1 for a summary of the perception process, and figures 3.2 and 3.3 for examples of the perception process.

As an adult the perception process is typically an unconscious process, until something happens that initiates the conscious mind. Factors that bring perception to the conscious level include:

- A sudden change or event
- Being faced with something unusual/strange/frightening
- An extreme change
- A smell/taste/sound that you were not expecting

The perception process is much different for children. They are creating many first-time experiences; therefore, there are many unexpected, strange, unusual, and frightening events. An interesting activity (maybe even as part of the research project in appendix C) would be to compare the perception process between children and adults.

There are three steps in the perception process: selection, organization, and interpretation.

Step One—Selection

We use **selection** to pick information, people, and experiences that we will pay attention to because it is impossible to pay attention to everything that is going on at any given time. For example as you are reading this section, try using all of your senses. First sit outside to *smell* the fresh air, while *listening* to the sounds around you, as you are *looking* at and reading the text, while *feeling* the material of your clothing, and having something with you to *eat*. What you will find is that (1) it is challenging to use all of your senses at the same time and (2) you have to make a conscious effort to even attempt to complete any or some of the tasks. We do not typically put that much effort into creating our daily perceptions.

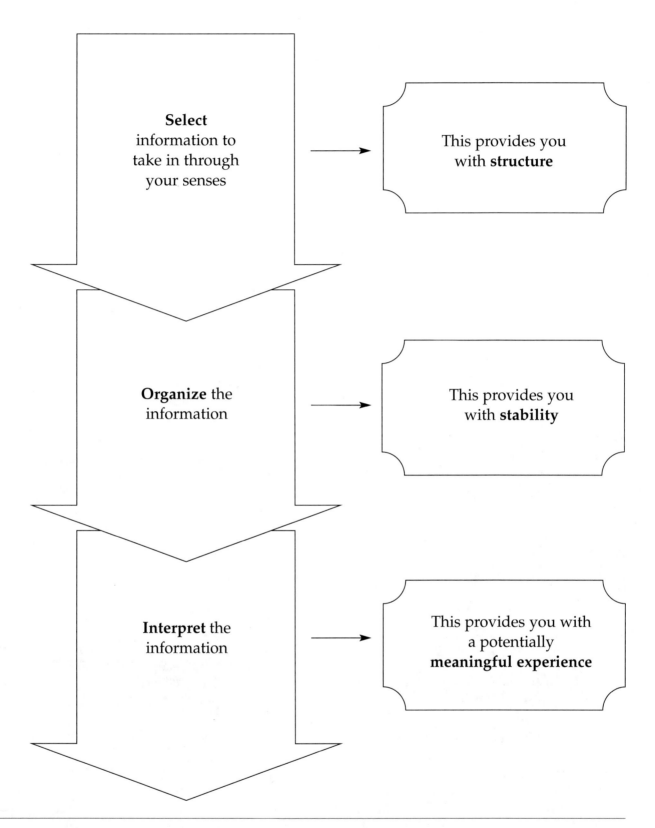

Select
information to
take in through
your senses

This provides you
with **structure**

Organize the
information

This provides you
with **stability**

Interpret the
information

This provides you with
a potentially
meaningful experience

FIGURE 3.1.
The perception process.

Typically we expose ourselves to people, animals, and environments that confirm what we know to be true; this is called **selective exposure.** For example, if you are very hungry and you are in a hurry, you are more likely to find a restaurant that you have been to before because you know what to expect. Another example is if you need to go to the grocery store, it is likely that you will get what you need from the store that you regularly go to, because you expect that you will know how to find the things that you need.

Another aspect of the selection process is selective attention. **Selective attention** is when you choose to listen or tune in to stimuli. For example, you may not realize that the radio is on until you hear a song that you like. Then you find yourself singing or tapping to the music; once the song is over you begin to tune out the radio and focus on something else. Another example is when you are talking on the phone and watching television at the same time. You can only consciously focus on or listen to one activity at a time; therefore, you will tune out either the television or the person on the phone until either one grabs your attention. A final example is when someone does something that is completely out of character for him or her. Your instructor may always be in a good mood, then one day you come to class and your instructor is in a very bad mood. Since this behavior is unusual, you choose not to pay attention to it or give it any merit.

The selection process ultimately provides you with structure, through selective exposure and selective attention. This structure is what creates your frame of reference. According to Gerald Wilson in his book *Let's Talk It Over,* a **frame of reference** is, "a set of interlocking observations, beliefs, values, and attitudes."

"This frame of reference is the basis for our understanding of people, events, and experiences. It has a structure in that we order our experiences to fit together in a way that is sensible to us. As we take in new information, we may use our frame of reference to process it in one of three ways: we may reject it because it doesn't fit with our frame of reference, we may use it to support the frame of reference, or we may use it to change the frame of reference," according to Wilson.

Step Two—Organization

The next step in the perception process is organization. In the **organization** step we are creating stability for each experience by arranging the information in a meaningful way. According to Peter Andersen in *Nonverbal Communication: Forms and Functions,* we organize our experiences into psychological, physical, role, and interaction constructs.

1. **Psychological constructs**—organizing people according to how you see their personality: generous, secure, smart, disability, etc.
2. **Physical constructs**—organizing people according to their appearance: beautiful or ugly, tall or short, fat, thin, or average, etc.

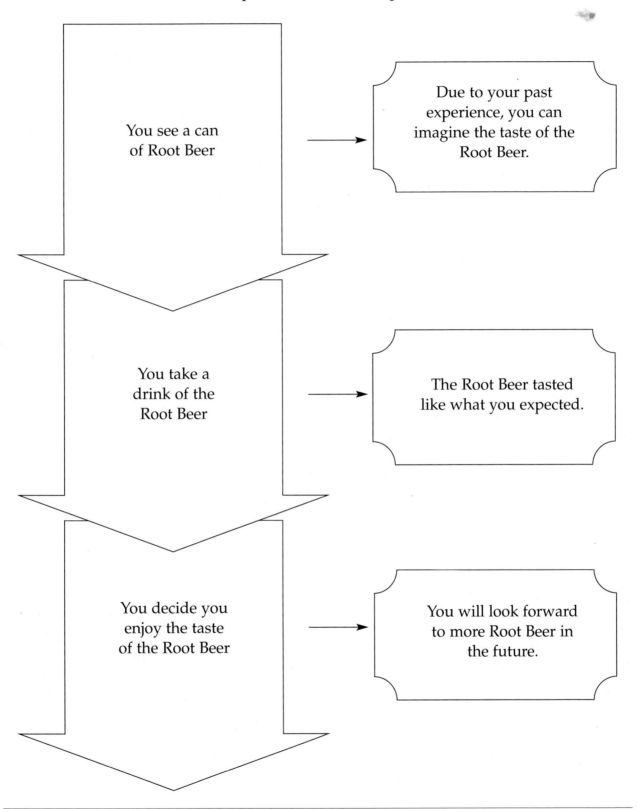

FIGURE 3.2.
Perception process example.

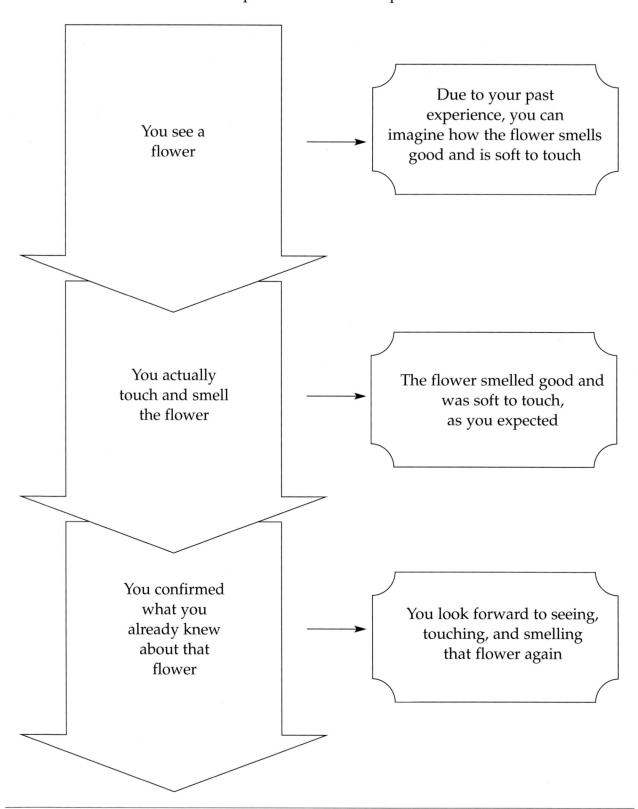

FIGURE 3.3.
Perception process example.

3. **Role constructs**—organizing people according to the role they play in your relationship: mother, father, teacher, doctor, etc.
4. **Interaction constructs**—organizing people according to your social interaction: kind, giving, boring, needy, etc.

When we organize people, animals, and environments in a way that creates stability for us, it makes the experience convenient, efficient, and easy to understand, and it nicely fits into our frame of reference. According to Wilson, "Frame of reference also provides stability for our perception. Rather than seeing our experiences as constantly shifting in response to various senses, perception within our frame of reference gives them a flowing quality."

Step Three—Interpretation

The final step in the perception process is **interpretation,** which is attaching meaning to our experiences. A major part of the interpretation step is evaluation, or creating some conclusions about what you experience, to add to your frame of reference. In turn you then know what to expect the next time you encounter that particular situation.

Another aspect of the interpretation step is closure. **Closure** is when you fill in the missing pieces or the gaps of information. Wilson tells us, "We are using closure when we add finishing touches to our perception of incomplete events by rearranging and filling in missing parts. We are also using closure when we draw inferences about an event from its bits and pieces, as when you finish another person's sentence or generalize about someone's character or behavior."

The final aspect of the interpretation step is to understand the attribution theory. The **attribution theory** says that we attempt to correlate specific behaviors and motives to what we experience. We have this need to understand why people do the things that they do. For example, men want to know why women go to the bathroom in groups; parents want to know why children break curfew knowing they will get disciplined; and tailgaters want to know why the people driving in front of them decide to drive 25 m.p.h. when the speed limit is 35 m.p.h. You probably cannot come up with a credible interpretation for any of the situations; regardless, people continue to try to explain the unexplainable.

SHARED PERCEPTION

If everyone sees things differently, then how can we ever get to a point where we communicate about the same experience? That is a good question. I am glad you were thinking about it (hey—it's my attempt at humor, give me a break). We can get to a point where we have a shared perception (see figure 3.4). With every experience that we have with other people, we both are processing information about one another in an attempt to create mutual understanding. The more we communicate with the other person and the more experiences we have with them, the larger our area of mutual understanding, or **shared perception.** Shared perception increases our stability and meaning in each relationship.

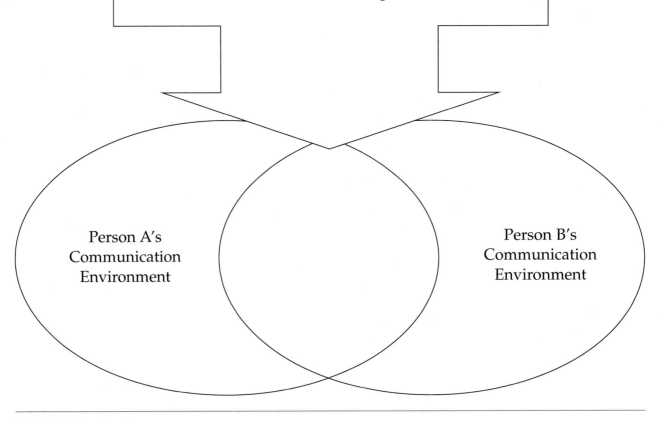

The area where the communication environments of person A and person B have overlapped, is the area where you have the highest chance for **shared perception.**

Refer back to chapter 1 for a complete diagram of the communication process.

Person A's Communication Environment

Person B's Communication Environment

FIGURE 3.4.
Shared perception.

 You are halfway done with this chapter; therefore, it is time to pause and reflect on what you have read. Consider the following questions and write down some notes in the space provided:

1. What didn't you know about the things you have read so far?

2. What surprised you the most about what you have read so far?

3. With what you've read so far, what don't you understand?

4. Is there anything you don't agree with, or is there anything you need more information about?

> "It is impossible to have 'perfect' perception because everyone perceives everything differently."
>
> —Ashley Kolp

CHECKING YOUR PERCEPTION

How many times do we actually take the time to check the accuracy of our perception? It is likely that you misunderstand something from a particular experience; however, are you willing to admit it? Perception-checking forces us to be accountable for our reactions to our experiences. Bill Marriott Sr., of Marriott Hotels, says, "People grow from making decisions and assuming responsibility for them."

Are you ready to begin assuming responsibility for the way you perceive other's behaviors and your experiences? Great! The perception checking process looks like this:

1. **Describe the behavior** or the experience—without judgment or evaluation.
2. **Provide at least two possible ways of interpreting** the behavior or experience.
3. **Ask for clarification** in interpreting the behavior or experience.

If you want to increase your shared or mutual perception of a behavior or an experience, you must practice perception-checking. Figure 3.5 has examples of the perception-checking process; however, I know it is important to have a variety of examples, so here are some more:

- When we were talking the other day I noticed that you seemed to have something else on your mind. Was there something you wanted to talk to me about or were you thinking about the big meeting you have tomorrow? Is there anything I can help with?
- For our trip to Texas I was thinking I would drive. If you want to drive you can, or we can share the driving. Do you have a preference?
- You have not called me lately. I figured you were working overtime or wrapped up in studying for finals. What's going on?
- When we went shopping today you bought the red dress. Did you buy it because I said that I liked it, because you liked it, or was there another reason?

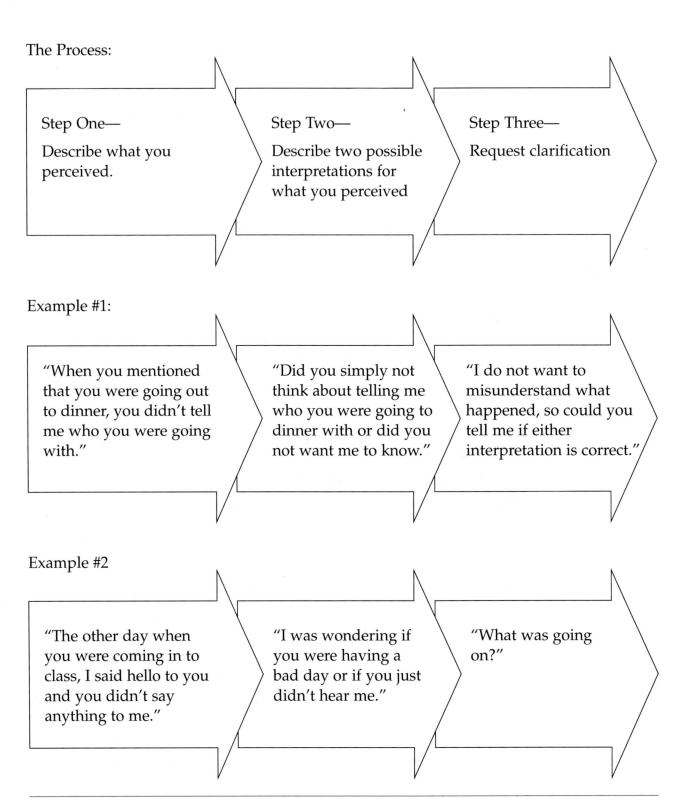

The Process:

Step One—
Describe what you perceived.

Step Two—
Describe two possible interpretations for what you perceived

Step Three—
Request clarification

Example #1:

"When you mentioned that you were going out to dinner, you didn't tell me who you were going with."

"Did you simply not think about telling me who you were going to dinner with or did you not want me to know."

"I do not want to misunderstand what happened, so could you tell me if either interpretation is correct."

Example #2

"The other day when you were coming in to class, I said hello to you and you didn't say anything to me."

"I was wondering if you were having a bad day or if you just didn't hear me."

"What was going on?"

FIGURE 3.5.
Perception checking.

THE GOOD, THE BAD, AND THE UGLY ON PERCEPTION

"It is obvious that, like everything else, money itself is neither good nor bad. To look at money as a moral issue is as absurd as it is to decide that airplanes are good or bad. We feel differently about airplanes when they are used to drop napalm bombs than when they are used to drop food supplies for starving people. Yet the planes are the same. The moral issue is in the intention of the user—not the plane itself," according to Ruth Ross in her book *Prospering Woman*.

Basically what Ross is saying is that *everything* has the potential to influence, limit, and hinder your perceptual experience. In her example she shows us how easy it is to blame money and airplanes when perceiving an experience, using your selective attention and selective exposure. However, remember that perception is primarily an intrapersonal phenomenon. Therefore, we need to look within ourselves as we try to understand our own reality. Let's examine areas that can potentially influence or limit our perceptual experiences; in an effort to change our frame of reference and improve our perceptual experiences. **Perceptual awareness** is the level of knowing or realizing how your perception is influenced.

What influences your perceptual experience?

1. **Physiological Influences.** How we feel on any given day affects the outcome of our day. If you have a headache, you're tired, stressed out, and so on, that feeling will influence how much or how little effort you will put into the communication process. I can recall spending the weekend at someone's house during a very stressful time. There was a lot of arguing going on and there were a lot a people who were very unhappy with one another. I had such a headache that entire weekend from the stress, that simply going to that town on future occasions instantly brought back the headache. Our bodies are a lot smarter than we give them credit for; they know how to tell us when we are hungry, tired, or stressed, and yes, our bodies react based on previous experiences we have had.

2. **Psychological Influences.** What your mind remembers about a situation, person, or animal affects how you will react when you are faced with a similar experience. Our emotions also greatly influence how we perceive situations, people, animals, experiences. If I come home from work in a bad mood, it affects my interactions with my family. If I accidentally snap at my son, he begins to wonder if he did something wrong. If I ignore my dog, as he is sitting there with a toy in his mouth ready to play, he gets annoyed with me too. This is why it is so important to take a conscious, mental shift from your mood at work to how you will behave at home. My family is excited to see me; my son wants to tell me about his day, and they all want to have time to just goof around for the rest of the night.

3. **Cultural Influences.** Your cultural background is another factor that influences your perception. The way you were raised, your values, and your expectations about how people in your culture should behave affect how you experience your reality. In today's society, the many people in our older generation have a hard time understanding why it has become unacceptable to spank your children. They were raised in a time where not only was spanking a way people disciplined their children, but it was also accepted to use a belt, switch, paddle, or whatever was handy. Our culture is different today; people use things like time out and redirecting the behavior as the new forms of discipline.

4. **Social Influences.** Your social status, job occupation, education, where you live, your social groups, and so on, all influence how you perceive your experiences. We create our own little worlds by going to the same job, the same stores, the same church, living in the same types of neighborhoods, spending time with the same people, and so on. Having these same social experiences limits how we view the world. If you have always lived in a safe, peaceful, and low-crime neighborhood, then you have no idea what it is like to live in a neighborhood where people always have to worry about the safety of their families. If you have always had enough money to pay your bills, then you have no idea what it is like to receive a disconnection notice from the power company. Developing empathy is the only way to bridge our experiences, without stepping out of our comfort zone. However, I would challenge you to try attending a new church in a different part of town, try shopping at other types of stores, try meeting different types of people and befriending them. I promise, if you try those new experiences, you will change your frame of reference.

What limits you from understanding a perceptual experience?

The Communication Research Associates in their book *Communicate!* discuss reasons why we overlook cues that we are presented with in our perceptual experiences. Some of those reasons include familiarity, complacency, and singularity.

1. **Familiarity.** Familiarity is when we take something for granted simply because we expect it to be there. For example, you may not notice certain sounds that your home makes until someone asks you about the sounds. Another example would be that you may not notice the trees growing on the side of the road on your drive home. Here's a good one—have you ever proofed your English paper, even used your spell check, and then you get the paper back and you are surprised at the number of errors? Since you wrote the paper, you may overlook some of the mistakes because you are familiar with it. This is why your instructors may suggest that you write the paper and then put it away for a few days. When you come back to it, you notice errors that you still have time to fix before submitting it for a grade.

2. **Complacency.** Sometimes we become complacent, or in a relaxed state, and our awareness of our environment is minimal. This can happen at the end of the day when we are extremely tired, it can happen when we have been drinking alcohol, and it can happen if we have taken medicine that makes us drowsy. With any of those examples we should not be driving a car, trying to study our homework, or trying to have an important conversation with someone, because we are not as perceptually aware.

3. **Singularity.** Singularity is when you have so many thought or concerns, to an almost obsessive state, on your mind that you cannot see or think about anything else. If you are studying for finals and a friend calls you, you may snap at him because you are so concerned about your finals. However, your friend may have been calling to help you study; you just may not have taken the time to find out. Another example would be if you are struggling with trying to pay your bills and you are extremely concerned with how you will pay the rent and eat, you will not notice other things that are going on around you. You may not be able to focus in the classroom; you may not see an opportunity to make some extra money, and so on.

> "The way in which I perceive a film, DVD, store, or even the town I live in is different from most people. I think this is what makes people truly unique."
>
> —Samantha Stream

What else hinders your perceptual experience?

1. **Halo Effect.** Halo effect is a way of describing why we seem to see some people as having positive qualities based on a first impression. For example, if someone creates a very positive first impression, we tend to think positively about their entire character. A job interview is a great example; the employer is looking for you to "wow" them. In other words, they want to find a great candidate, who has almost angelic qualities.

2. **Horn Effect.** The horn effect is the opposite of the halo effect. If someone creates a negative first impression, then we tend to see them as having an unpleasant character. That person may have been having a bad day, and we have decided not to like that person based on one experience with him or her.

3. **Expectations and Assumptions.** As we have discussed throughout this chapter, you have a lot of expectations and assumptions regarding everything you experience. If a dog bit you when you were five years old, you may expect that all dogs will bite you. If you were in an abusive relationship, then you may expect future relationships may become abusive. All of our expectations and assumptions have the potential to hinder your future experiences. We have to make a conscious effort to change our frame of reference in order to change our expectations and assumptions about people, animals, and situations. This is a process that takes time and, depending on the depth of a painful experience, you may need to see a therapist to help you change your frame of reference.

4. **Demographics.** Many times our own demographics affect our perceptual awareness, and how we see others simply because of their demographics. Demographics include age, height, gender, race, and so on. This may shock some of you, but we cannot change our demographics and neither can anyone else; however, we will judge or evaluate people because of things that they cannot change. If you are Caucasian, you cannot change that; if you are African-American, you cannot change that. However, racism still happens in our country today. Another thing we like to judge or generalize is gender. Have you ever said, "All men are sexist," or "all women are stupid drivers?" Making these judgments or generalizations will hinder your perceptual awareness.

5. **Ignoring the Details.** Our perception is influenced when we do not listen to someone's entire perceptive. For example when someone is telling you how to do something and as soon as you think you have it figured out, you may tune them out. How about when you are reading the directions to put together a bookcase you just bought? As soon as you think you understand how to put it together, based on skimming the directions or looking at the pictures, you stop reading the details of the directions. Another example that consistently amazes me, is my online courses; I am amazed at how many students do not read the directions completely. They ignore some of the details and then do not understand why they missed something important. If you ignore the details or do not read things thoroughly, you will hinder your perceptual experience.

6. **Inconsistent Behaviors.** When our behaviors or others' behaviors are inconsistent, it makes each experience challenging to adapt to. There are those who act differently around their significant other, their parents, their friends, their employer, and so on; and because that person acts differently depending on who is around, other people may call him or her "fake." This is because people do not know what to expect from that person. Another example is the person who can be hot or cold on any given day; other people can become hesitant to spend time with that person because they do not know what to expect.

BECOMING MORE PERCEPTUALLY AWARE

Becoming more perceptually aware is the challenge for all of us. We need to learn how to face each new experience with an open mind and a conscious effort.

The following quotation presents an interesting perceptive on gratitude and how we need to become more perceptually aware. "Gratitude is like a flashlight. If you go out in your yard at night and turn on the flashlight, you suddenly see what's there. It was always there, but you couldn't see it in the dark," according to Dawna Markova as she was quoted in the book *Attitudes of Gratitude* by M.J. Ryan.

If we want to increase our areas of shared perception, we need to start by "turning on the flashlight." Then maybe we can open our minds enough to feel like we are not in the dark. If you don't feel like you are in the dark, kudos to you. Now it is time to teach others.

 In closing, it is time to pause and reflect on what you have read. Consider the following questions, and write down some notes in the space provided:

1. What didn't you know about the things you have read so far?

2. What surprised you the most about what you have read so far?

3. With what you've read so far, what don't you understand?

4. Is there anything you don't agree with, or is there anything you need more information about?

Chapter 1

I walk down the street. There is a deep hole in the sidewalk.
I fall in. I am lost . . . I am helpless.
It's not my fault.
It takes forever to find a way out.

Chapter 2

I walk down the same street. There is a deep hole in the sidewalk.
I pretend I don't see it.
I fall in again. I can't believe I'm in this same place. But it isn't my fault.
It still takes a long time to get out.

Chapter 3

I walk down the same street. There is a deep hole in the sidewalk.
I see it is there.
I fall in . . . it's a habit . . . but my eyes are open. I know where I am.
It is my fault. I get out immediately.

Chapter 4

I walk down the same street. There is a deep hole in the sidewalk.
I walk around it.

Chapter 5

I walk down a different street.

—Anonymous

WHEN TO SHUT UP

Peter D. Kramer

Of all the advice that has drifted from psychotherapists' offices into couples' daily lives, the most overworked—and, I suspect, the most destructive—is the injunction to communicate. Be open, be honest, speak your mind, demand to be heard . . . well, yes, sometimes, maybe—if simple misunderstandings are at the root of your frustrations.

But how often, really, does one partner have no notion what's on the other's mind? When I evaluate a couple, it's not at all unusual for them to cite "communication" as a problem: "He'll say anything—he has no notion how he undermines me."

Rarely is the impasse caused by lack of information. Think how hard it is to keep a secret in an intimate relationship. But it is common for thoughtless speech to stir up discord. There may even be instances where silence is, as advertised, golden.

I am thinking of a story a husband told me in praise of his wife. He had come home on a Friday griping about his job. The managers were ratcheting up the pressure, and now an immediate supervisor was hinting that a promised promotion might not come through. His wife looked annoyed, but instead of speaking her mind, she puttered and listened and offered vague encouragement. On Saturday, she said, "About that supervisor—" And the husband interrupted: "I know. I'm going to have to confront him or go over his head."

"She could have laid it out for me the night before," the man told me. "She may have been thinking that I'm timid and inse-cure. Other women have said as much. But she was patient. She let me vent, let me spend a night mulling it over."

I asked him what his wife's silence meant. He said, "She has faith in me. She knows I'll do the right thing."

I like this story because it indicates where communication lies.

Communication is not just putting ideas into words. It's getting ideas across, preferably in a way that allows them to be used. Timing is crucial.

But what of spontaneity? Many people believe intimacy means being able to say what you think: "I'm through repressing my feelings. What good is a relationship if I can't express myself?"

I see the point in this objection. Women have been forced for too long to control their responses. We may admire Jane Austen's shrewd heroines, but we wouldn't want to live in a world that demands such extremes of social calculation. No one should have to weigh every syllable.

All the same, self-expression often bene-fits from forethought. That's why writers revise. Sometimes I think therapists have done great harm by overemphasizing imme-diacy in communication, as if the ideal mar-riage were like psychoanalysis from the patient's position, where you say whatever comes to mind without censorship.

It is worth noting that psychotherapy from the therapist's standpoint is very much a matter of timing. Trainees often lie in wait for moments when emotions run high, hoping to express an insight when it will have the most impact. This strategy works for some patients but leaves others feeling ambushed. The point of therapy—or of fruitful communication in marriage—is not for one party to look clever or to humiliate the other. Many years ago, a psychoanalyst I admire, Fred Pine, of Albert Einstein College of Medicine in New York, wrote an essay titled "The interpretive Moment" about communication techniques that leave the other person feeling respected. I like to remind overeager trainees of an adage from that paper: Strike while the iron is cold.

There are moments when speech is likely to damage intimacy. The heart-to-heart that seems so appealing when you've had too much to drink won't do anybody any good. Nor is it a useful strategy to mention one more annoyance as the two of you are headed to bed.

Sometimes bad moments declare themselves in the middle of a discussion. If you find yourself making the same point five times, maybe the problem is not that you've failed to make your opinion clear. He knows what you've said. He disagrees, or emotionally he can't afford to agree right now. Perhaps your insistence carries a secondary message, that you find him disappointing in an important way, and you may need to think through the larger problem separately, and perhaps on your own.

Psychotherapists pay attention to what they call the working alliance. You can't bring up hurtful issues, can't hope to change things for the better, if you're not on the same team. Early in a relationship, all that counts is creating trust and comfort. Solving problems through explicit negotiation makes sense only if the effort serves the prior goal of relationship building. Nonverbal communication might serve the purpose best: working side by side, sharing pleasures, touching, being there.

Particularly in times of stress, you need to have faith that the two of you can tolerate a little unclarity and muddle through, and not just with the small issues. The big, ongoing struggles—about time, money, and the expression of affection—may need to be postponed.

In hard times, it's worth considering a role for simple curiosity. *What exactly is he trying to say?* People like to be understood with precision, especially if they are hurting. It is said that rather than listen, men suggest solutions, but women can do that, too. The motive may be less to fix the problem at hand than to reform the other person, or to insult him: "Stop whining about your boss! Be a man!"

Even constructive suggestions can come across as undermining. What many people need is a response that suggests they are capable of finding their own solutions. Or—if they're asking for advice—an acknowledgement that the dilemma is as complex as they feel it to be: "That is complicated. I'll want to think it over."

Couples may actually be energized by letting an issue remain unsettled for a while. The ability to tolerate ambiguity implies confidence in the relationship as a whole. It may be enough to say, "You're right, that's a problem, and sooner or later we'll need to address it." To be sure, this approach works best if you actually intend to sit down on a quiet afternoon and put in your two cents.

None of this is to say that couples can't be spontaneous or that they must suppress annoyance. One of the great problems of self-help prescriptions is that they equate shaky couples with all couples. If the two of you are resilient, smart-mouthed street fighters, you may amuse each other by saying whatever comes to mind. You may even both learn something from what pops out of your mouth. But if your relationship is strained, or if it is just young and untested, you might consider paying attention to the timing of squabbles and, if you need to strike, waiting until the iron is cold.

Name: _____ Date: _____

QUESTIONS FOR DISCUSSION—

WHEN TO SHUT UP
by Peter D. Kramer

1. What are your top 3 reactions to this article?

2. How does this article relate to what you have learned thus far about Interpersonal Communication?

(Questions continued on back)

3. Do you agree with Kramer's idea of letting issues remain unsettled for awhile? Explain.

4. What communication techniques, do you think, are most helpful for couples?

5. Other thoughts about the article?

"WE CAN'T STOP FIGHTING OVER MONEY"

By Margery D. Rosen

"I hate being treated like a child who has to be constantly monitored," said Becca, 37, a pediatrician and mother of two boys, Alex, 6, and Jake, 3. "Adam interrogates me every time I buy a pair of shoes or a new toaster. 'What's wrong with the one we have?' he'll say in his holier-than-thou-voice. Yes, the old toaster works—but it burns everything to charcoal unless you stand there and watch it, which I have no intention of doing. And then there's his lecture: 'What kind of message are you sending our children?' As if buying a toaster is irresponsible and unethical!

"Money fights dominate our life, and they get heated. Adam has strong views about what he considers wasteful spending. He can be downright self-righteous about it. When he's upset with me, he sulks for days. I spend a lot of time wooing him back.

"I'm very fortunate to have a family trust fund, so unlike so many families, we're not frantic about having enough to pay the bills. Instead we fight about how to spend the money we do have. I'm no extravagant—I don't buy jewels or book exotic vacations. And I'm not getting us into debt. But I believe that if you work hard, you deserve to enjoy the fruits of your labors. I shouldn't be reminded every time I buy something that there are children starving in Africa!

"Adam gets particularly hostile on holidays. I admit my relatives go overboard with gifts. Adam wants me to weed out stuff that duplicates what the kids already have or what he deems unnecessary. But how do I explain to my mother that I didn't give the boys the train set she sent? How do I help my kids write a thank you note for a gift they didn't receive? Last year, Adam sent my mom a curt e-mail telling her that her abundant gift-giving was ridiculous and that he was sending the presents back to Amazon.com and having her account credited. That was plain rude.

"Our house is another source of conflict. When we moved to Denver seven years ago, we bought a 100-year-old colonial. I want to renovate the attic so the boys can have separate bedrooms. The bathroom upstairs has no shower, so I'd like to fix that, too, but Adam is putting the kibosh on both projects, saying they're too expensive and unnecessary. I'm tired of being made to feel like a spoiled brat because I want our home to be nice.

"While my family wasn't Rockefeller rich, we were very comfortable—my father was a lawyer, and I grew up in a big house outside of Boston with my older brother, Jake. My parents divorced when I was 10, and both remarried quickly; I was devastated. Mother was very involved in volunteer organizations and her social life, and she spent little time with us. Jake and I were closer to our nanny than to our parents.

"As a teenager, I was depressed and anxious and fought with my mother and stepfather on just about every issue. After high school, I went to college and medical school in San Francisco. Back then, we were all living a kind of student-Bohemian life, with no money, and furniture that was Salvation Army cast-offs. Adam and I met through mutual friends when I was in my last year. He's so smart, a Renaissance man who can do just about anything he sets his mind to do. I loved the mixture of playfulness and social responsibility I saw in him. We'd stay up late dinking coffee and having philosophical discussions about all sorts of things.

"When I was offered a residency in Denver, we decided to get married. Though I'd told Adam my family was wealthy, I think it went in one ear and out the other. We certainly never discussed money before we married. In fact, the subject didn't really come up until I learned I was pregnant and we had to figure out child-care arrangements. Adam wanted to stay home with the baby. Some day, he plans to teach business in high school or college; but for now, we both feel strongly about not having someone else raise our kids. Adam is totally committed to being an at-home dad, and he has no ambivalence about his choice.

"We have friends who fight about household chores, disciplining the kids, sex, or even what movie to see. We agree on those things—so why do we get so hostile over money issues?"

"I never thought money would come between us," said Adam, 41, who, in his jeans, work boots and a college sweatshirt, still looks like a graduate student. "In our social circle in San Francisco, money was irrelevant. If wealth was measured at all, it was by the kind of mountain bike you had, not whether you drove a fancy car or had granite kitchen countertops. Even after Becca told me about her parents' money, it never dawned on me that anything would change between us.

"When I first met Becca, I fell in love with her immediately. She not only was beautiful, she was intelligent, independent and interested in so many of the things I thought were important. We had a great time together and our values seemed in sync. But in my mind, ripples of conflict surfaced soon after we mar-

ried. I'd assumed we'd continue to live the rather minimalist lifestyle we had at school. But Becca started to insist on eating at fancy restaurants and traveling first class—and she pointed out that she could afford to do so. But living that kind of lifestyle was not the way I was raised.

"I'm the oldest of four kids, all about a year apart. I was born in Rome, where my parents were foreign correspondents for an American news service. Mother stopped working after her second child has born, and we lived in several cities in Europe and the Middle East. When I was 12, we moved back to California, near my mother's family. We were middle class: We always had enough, but we were taught to be frugal. If I wanted something, I had to earn the money to pay for it. I remember at 14 really wanting a TV. We didn't have one because my parents thought most of the programs were garbage, so I got a paper route and saved for two years to buy my own set. I also shared a room with my two brothers; it was tight, but we learned how to cooperate. Now, just because we have a big house doesn't mean we shouldn't stick to our values. I don't believe my thinking is 'extreme'; I believe it is totally justified.

"When the kids are older, I plan to teach—I have a master's in education. But right now, I love being a stay-at-home dad. That decision was a natural evolution for us. I've never regretted that choice.

"But I have started to get increasingly upset about living this life of 'indefensible affluenza' as I like to call it. I'm repulsed by such crass consumerism. Plus, every time Becca wants to buy something or make a few changes in the house, it always turns into a huge project that has consequences for me. If she buys a new DVD player or computer, I have to set it up or deal with the tech support people. I'd rather be reading to my kids or hiking in the woods.

"The bathroom renovation put me over the edge. Initially, Becca was just going to install a shower unit. Now she wants a new sink, vanity, and to re-tile the whole bathroom. I don't want workmen streaming in and out of the house. It's disruptive. But when Becca gets a plan in her head, she's unyielding. We reach an agreement, then she goes right ahead and does what she wants anyway. It makes me think she hasn't heard one thing I've said.

"I'm particularly offended by what happens at Christmas. Last year, we came home after a weekend away and there were 24 UPS boxes from her relatives on the front porch. I lost it. I wanted her cooperation in sending the stuff back or giving it away.

"The truth is, Becca and I hardly ever fight or raise our voices except when it has to do with money. But that's been happening enough that we both want to figure out why."

"When they first met, money was a non-issue for Adam and Becca and neither saw any reason to discuss it," says the counselor. "They should have. Assumptions and expectations about money can change dramatically over the lifetime of a relationship, particularly when children enter the picture. However, because money was such a loaded issue for Becca and Adam, they weren't flexible enough to accommodate those shifts. And they didn't understand how much their arguments were rooted in their unique family histories.

"Becca's family was wealthy but emotionally distant. Money was a way for Becca to fill her emotional needs. Living a certain lifestyle and making her own decisions about spending gave her a sense of love, comfort and control.

"Adam's family, however, had prided itself on its frugality. As the oldest child, he took comfort in his parents' rules and felt obligated that his children carried on those firm beliefs.

"We spent a considerable amount of time talking about how their feelings about money had developed. These conversations were eye-opening, particularly for Adam, who had never heard Becca speak so movingly and tearfully about the emptiness she'd experienced as a child and how controlled she felt by his treatment now. The counseling process takes time, and can involve repetitive discussions as each partner begins to pull apart the threads of beliefs and analyze his or her feelings. At one point Adam conceded: 'I love Becca; I never meant to hurt her. I can see that our different financial objectives can be a plus: My goal to spend less will be crucial as our expenses grow, and I also understand that Becca's push for renovations will make the house feel more like a home.'

"This was a significant step to resolving their problems. As with many couples. Becca and Adam were operating on right/wrong, your way/my way assumptions that are self-defeating. No one likes to have his or her ideas denigrated; when they are, the response is to dig in your heels and defend your position. 'When you stop fighting so hard to change your spouse,' I told them, 'you open the door for solutions.'

"I suggested they think in terms of acceptance and respect, which would lead them toward discussion and negotiation. 'What is more important—the kind of restaurant you go to for dinner or harmony in your marriage?' I asked. They agreed harmony was their goal, so we focused on fine-tuning their communication skills. Adam's insulting comments shut down productive discussions. Similarly, Becca's persistence in doing whatever she wanted made Adam feel unheard.

"I told Becca, 'Once you make an agreement, you have to follow through on it. If you don't, Adam will feel disregarded.' In turn, I told Adam that he had to watch his dogmatic tone and listen more empathetically without cutting off Becca with a lecture.

"As conversation in general became more fluid, they brainstormed alternatives to their previously rigid stances on a variety of hot-button money issues. After hearing each other's points of view in a calm, rational discussion, they agreed that putting a cap on the kids' Christmas gifts was important, so together they wrote a letter to family members, graciously thanking them for their generosity and explaining that they would appreciate it if they limited their gift-giving to only one present per child. 'That note was well received,' Becca said. 'So I hope this year, we won't be inundated.'

"Next, they tackled the issue of renovation. Becca decided that for now, Adam was right about the boys sharing a room. 'As they get older, if we feel it's in their best interests, we can always fix up the attic.' She explained. 'As for the bathroom, I know construction is disruptive, so I'll talk to the contractor about doing most of the work over the holidays when we'll be away.' Since she was acknowledging his concerns, Adam conceded that the bathroom did need work. 'I see now that Becca isn't being princess-y about this. We need a shower installed anyway, so why not make the bathroom look as nice as possible?'

"Adam and Becca know that their rapprochement on money matters is a work in progress. Undoubtedly, they'll knock heads again but they both now feel confident in their ability to handle disputes as a team."

Name: _____ Date: _____

WE CAN'T STOP FIGHTING OVER MONEY
by Margery D. Rosen

1. What are your top 3 reactions to this article?

2. What metacommunication should this couple have been doing early on to prevent their different perceptions about money?

(Questions continued on back)

3. Describe some perception checking this couple should have been doing, to minimize their assumptions and expectations.

4. What do you think about the counselor's suggestions? (the last 3 paragraphs)

5. Other thoughts about the article?

INDIVIDUAL ACTIVITY #1
Create a Perception Box

PURPOSE—

To turn an ordinary box into a visual representation (a collage) of who you are and how you view the world. This is a perception and self-disclosure activity.

PROCEDURE—

Decorate a box following the instructions below for the outside of the box, the inside of the box, and the "secrets" envelope. The box should be no smaller than an adult size shoe box.

The outside of the box—

Use magazine pictures, words, and objects to show how you believe others see you. Consider your values, beliefs, attitudes, and behaviors. Ask coworkers and/or classmates to give you ideas about how they see you. Maybe they can pick out words or magazine pictures that they think fit your personality. You may want to use each side of the box for different parts of your personality— i.e., social, intellectual, recreational, etc. Be creative!!

The inside of the box—

Use magazine pictures, words, and objects to show the more private and personal sides of your personality—the areas that you don't show most people until they get to know you. I suggest that you ask your closest friends and loved ones, the people who really know you. This part of your box should include your biggest dreams, greatest fears, your "if only I had time and/or money I would do this" and goals for your life, etc. Be creative!!

The "secrets" envelope—

Inside your box you should have an envelope that contains a list of your most private secrets. You will **NOT** have to open the envelope and share the contents with anyone. However, even though others may not know what is in the envelope, it is important to honor this piece of yourself. When we honor our secrets we are able to deal with them more effectively in the future, and they are less likely to do more harm to our life.

From Michelle Burch, *Interpersonal Communication: Building Your Foundations for Success.* Copyright © 2005 by Kendall/Hunt Publishing Company.

Things to consider—

      1. The entire box should be covered.

      2. You need to be creative and make something you are proud of.

      3. You need to know *why* you are putting things on your box and *what significance* each item holds for you.

      4. Don't put anything on or in the box that you do not want disclosed to the class (except the envelope).

FOLLOW-UP—

Discuss the activity in small groups or with the entire class. Discuss why you put the items on the box and what significance the items hold for you. Finally, discuss how you felt creating this perception box and what you plan to do with the "secrets" envelope.

Name: _____ Date: _____

INDIVIDUAL ACTIVITY #2
Checking Your Perception

PURPOSE—

To understand how the perception process works, and to pick out effective ways to check your perception.

PROCEDURE—

After reading each of the following situations, create your responses, using the perception-checking method. Remember, perception-checking includes: (1) describe the behavior, (2) provide at least two possible interpretations, and (3) seek clarification. Write your responses in the space provided.

Scenario #1

You made plans with your significant other (you have been dating about six months). Together you decided on meeting at 6:00 p.m. to go to dinner and then to a movie. Your significant other has been known for forgetting plans that were made, and you are usually very forgiving. However, the forgetfulness is beginning to wear on your nerves. You are trying to be understanding; after all, s/he is working full-time, taking 18 credit hours, volunteering at the local animal shelter, and helping out at home. It's 7:00 p.m. and your significant other isn't there yet and has not called. At 8:00 p.m. s/he stops by your place and doesn't refer to missing your date. What do you say?

(Questions continued on back)

Scenario #2

You tell your mother that you are moving out of the house and moving in with your friends. You know that she doesn't like your friends and, as you have anticipated, she is very angry. She begins yelling at you, telling you that this is a bad decision, that she will not help you out with your finances, and that your friends are not going to lead you down a very positive path. You knew this is how she would respond; therefore, you are prepared to discuss the behavior. What do you say?

Scenario #3

Your teenager missed curfew for the third weekend in a row (a half-hour late each time). You have talked to him/her but each time it's late, you are both tired, you end up yelling at each other and going to bed angry with one another. You decide it's time to discuss the behavior of coming home late and how you both handle your emotions. What do you say?

Scenario #4

Create your own scenario here and then describe how you would check your perception.

FOLLOW-UP—

As a follow-up your instructor may ask you to turn this in for review and/or grading. You may also be asked to discuss your responses, as a class.

From Michelle Burch, *Interpersonal Communication: Building Your Foundations for Success.* Copyright © 2005 by Kendall/Hunt Publishing Company.

Name: _____ Date: _____

GROUP ACTIVITY #1
Trying Walking in My Shoes

PURPOSE—

To experience the world from another's perspective.

PROCEDURE—

The following statements are ideas to get the class thinking about how to experience the world from someone else's perspective. Each idea addresses a variety of people, with a variety of needs. Each idea suggests that you "spend time" doing something that will help you understand; how much time depends on your class and how much time you think you need to truly understand each particular perspective.

1. To experience the world of a person with arthritis: Try walking with popcorn in your shoes.

2. Try another experiment to experience the world of a person with arthritis: Try playing catch with your hands wrapped in bandages to limit your hand movement.

3. To experience the world of a physically impaired person: Try spending time in a wheelchair.

4. To experience the world of a person with one arm: Try spending time with one arm tied behind your back.

5. To experience the world of a person without any arms: Try spending time with both of your arms tied behind your back.

6. To experience the world of a person who is blind: Try spending time with a blindfold covering your eyes.

7. To experience the world of a visually impaired person: Try walking with butter smeared on a pair of glasses.

8. To experience the world of a hearing impaired person: Try spending time with ear plugs in your ears (be sure to use ear plugs that really block hearing—some are better than others).

From Michelle Burch, *Interpersonal Communication: Building Your Foundations for Success.* Copyright © 2005 by Kendall/Hunt Publishing Company.

9. To experience the world of a person who lacks peripheral vision: Try playing catch with "tunnel vision." To create "tunnel vision" get a piece of heavyweight paper, create an oval shape, and affix it to your head so you cannot see out of the corners of your eyes. I suggest a rubber band to make the paper stay.

10. To experience the world of a person who is of small height: Try spending time on your knees, walking around, trying to talk to people, etc.

11. To experience the world of a person who is extremely overweight: Try spending time in a "fat suit." Many colleges and/or hospitals have them and may let you borrow one.

12. To experience the world of someone from another culture: Try wearing traditional African garb or a traditional dress from India (including the sari, henna, and bindi).

FOLLOW-UP—

As a class, discuss what you now understand about how someone else perceives. Next discuss how your perception process was affected by this experience.

From Michelle Burch, *Interpersonal Communication: Building Your Foundations for Success.* Copyright © 2005 by Kendall/Hunt Publishing Company.

Name: _____ Date: _____

GROUP ACTIVITY #2
What Do You Perceive?

PURPOSE—

To analyze how perception works from one person to another.

PROCEDURE—

Using the pictures below, write down your first and second reactions to each picture or situation. Don't discuss your reactions with your classmates until everyone has had the opportunity to write down their reactions.

Photo 1   Photo 2

(1) _____   (1) _____

(2) _____   (2) _____

(Continued on back)

Photo 3

(1) _____

(2) _____

Photo 4

(1) _____

(2) _____

Photo 5

(1) _____

(2) _____

Photo 6

(1) _____

(2) _____

FOLLOW-UP—

1. Compare your reactions to your classmates.

2. Discuss why our perceptions vary from person to person.

WORD SEARCH
Reviewing the Terms

```
E F Y L B U K S H G V I X F Q Y S S S J
C A T L N X R V L Z D S K U C Z S E E J
N M I W F V H Q Y S M N H F F N E L L I
E I R C F K F O F T O J A V O X N E E X
R L A N L W A M R I E E I W I E C C C
E I L Y R O E H T N O I T U B I R T T A
F A U B O O E P C C E A Q R K V A I I H
E R G M A D E C L W T F Q E P U W O V M
R I N W R C J O G E E E F T O C A N E D
F T I Y R U S U R D H K B E E X L Y E O
O Y S E M U T P H H J C J Y C B A J X T
E I P J R F R L E O S T X Q E T U T P Y
M M S E L E C T I V E A T T E N T I O N
A U R G T Y C N E C A L P M O C P R S V
R P Q N O R G A N I Z A T I O N E W U V
F X I H A L O E F F E C T Y Q T C P R W
D T I M Y O L Z G G X K A N X E R L E D
L M X S D M V L M V Z Q D O B W E P F H
T C B R C W T B W G D T Q O H F P X Y F
B K Y X A L E N N J P Z E K O B K V K M
```

1. a process of developing awareness through your senses

2. to pick information, people, and experiences that you will pay attention to

3. we expose ourselves to people, animals, and environments that confirm what we know to be true

4. when you choose to listen or tune in various stimuli

5. a set of interlocking observations, beliefs, values, and attitudes

6. creating stability for the experience by arranging the information in a meaningful way

7. attaching meaning to our experiences

8. fill in the missing pieces or the gaps of information

9. correlating specific behaviors and motives to what we experience

10. we take something for granted simply because we expect it to be there

11. a relaxed state of mind and body where our awareness of our environment is minimal

12. so many thought or concerns, to an almost obsessive state, on your mind that you cannot see anything else

13. the level knowing or realizing how your perception is influenced

14. a positive impression of someone's entire character

15. a negative impression of someone's entire character

Name: _____ Date: _____

CHAPTER QUIZ
Reviewing the Chapter

1. We ignore a message because we think we know what the person is saying, so we take it for granted.
   (a) complacency (b) singularity (c) familiarity (d) none of them.

2. Thoughts or concerns which are near-obsessive tend to override other stimuli.
   (a) complacency (b) singularity (c) familiarity (d) none of them.

3. A relaxed state of mind or body can diminish our awareness.
   (a) complacency (b) singularity (c) familiarity (d) none of them.

4. Perception is primarily what type of phenomenon?
   (a) Interpersonal (b) Intrapersonal (c) Extrapersonal (d) none of them

5. We can eliminate all distortion in our perception by:
   (a) perception checking (b) communicating effectively (c) listening and offering feedback (d) all of them (e) none of them.

6. The following factors affect our perception except:
   (a) occupation (b) age (c) gender (d) height (e) all are factors that affect perception.

7. The perception process is:
   (a) structure, organize, interpret (b) interpret, organize, structure (c) structure, interpret, organize (d) none of them describe the perception process.

8. Your perception is your reality.
   (a) true (b) false

9. The perception process provides us with:
   (a) structure (b) stability (c) meaning (d) closure (e) all of them.

10. We organize information by using the following constructs:
    (a) psychological (b) physical (c) physiological (d) both a and b (e) none of them.

11. You can increase your perceptual awareness by:
    (a) having inconsistent behavior (b) evaluating someone based on his gender
    (c) assuming you know what someone will do (d) none of them (e) only b and c.

12. The horn effect is when you create a negative impression of someone's character based on one meeting.
    (a) true (b) false

13. The halo effect is when you create a positive impression of someone's character based on one meeting.
    (a) true (b) false

14. Organizing people according to the role they play in your relationship is:
    (a) role constructs (b) social constructs (c) physical constructs (d) psychological constructs (e) none of them.

15. Organizing people according to their appearance is:
    (a) role constructs (b) social constructs (c) physical constructs (d) psychological constructs (e) none of them.

16. Organizing people according to your social interaction is:
    (a) role constructs (b) social constructs (c) physical constructs (d) psychological constructs (e) none of them.

UNIT II

UNDERSTANDING HOW YOU COMMUNICATE

Chapter 4—Verbal vs. Nonverbal Communication

Chapter 5—Understanding the Self

Chapter 6—All About Emotions

CHAPTER 4

VERBAL VS. NONVERBAL COMMUNICATION

KEY TERMS

Affect display

Connotative

Denotative

Emblem

Illustrator

Manipulator

Meanings

Nonverbal communication

Nonverbal communication
   disability

Paralanguage

Regulator

Verbal language

Words

CHAPTER OBJECTIVES

1. Understand the major aspects of verbal communication.

2. Examine the intentional and unintentional meanings behind words.

3. Describe the meaning within language.

4. Build your vocabulary with more effective language.

5. Understand the major aspects of nonverbal communication.

6. Describe specific types of nonverbal communication.

7. Determine how to develop your nonverbal awareness.

8. Practice skills for improving your verbal and nonverbal communication.

I wanted to listen to what she was saying, but I was distracted. Her body was covered with tattoos and her face had so many piercings. I wanted to look at her tattoos and her piercings, but I needed to be listening to her; after all, I didn't even know her and she was trying to talk to me. I am so distracted. She was getting offended; I could tell because the smile had left her face and her eyes were beginning to fill with frustration. I think she assumed that I was judging her; how could I tell her that the opposite was true. I don't want to sound stupid—I wish I could clearly get my ideas across to her. "I admire your tattoos." That was simple enough. Her smile was returning. "I hope you don't mind my looking at them." That sounded smooth enough. She smiled and her posture began to move toward me. Finally, we understood each other. What was she talking about, again? Oops.

DEFINING VERBAL AND NONVERBAL COMMUNICATION

Our language is the essence of the entire communication process. Our **verbal language,** or the actual words that we communicate, provide us with the ability to express who we are, what we want, what we need, and what we desire. With the definition in mind, verbal language is the actual words that we communicate; do you think American Sign Language is verbal or nonverbal communication? If you said verbal communication, you are correct. A person with a hearing impairment communicates words through the signs they create with their hands. A person with a hearing impairment can communicate nonverbally, as you will understand after reading this chapter.

We began learning about verbal language from birth, and our teachers spend a lot of time teaching us the rules for proper English. However, for some reason verbal language is still extremely challenging for many people. Therefore, in this chapter we will not explore the rules for proper English; rather, we will look at words and their meanings, the major aspects of verbal language, and the intentional and unintentional meanings of words; at the end of the chapter we will look at how to create more effective verbal language.

Though verbal language is important to the communication process it actually only makes up a small percentage of our total communication. **Nonverbal communication** is anything we communicate, intentional or unintentional, without using words. Nonverbal communication constitutes 75 to 95 percent of our total communication. According to Mark Knapp and Judith Hall in their book *Nonverbal Communication in Human Interaction*, "Clearly nonverbal signals are a critical part of all our communication endeavors. Sometimes nonverbal signals are the most important part of your message. Understanding and effectively using nonverbal behavior is crucial in virtually every sector of our society."

Let's begin this chapter with examining how verbal communication works in the communication process.

WORDS & THEIR MEANINGS

"Language is a complex system for communicating ideas, thoughts, and feelings to others. Words, with their associated meanings, are the foundation of language, but the ways in which the words are selected and used communicate also," according to Margot Olson and Mary Forrest in *Shared Meaning*.

Olson and Forrest define **words** as "the symbols for objects, events, and feelings; they are not the objects, events, and feelings themselves." They continue to then describe **meanings,** "Words themselves do not possess meaning. The meanings attached to words exist within the person who is perceiving the words. Many words, in fact, are associated with several meanings, and the same object, event, or feeling may be described in a variety of ways. Words have no meaning until the individuals who use them attach some meaning to them. Each person, through past experiences with a word or combination of words, attaches a unique and personal meaning to every message."

To help clarify this concept, let's look at the triangle of meaning. Researchers Ogden and Richards created the Triangle of Meaning model, (see figure 4.1) to show the relationship between meaning and words. The triangle demonstrates, in a very simplistic way, that meanings are in people—not words. Remember that this is one theory to help us understand the mysteries of language; this theory is just the beginning in your journey of trying to understand language. There are three parts to the triangle of meaning:

1. First there is the *symbol*, in the lower left corner of the triangle. The symbol is the actual words that are being communicated.
2. *Referent*, in the lower right corner of the triangle, is the subject the communication. It could be a person, place, object, or an event. This should be a clear mental image of the symbol. In figure 4.1 you will notice the broken arrow between the symbol and the referent; this is

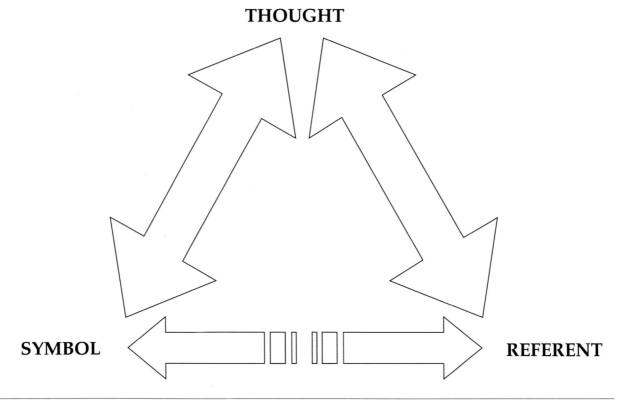

Ogden J. Richards Triangle of Meaning

THOUGHT

SYMBOL   **REFERENT**

F I G U R E   4 . 1 .
The Triangle of Meaning.

a reflection of how the meaning (or the referent) is within the word or it is a direct reflection of the word.

3. Next is the *thought,* on the top of the triangle. The thought is the image in our mind that we have when discussing the referent. It is our perception, our feelings, our experiences, our ideas, and how we relate to it. The thought is at the top of the triangle because it is an implication of both the symbol and the referent.

Here are a couple of examples using the Triangle of Meaning:

(1) Jane said, "I talked to your mother (symbol)."
Dave saw an image of his mother (referent).
Dave began thinking about why Jane is telling him that she talked to his mother and how he feels about her doing that (thought).

(2) The professor told her students, "There will be a test (symbol) tomorrow."
Bill, a student in the class, had an image of his cramming for the test (referent).
Then Bill began to sweat and feel extremely stressed (thought).
Tyler, another student in the class, had an image of himself taking the test the next day and doing well on the test (referent). Tyler felt calm and thought about how much he enjoyed the class (thought).

> "Although the spoken or verbal language is a powerful tool,
> nonverbal communication is also a way to effectively explain
> in more detail what you are trying to say."
>
> —Diana Shirk

INTENTIONAL VS. UNINTENTIONAL MEANINGS OF WORDS

Jerome Bruner in his book *Actual Minds, Possible Words* suggests to his audience that, "language cannot be neutral; that imposes a point of view not only about the world to which it refers but toward the use of mind in respect of this world. Language necessarily imposes a perspective in which things are viewed, and a stance toward what we view. It is not just, in the shopworn phrase, that the medium is the message. The message itself may create the reality that the message embodies, and predispose those who hear it to think about it in a particular mode. If I had to choose a motto for what I have to say, it would be that one from Francis Bacon, used by Vygotsky, proclaiming that neither mind alone nor hand alone can accomplish much without aids and tools that perfect them. And principal among those aids and tools are language and canons of its use."

Basically what Bruner is telling us is that every time words come out of our mouth there is meaning; that meaning has intentional or unintentional repercussions. Let's examine denotation vs. connotation, the power we give to our words, and our internal verbal limitations.

DENOTATION & CONNOTATION MEANINGS IN WORDS

The dictionary definition of a word is the **denotation** meaning. The dictionary may have several definitions for the same word, all of the definitions relate to the direct and universal meanings of the word. Here's where things get tricky. The **connotative** meaning of a word is the feeling we have when we hear the word or what we associate the word to. Connotative meanings are ever-changing, based on how we feel and our experiences.

Here are some examples of denotation vs. connotation:

- The word "college" is denotatively defined as a place of higher learning. The connotative meaning for Monica is, "A place I enjoyed attending. I may even go back for another degree someday." The connotative meaning for Leanna is, "A place that is very stressful."
- The word "father" is denotatively defined as a man that one is biologically related to." The connotative meaning for Chris is, "A man I don't know and I don't like." The connotative meaning for Chung Li is, "A man I admire and someone I want to be like.

When you are engaged in conversation, it is very likely that something you say could trigger a connotative meaning within the other person. That trigger could cause that person to lose focus, have an emotional reaction, or stop listening altogether. Sometimes we intentionally say things to someone in hope that they will connect with the connotative meaning of a word; other times, this can unintentionally distract the person and then you may get frustrated because the person is no longer listening to you.

> "I never know how much we used nonverbal communication. It really makes me appreciate the quote, 'Actions speak louder than word." It also makes me want to pay more attention to people's gestures, posture, and facial expressions."
>
> —Samantha Stream

THE POWER WE GIVE AND TAKE AWAY FROM WORDS

Through meaning we have the ability to give a lot of power to our words. Language has power when it is direct, straightforward, and to the point. This will limit the amount of misinterpretation, or connotative meanings, and it can make a person sound confident and knowledgeable. Language can intentionally or unintentionally have power. Lawyers, public officials, and police officers are examples of people we hear use powerful language. Discuss in class or online how people use words to sound powerful.

Language can also have the opposite effect by sounding powerless. Richard Weaver, in *Understanding Interpersonal Communication*, summarizes some of the characteristics that can make language, and in turn the person, sound powerless:

1. *Hedges/qualifiers.* When you qualify a sentence with "I guess" or "I think," you are taking away from the overall impact of the statement.
2. *Hesitation forms.* You will hear this a lot in public presentations when someone is nervous or lacks confidence. It could be "uh," "um," or "well."
3. *"You knows."* This phrase is becoming more and more popular. You hear it in conversations among friends, on television, and in speech class. Similarly to hesitations, this makes the person sound less confident or naive; it assumes that other people know something that they probably do not know.
4. *Tag questions.* A tag question is adding a question to the end of a statement. For example, "I think we should go to lunch, don't you?" It implies that you need someone's reassurance.
5. *Disclaimers.* Finally, there are disclaimers, which are introductory phrases that ask the listener to not hold the speaker responsible for what s/he is about to say. For example, "I know you won't agree with me, but . . ." or it could be more direct disclaimer like this, "Don't blame me, but . . ."

OUR INTERNAL VERBAL LIMITATIONS

Whether it is stereotyping, gender biases, racism, homophobia, ageism, or other biases, we all have internal limitations. Our experiences, our political opinions, and of course, our mood can inhibit our ability to communicate with others. When you are driving and the person in front of you is driving "too slow," according to you, what do you do? Do you begin cursing at that person? Do you become aggressive? Do you shout out names at that person? Or are you calm, understanding, and open to the experience? How you react to this situation can affect your communication with other people that you associate with the slow driver.

As you continue working through this textbook, consider your internal limitations. If you think that you don't have any limitations, that is wonderful; however, be open to the experience. Maybe you have limitations and you are not consciously aware of it. If you know what your limitations are, try to understand where they come from and what you would have to gain by letting go of them.

You are halfway done with this chapter; therefore, it is time to pause and reflect on what you have read. Consider the following questions and write down some notes in the space provided:

1. What didn't you know about the things you have read so far?

2. What surprised you the most about what you have read so far?

3. With what you've read so far, what don't you understand?

4. Is there anything you don't agree with, or is there anything you need more information about?

SPECIFIC AREAS OF NONVERBAL COMMUNICATION

All behaviors have communicative value; whether we are consciously or unconsciously aware of the messages we are sending, it does not change the significance of our behaviors. Let's look at four areas of our nonverbal behaviors:

- communicating your identity
- exemplifying your personality
- creating your persona
- expressing your mood

As you read about the specific types of nonverbal communication and the categories they are listed under, keep in mind two things: (1) some types of nonverbal behaviors can fit into more than one category, and (2) there are more examples of nonverbal behavior than the ones discussed here. Try to come up with your own examples as you are reading.

Category 1—Communicate Your Identity

The first thing people tend to recognize is your basic identifying features, and just like with all nonverbal communication, people begin to draw conclusions immediately about who you are. Some of your identifying features include the following:

- Race
- Culture
- Gender
- Age
- Height
- Weight

Category 2—Exemplify Your Personality

Knowing that people are drawing conclusions about us, we tend to then create our own identifying features by using our physical appearance and body language to exemplify our personalities. Here are a few:

- Physical appearance
  - Hair—the color and the style of your hair.
  - Face—wearing or not wearing makeup, your eyebrows plucked, left natural, or plucked but not maintained, a shaven or unshaven face.
  - Style of clothing—how you wear your clothes, the type of clothes you wear, etc.
  - Tattoos
  - Body Piercings
- The scent we give off. Whether it is our deodorant, our perfume or cologne, or it is a fresh-from-the-shower smell; or maybe you haven't seen a shower in days, all types of scents tell people about your personality.
- Use of time. Another aspect of exemplifying our personality is how people use and structure their time, which gives off intentional or unintentional messages about what you value within yourself and how you value others' time. Many people will draw conclusions about how much or how little you respect them, depending how you use your time when you are with them and if you are prompt or tardy. This is an example of a nonverbal behavior that fits easily within two categories. Time can also show others about your culture, as all cultures have a different perspective on how to use time.

- Touch. How we touch people, how often, or how little we touch others tells a lot about our personality. Women have ten times as many touch receptors on their skin as men do. Joseph Devito in *The Interpersonal Communication Book* describes the five meanings behind touch. They include:
  - **Positive emotions.** This tells other people we are interested in them, we appreciate or support them, we empathize with them, etc. This form of touch often indicates that an interpersonal relationship is developing or has developed.
  - **Playfulness.** This form of touch is light and tells the other person that you are trying to have some fun or trying to be affectionate.
  - **Control.** This form of touch is used to get someone to do something for you—get out of their way, hurry up, be quiet, etc. It is also used to dominate someone by grabbing an arm, pushing, pointing your finger, etc.
  - **Ritualistic.** This form of touch is used to recognize someone's presence or to initiate a conversation. It may be a handshake, a kiss on the cheek, or a hug.
  - **Task-related.** This is a form of touch that relates to performing a task. It can be when your doctor puts his hand on your shoulder to discuss a serious matter with you; it can be someone picking lint off of your shirt, or someone helping you up when you have fallen down.

Category 3—Create a Persona

Everyone creates a unique persona or an outer personality to present to the world. Some consider this a way to show their social status, education level, economic status, moral character, level of sophistication, etc. You will notice that physical appearance fits in this category as well.

- Physical Appearance
  - Hair—the haircut is well-maintained or it is not; the hair is colored to hide the gray or in bright colors to show eccentricity, etc., or the hair has its own style.
  - Style of clothing—name brand clothing or Goodwill store; your shirt tucked in or untucked; type of shoes and/or the brand name, etc.
- Environment and Territory
  - The type of home you live in, how you keep your home (clean or dirty, organized or lived in), and how you decorate the inside and the outside of your home.
  - The type of car you drive and how you keep your car on the inside and on the outside.
  - The type of neighborhood you live in and the area of town you live in.
- Posture—How do you stand? Are your shoulders back or are they slouched over? Someone who stands up straight gives the illusion that s/he is confident. Isn't that great! You don't actually have to be confident; you can just create a persona that you are confident.
- Proximity. Proximity is the amount of space or distance between people. Edward T. Hall developed a theory about proximity, he called them "zones" and there were four of them—intimate, personal, social, and public.
  - **The Intimate Zone.** This zone is having someone as close to you as possible and up to 18 inches away. We only allow people in this zone with whom we have a close,

interpersonal relationship—our significant other, our children, our parents, our brothers and sisters, etc. The closeness is for wrestling around with each other, making love, or nurturing someone. There are occasions where people have to get this close to us, on a bus or in an elevator; however, we typically ensure there is no touching and minimal eye contact to make us feel like they are not as close as they are to us.

- **The Personal Zone.** This zone is also referred to as your invisible "bubble" or the area around you that protects you from others. The zone is from 18 inches to 4 feet. We allow people in this zone with whom we want to interpersonally communicate; for example, our friends, our neighbors, our relatives, etc. We will allow them to step into our intimate zone for a handshake or a hug, and then it is back in our personal zone (or out of our bubble).
- **The Social Zone.** The zone is 4 feet to 12 feet. In this zone we conduct business, attend meetings, parties, class, etc. Communication occurs in this zone; however, it is typically impersonal. We are also typically using more formal English in this zone.
- **The Public Zone.** This zone is 12 feet to 25 feet. This zone is to acknowledge the communication that goes on in much larger arenas. It may be a large lecture hall, a public presentation, or an actor on a stage. Communication is going on; however, there typically isn't a relationship between the parties involved.

> "I know what to say, I only wish the words come out like they sound in my mind. I am doing better now that I have taken this class. I finally stop, think, and organize my thoughts before I open my mouth."
> —Anonymous

Category 4—Express Your Mood

Everyone uses nonverbal communication to express their moods to others. We use it to say what we are not willing to verbally communicate, we use it to start or end a conflict, we use it to vent or let out some of our pain, and so on. Here are just a few examples of how we express our mood through our nonverbal behaviors:

- **Paralanguage,** or the fluctuation in our vocal tones. For example, we use paralanguage to raise our voice and yell at someone, to emphasize a certain word in a sentence, to whisper a message, to persuade someone to do something for us, to act innocent, etc.
- **Silence.** We use silence in a variety of ways; to let someone know it is their turn to talk, to give someone a moment to think, to punish or hurt someone, to play a "power" game, to add emphasis to something you are about to say, etc.
- **Facial Expressions.** We use our facial expressions most often when expressing our mood. We express fear, surprise, anger, disgust, interest, bewilderment, happiness, determination, etc. With our facial expressions we do things like intensify or de-intensify our emotion, mask or fake our true emotion, and use our "poker" face or try not to show any emotion. However, many experts tell us that our facial expressions are the most difficult to control. As a matter of fact, a University of Pennsylvania study found than men are 25% less accurate in identifying someone's emotional state based on their facial expressions. You probably agree that your facial expressions are difficult to con-

trol; if people have told you that they know exactly how you are feeling, from the expression on your face. It does take a lot of work to control our facial expressions, and there are definitely times when we cannot control them.

- **Eye Contact.** As with other nonverbal behaviors every culture has different "rules" for the appropriate use of eye contact. In our culture, we use eye contact to show interest or lack thereof, to express feedback, to intimidate or to dominate, to initiate a conversation, and to flirt with someone. We use our eyes to stare, to look away, to show surprise, to roll our eyes in disgust, etc. The size of our pupils can even communicate— yep it's true! Your pupils enlarge when you are interested or attracted to someone; your pupils get smaller when you are disgusted or lying to someone.

- **Body Movement.** How you sit, how you stand, and how you move your body, all communicate something about how you are feeling. Many times you are unintentionally giving off messages about your mood. For example, if you are slouched over, someone may conclude that you are bored; however, that may not be the case; rather, you may be tired or simply trying to get comfortable. An interviewer spends a significant amount of time watching an interviewee's body movement. The interviewer is typically trying to conclude if you are professional, nervous, interested, etc.

- **Gestures.** There are those who "talk" with their hands, especially if they are excited about something. Using too many gestures can become a distraction to your overall message; therefore, you need to make a conscious effort to try to control or be aware of your gesturing. We use gestures to express our mood; however, gestures do have purposes other than ones that fit neatly into the four categories discussed thus far. Those purposes include the following:

  - **Affect display.** This is the one purpose that does relate to expressing your mood. We use gestures to show our excitement, happiness, anger, sadness, etc. It could be making big gestures, throwing your hands in the air as if to give up, wiping your tears from your face, or hitting a pillow or hitting your fist in the palm of your hand in anger.

  - **Regulator.** Here we are using our hands to monitor, encourage, or control a conversation. We may put our hand up to say "stop," or wave our hand to encourage someone to "keep talking," or we may point to someone to let him know that it is his turn to talk.

  - **Illustrator.** In this case we are trying to add meaning to the verbal message. We may move a hand up to show how tall someone is, or make circles with our hands to show something rolling in circles.

  - **Emblem.** This is a gesture that clearly has verbal meaning. It may be the "Ok" sign to say I understand you, or a wave to someone to say hello, or a "thumbs up" to say good job.

  - **Adaptor.** The final purpose for gesturing is the adaptor which is simply a gesture to relieve tension. It could be scratching your head, biting your nails, or rubbing your hands.

NONVERBAL COMMUNICATION DISABILITY

An area of nonverbal communication that is not often discussed in interpersonal communication textbooks is **nonverbal learning disability (NLD).** People who have NLD have great difficulty organizing, sequencing, and synthesizing information. They also are extremely stressed in social situations due to all of the interacting that goes on simultaneously. Much of the disability comes from neurological limitations, and therefore the disability can greatly affect the person's capacity to communicate with others. The average person may not even know that one has this disability. To that end, this is a perfect example of why we need to be aware of how we communicate nonverbally. Someone who does not have NLD can watch another person's posture, facial expressions, and gestures while listening to him communicate at the same time. This same situation is troublesome for someone with NLD because they have a hard time grasping the "big picture."

NLD is a specific sub-type learning disability, and sometimes it is a characteristic of someone with Asperger Syndrome. Bryon Rourke and Katherine Tsatsanis wrote "Nonverbal Learning Disabilities and Asperger Syndrome" in the book *Asperger Syndrome*, where they discuss the difficulties people with NLD have in adapting to social situations. The challenges they face include:

1. Difficulty assessing someone's emotional state, for example, someone's tone of voice and the emotion she is trying to convey.
2. Difficulty assessing cause-and-effect relationships, for example, the relationship between a gesture and the verbal message.
3. Difficulty understanding and appreciating humor in social situations.
4. Misinterpreting a variety of nonverbal behaviors.

"Social competence also requires adaptability to novel interpersonal situations and a constantly shifting pattern of exchange. A basic deficit identified in persons with NLD is coping with novelty, which is exacerbated by poor problem-solving and hypothesis-testing skills. This constellation of difficulties conspires to render a smooth adaptation to the constantly changing milieu of social interactions all but impossible for the child or adult with NLD," according to Rourke and Tsatsanis.

A final word on NLD is a story by Lori Shery. In the book *Asperger Syndrome* Shery has a chapter entitled "A View from Inside," where she discusses her life as a parent of a child with Asperger Syndrome. Her son, Adam, also has the sub-type NLD. Here is an excerpt from her chapter:

Adam still had difficulty with social situations, but he has made great progress. The boys in the social skills group he has attended for the past two years have become his good friends. Last year, on a flight home from Disney World, Adam was seated next to a boy that he didn't know. As the plane took off, I could hear Adam making conversation with the youngster.

"Hi, my name is Adam. What's your name?" and then
"Nice to meet you, Tommy. I'm in fifth grade, what grade are you in?" and then
"You're also in fifth grade? What's your favorite subject?"

I smiled to myself. No one but Adam and I knew that this was a well-rehearsed script that he had learned in his group. To anyone listening, it sounded completely natural and spontaneous. They couldn't have known how proud I was of him.

If you want more information about NLD, check out the following websites: *www.nlda.org*, *www.nldonline.com*, or *www.ldonline.org*.

INCREASING YOUR VERBAL AND NONVERBAL COMMUNICATION SKILLS

Do you ask for what you need? Do you feel powerful or powerless around strangers? Are you intimidated easily? Many of you are probably saying, "Well, it depends on who it is and what I need." My question for you is—Why? It shouldn't matter if it is your mother, your best friend, a stranger, or even the president of the United States. Here's an example for you—In 1995, I was presented with the opportunity to meet and spend some time with President Bill Clinton. I was asked to join 10 other people and discuss the value of financial aid (specifically the federally funded Pell grant) for students. Of course I jumped at the chance. I knew how important financial aid was to a lot of people, myself included! It wasn't until the night before the big day that I realized—I am going to meet with the president of the United States! Fortunately I had already said yes to the opportunity before I realized that I was feeling powerless, tongue-tied, and intimidated. I tried calming my nerves at the local bar, that didn't work. I tried drinking a half a bottle of Pepto-Bismol, that didn't work. Here is what worked—realizing that there was no reason to feel intimidated or powerless. I had a voice and it was my turn to use it. I am so thankful that I participated in that discussion because it was then that I decided to never feel powerless or intimidated, and to always take the opportunity to share my ideas. I am worth it and so are you.

There are a few things you can do to increase your verbal and nonverbal communication skills. They include the following:

1. Always, always, always think about what you want to say prior to saying it.
2. Never assume that people are going to completely understand you. Learn how to read nonverbal communication to check for understanding, and ask someone to repeat what you said to ensure understanding.
3. Check to make sure you understand the intention of the verbal and nonverbal messages. Never assume you have completely understood what someone is trying to tell you—ask if you are correct.
4. Keep in mind that your perception of the communication situation is not necessarily the same as the other person.
5. Evaluate how you verbally and nonverbally communicate with others. Talk to your significant other, family, and friends about your communication.
6. Try role-playing in the classroom or with a friend. This gives you an opportunity to work on becoming more comfortable. This is a great tool to use prior to a job interview. If you have a video-tape, try recording the activity to assess how effectively you communicate.

In closing, it is time to pause and reflect on what you have read. Consider the following questions and write down some notes in the space provided:

1. What didn't you know about the things you have read so far?

2. What surprised you the most about what you have read so far?

3. With what you've read so far, what don't you understand?

4. Is there anything you don't agree with, or is there anything you need more information about?

PLEASE TOUCH!
HOW TO COMBAT SKIN HUNGER IN OUR SCHOOLS

Sidney B. Simon

You can see them in any junior high school. They're the ones who shove and push. They knock one another down the stairwell and slam the locker door on each other's head. And behind every push and shove, they are crying out their skin-hunger needs.

The shovers and trippers aren't your disruptive discipline problems. They're not the window breakers, either. The ones I have in mind are your nice kids from nice families. They abound in those suburban orthodontia belts ringing our major cities.

They are kids with a severe form of malnutrition—a malnutrition of the skin. Their disease is called skin hunger, and it has reached almost epidemic proportions in all of our schools.

It is shocking that we have allowed this disease to persist despite research which shows that infants who weren't touched and handled and fondled when they were fed by their orphanage attendants simply withered up and died. Today, no orphanage or child-care agency would think of putting a baby down with a bottle propped up to work on gravity feed.

There are dozens of animal studies which support what so many of us instinctively know. Researchers found that laboratory rats from the cages of certain keepers were smarter than other rats. What was the difference? The smarter rats had keepers who fondled them, stroked them, or touched them when they cleaned their cages or fed them.

Not only were the rats smarter, they were less vicious, had larger and healthier litters, and took care of their young with much more tenderness and warmth. The research was overwhelmingly clear: when we touch and caress and stroke, life is better for rats.

There are enormous implications here for people: Touch! But don't do it in school. No way. There, the rules are clear. *No* one touches anyone else. No hand holding. No hugging. No recognition that touching and being touched are vital to the well-being of all of us.

Woe to the teacher who should dare break the icebound tradition. You can predict the responses—"Say, what are you? A dirty old woman?" (Or a dirty old man?) "Hey, aren't you getting enough at home?" Schools have people memorize research but act as if they don't believe that research since they don't apply it.

Oh, there are exceptions to the no-touch rule. Kindergarten children can be touched. And some first grade teachers might still hold kids on their laps and read to them. But by the end of the third grade, touching has just about dried up in most of our schools, replaced by the onward push of the college-entrance curriculum.

We have conveyed the message very clearly: Don't touch! There are some kids who even flinch when you reach out to them. They somehow have read us to say, "Touch is very dangerous. It can lead to sex." And in our schools, dominated by minds which are somehow third-sex neuters, we can't have any of that.

So, instead, we have the shovers and the pushers and the trippers. For some of these kids, violence becomes a way of getting the touching they need. Sometimes I think contact sports were invented to provide what a saner society would have supplied in a saner way. One wrestling coach told me, "My wrestlers don't have skin hunger. They get lots of touching, every day." In some ways, the coach is right. They do. But it is underground, not owned for what it is—a rather convoluted way of getting what we need naturally, daily and with open recognition of our need.

As you read this, you may be thinking: "What's all the furor about?" I didn't need touching when I was in school, and these kids don't need it either. We've got other more important work to be done."

Well, I certainly hope you did get the touching you needed when you were younger and that because you did, you don't recall needing it in school. I do hope you came from a family which routinely gave each other back rubs and that hugging each other warmly and at some length was also a part of your family pattern. Clearly, there are thousands of adults roaming this pornographic society who were not touched by their families, and so they don't touch their own children, who will not touch their own children—and so on. Adults spread and dump onto children their own confusion and conflict about love and sex, touch and caring, and the difference between hands which touch to heal and hands which touch to turn someone on.

In this slightly cockeyed world, there doesn't seem to be provision for someone to get touched without having to go to bed with whomever does the touching. Think about that. We have mixed up simple, healing, warm touching with sexual advances. So much so, that there seems to be no middle road between, "Don't you dare touch me!"

and, "Okay, you touched me, now let's make love."

Some of this confusion shows up in our high school kids today. In the spirit of the new freedom, many of them are experiencing intercourse years before they really are ready for it. Lovemaking involves such complex feelings and responses, requires so much more than merely being stroked; it's no wonder some youngsters remain baffled with the question, "You mean, that's all it is?" Of course it's a whole lot more. What many of these young kids really, truly want is simply to be held and rocked and stroked. They are suffering from skin hunger. And it is a need as strong as the need for water or food—and quite different from the need for sex. If touching were permitted—even tolerated—in our schools, how much less grief and anxiety and deep feelings of inadequacy we would find in our young people. How much less jumping into bed with the first person who strokes them gently.

I feel the schools should face this problem and begin to find ways to deal with the skin-hunger needs of the youth they serve. It is that simple. We are deeply involved these days in providing students with all kinds of help. We have budgets for helping students gain college entrance. We pour enormous resources into fostering athletic programs, preventing drug abuse, and aiding disabled children. But there is little attention paid to the children who are starving from skin malnutrition.

Since their skin-hunger needs are not being met in other ways, some students get pregnant, or cruise the highways at diabolical speeds—indifferent to life or start trafficking in drugs. Many of these cases are skin hunger related. The loss of human joy and potential is just too great for us to sit by and remain quiet while our students wither and die from skin starvation.

When you teach, you can see the difference. Children from homes which are well aware of skin-hunger needs tend to be more open and warm and less touched at home, often seem more withdrawn, more fantasy ridden, or more aggressively hostile. I feel they tend to have a lesser sense of their own worth and beauty. In children who are getting lots of skin-hunger care and comfort, you can see clear eyes and energy which seems to flow effortlessly throughout more brilliant eyes, looking out less afraid. Then there are the furtive eyes of those who don't get touched at all. Or the more glassy eyes of the ones who get touched a lot, but only for sex. The difference is marked.

Name: _____ Date: _____

PLEASE TOUCH:
HOW TO COMBAT SKIN HUNGER IN OUR SCHOOLS
By Sidney B. Simon

1. What are your top 3 reactions to this article?

2. How does your local public school system handle touching between students and student/teachers? Do they have a no-touch rule?

(Questions continued on back)

3. How do you feel about the way our society is reacting to the negative side of touch? Are they going to far when they create new rules and laws? How can we find a balance?

4. Does touch typically lead to negative behaviors?

5. This article was written in 1974. Explain how it relates to today's schools.

6. Other thoughts about the article?

ARTICLE FOR DISCUSSION—

"What Are You Telling the World?"
by Kare Anderson

How do others perceive you? How soon do you realize that you are getting tense? How well do you anticipate their unspoken feelings? Your ability to understand these signals has an enormous impact on how well you get along with others.

"The secret is all in understanding a code. It is a most elaborate code that is written nowhere, known by none and yet understood by all."

Tour Your Body for Vital Signs

Your body is a hologram of your being; a three-dimensional movie that is constantly on, showing others how you feel about yourself and the world. As you walk through life, is your body saying what your words are saying? Your body is a three-dimensional "full motion" billboard you are constantly showing the rest of the world. Even if people are consciously reading your body language, they will subconsciously react to your bodily signals.

For example, if you are literally uptight, that is rigid in any part of your body, especially your face, where most people focus most of their attention in conversation, people will instinctively resist or react against you and your comments. This phenomena is akin to bouncing a hard rubber ball on a concrete surface and then on a soft carpet. The ball will bounce higher and faster against the hard surface than the soft one of course, just as others react against your "hardened surface." Suggestion: Whenever you are entering a potentially volatile or even new situation, loosen up physically. Walk, stretch, and

work on the areas you tend to hold most of your tension.

For example, if you are like many conscientious, hard-working people, you probably hold your shoulders higher and slightly more forward than is natural and one of the tendons in your neck has tightened up even more than the other. If someone will give you a quick ten or fifteen minute shoulder and neck massage, you will enter the situation more relaxed and others will respond more softly to you.

It's time to get to know your body. If you don't know where you hold your tension, and most people don't, take a tour of your body, so you can know what needs the most loosening—and exercise. Are you shouldering the world's responsibilities, or perpetually drooping? Or, in your determined drive toward success, do you plant your feet solidly on the ground in a life gesture of hostility, defiance or taking ground? Perhaps you have a forward leaning posture, with the head tilted slightly forward, as if you are ready to spring into action, expressing a lifelong pattern of flight away from psychologically threatening situations, when you thought it as part of your make-up to leap forward to new opportunities.

To be depressed is, in fact, to press against yourself. To be closed off is to hold your muscles rigid against the world. Being open is being soft. No instinctive muscle clenching, such as in the jaws, a growing pattern in Americans, even into their sleep. Hardness is being uptight, cold, separate, giving yourself and others a hard time. Softness is synonymous with pleasure, warmth, flowing, being alive, drawing other people toward you rather than forcing them away.

Are you itching to get at someone? Is your colleague a pain in the neck? Are you sore about something? What is your aching back trying to tell you? Is there someone or thing on your back? What about your ulcer, allergy, muscle spasms? Is there someone you cannot stomach? What is it that you would like to get off your chest, or your back? Your body speaks to you all the time, telling you what your own needs are. Listen there. It is your free and most sophisticated medical feedback testing system. It is constantly showing you your inner tensions, state of mind and habitual life attitudes.

When you are misaligned and tense, you expend outrageous sums of energy doing the everyday gestures of life. Since the body is a high viscosity substance, that is 60 percent to 80 percent water, the bonds are floating in a relatively fluid environment. Yet, over time, despite that apparent fluidity, you have tightened the muscles around every major experience of pain, fear or anger, and continue to tighten them each time you think you are experiencing similar situations, thus guaranteeing that you make your own pattern of uptightness familiar and increasingly habitual, until it becomes a permanent condition you no longer recognize as not normal.

We all hold great muscle tension around certain bones in blind remembrance of fearful events, long after the actual events are often long forgotten. You may never recall what initially made you afraid, but you can note where your body reacted to protect itself and spend more time in your exercise and massage or other body work to relax and loosen those muscle groups.

In Western society, we usually hold the tension somewhere in our upper body whereas in many Eastern cultures the tension tends to be held in the lower body.

If you don't begin a regular practice of exercise and stretching, you are guaranteed to lose mobility sooner as you age and rob yourself of the most positive and alive personal presence you could offer the world every day.

We go through life making decisions, closing down and limiting ourselves unconsciously. Stay open literally by getting in motion more frequently. Stand and stretch at least every twenty minutes when you are sitting and working. Try to talk, hopefully in sync with someone else, in fresh air and sunlight, at least thirty minutes a day. As Dr. Dean Ornish wrote in his most recent book, Love and Survival: The Scientific Basis for the Healing Power of Intimacy, ""our survival depends on the healing power of love.

One of the safest and most natural ways to move closer to others is to walk with them. Walk further to the restaurant. Walk and talk on the way to the meeting. Walk with your loved one, rather than sitting at home, to come down from your day, and come together. Motion is emotional and makes every event more vivid and memorable. Literally move towards the one you want in your life and loosen up together. Your life may depend on it. In fact, why not get up right now and take a stretch, look around, call someone and suggest a walk.

Want to learn more about the importance of cultivating intimate relationships to keep healthy? Consider reading, in addition to Ornish's book:

Cortis, Bruno, Heart and Soul, Villard Books, 1995

Dossey, Larry, healing Words, HarperCollins, 1993

Goleman, Danile. Emotional Intelligence. Bantam Books, 1995

Keen, Sam. To Love and Be Loved. Bantam Books, 1997

Lynch, James J. The Broken Heart. Basic Books, 1977.

Pert, Candace. Molecules of Emotion: Why We Feel the Way We Feel. Scribner Books/Simon & Schuster, 1997.

Remen, Rachel Naomi. Kitchen Table Wisdom, Riverhead Books, 1996.

Scarf, Maggie. Intimate Partners. Ballantine Books, 1987.

Weil, Andrew. Spontaneous Healing. Knopf, 1995.

Name: _____ Date: _____

QUESTIONS FOR DISCUSSION—

"WHAT ARE YOU TELLING THE WORLD?"
by Kare Anderson

1. What are your top 3 reactions to this article?

2. Do you agree that your body is "a three-dimensional movie"? Support your answer.

(Questions continued on back)

3. Do you feel like you know what your body language tells others? If yes, describe what you are telling people. If no, describe what you can do to get to a point of understanding what you are telling people.

4. Describe an incident where you completely misunderstood someone's body language.

5. Other thoughts about the article?

GENDER DIFFERENCES IN NONVERBAL COMMUNICATION

M.A. Griffin, D. McGahee, and J. Slate

A study was conducted at Valdosta State University in Valdosta, Georgia, during Fall Semester, 1998, to determine students' perceptions of gender differences in several areas of nonverbal communication. Specifically, the areas of eye contact, gestures, smiles, personal space, touch, and interpretation of nonverbal cues were examined.

To collect data, a survey instrument was administered to 387 undergraduate students in 18 sections of classes. In addition to demographic information, the students responded to 28 items. Data were analyzed using the SPSS statistical package.

Who established more eye contact? The females surveyed thought they do; 67.5 percent agreed that females typically establish more eye contact than men do. Burgoon, Buller, and Woodall (1996) concluded that North American women engage in more eye contact during conversations than men. Ivy and Backlund (1994) suggested that women (more often in a subordinate role) make more eye contact than a person in a dominant position. In addition, Ivy and Backlund found that women were more comfortable giving eye contact than men (1994).

Who used more gestures? The majority of the females surveyed (74.5 percent) felt that they typically use more gestures than a male. However, the opinions of experts in literature were mixed. For instance, Hanna and Wilson (1998) felt that women used fewer gestures than men. These authors also stated that women use fewer gestures when they are with other women but more ges-

tures with men. However, Burgoon, Buller, and Woodall (1996) felt that the difference was in the types of gestures used rather than in the frequency of use.

A very large majority of the female respondents (83.7 percent) felt that they typically smile more often than a male does. However, almost everyone surveyed said they would automatically return a smile if someone smiled at them first. Our experts agreed with the survey findings. Hanna and Wilson (1998) not only said women smile more than males, but they were also more attracted to others who smiled.

Who required more personal space? Fifty-six percent of the female respondents felt they require more personal space than a male. However, all the experts in literature agreed that males used more personal space than females.

When asked who touches more, 57.8 percent of our female respondents agreed that they touch others more than a male does. However, the experts had mixed opinions on the subject. Hanna and Wilson (1998) felt that women touch others less than men do. But Burgoon, Buller, and Woodall (1996) conclude that women give and receive more touches than men (except when initiating courtship). They explain how touch is considered a feminine-appropriate behavior and a masculine-inappropriate one. Mothers touch female infants more than male infants, and female children desire and offer more nonaggressive touch than male children. Another important point made by Burgoon, Buller, and Woodall is that touch initiation may depend not on gender alone but also on the intentionality of the touch, the age and relationship of the participants, and the setting where the touch occurs. Of course, teachers must be very careful about touching students in today's school environment.

Which gender was able to interpret nonverbal cues better? Of the female respondents, 73.7 percent agreed that they can interpret another person's nonverbals better than a male. From the review of literature, all experts agreed that, in fact, females are better interpreters of nonverbals. Burgoon, Buller, and Woodall (1996) described women as being more sensitive communicators. And Ivy and Backlun (1994) conclude that women more actively communicate the importance of relationships by using a number of verbal and nonverbal channels.

Teachers should be aware of gender differences in the classroom to help students develop an awareness of nonverbal communication—particularly what is appropriate nonverbal behavior in the workplace.

References

Burgoon, J. K., Buller, D.B., & Woodall, W.G. (1996). *Nonverbal communication: The unspoken dialogue* (2nd ed.). New York: McGraw-Hill Companies, Inc.

Hanna, M.S., & Wilson, G.L. (1998). *Communicating in business and professional settings* (4th ed.). New York: McGraw-Hill Companies, Inc.

Ivy, D.K., & Backlund, P. (1994). *Exploring genderspeak*. New York: McGraw-Hill Companies, Inc.

Name: _____ Date: _____

QUESTIONS FOR DISCUSSION—

GENDER DIFFERENCES IN NONVERBAL COMMUNICATION
by M.A. Griffin, D. McGahee, and J. Slate

1. What are your top 3 reactions to this article?

2. What do you think are the major gender differences between men and women? Explain your answer.

(Questions continued on back)

3. What do you think about the Valdosta survey results? Are the results consistent with what you believe to be true? Are the results consistent with any other gender surveys that you have read about? Explain your answers.

4. Other thoughts about the article?

Name: _____ Date: _____

INDIVIDUAL ACTIVITY #1
Nonverbal Observations
(adapted from the Nonverbal Cafeteria Exercise in Communicate! by CRA, Kendall/Hunt Publishing)

PURPOSE—

To demonstrate the lack of credibility when making assumptions based on nonverbal communication alone.

PROCEDURE—

First, find a place where you can sit and observe people.

> *Option:* If you don't know your classmates very well, you could potentially conduct this activity in the classroom.

Second, find someone that you don't know and observe that person for as long as possible. Third, use the chart below and fill out the column entitled, "Assumptions."

Finally, after you have completely filled out the assumptions chart it is time to find out your level of accuracy. In order to do this you need to go up and introduce yourself to the person you were watching. Let the person know why you were observing him or her. Most people will be open to assisting you complete your activity.

Nonverbal Description	Assumptions	Actual
1. Age?		
2. Racial make-up?		
3. Single, married, widowed, or divorced?		
4. Children? How many?		

(Chart continued on back)

Nonverbal Description	Assumptions	Actual
5. Like animals? Have any? What type?		
6. Good relationship with his or her mother?		
7. Good relationship with his or her father?		
8. College degree? What is or was his or her major?		
9. Like to give gifts to others whenever s/he can?		
10. Environmentalist?		
11. Favorite type of music?		
12. Hobbies or interests in what area?		
13. Ever in the military?		
14. Comes from a large family?		
15. Introvert or extrovert?		

FOLLOW-UP—

1. Discuss your experience with your classmates.

2. Discuss how you came up with your assumptions.

3. Discuss how you feel about making assumptions based on everything you have learned in this chapter.

Name: _____ Date: _____

INDIVIDUAL ACTIVITY #2
Taking Responsibility for What You Say—Even on the Internet

PURPOSE—

To assess the importance of taking responsibility for your verbal communication, by evaluating Internet communication.

Most of my students agree that it is easier to communicate on the Internet. Their reasoning is because they don't have to see the other person; therefore, they feel as though they can say whatever is on their mind. With that in mind your challenge for this activity is to learn to say what is on your mind with two rules: (1) think about what you want to say before you say it, and (2) apply the tools you have learned in this chapter about verbal and nonverbal communication.

PROCEDURE—

Step 1—Pick a minimum of three interpersonal communication situations, with at least one of the situations to take place via Internet communication (email, chat, or instant messenger), where you need to talk to someone about something that has been on your mind.

Step 2—In the space provided, write down a summary of what you need to discuss with someone else. Some examples are:

- I need to tell my professor that I do not like the way she talks to me.
- I need to tell my father that I am engaged to a guy whom he is not very fond of.
- I need to tell my best friend that she is making a big mistake.
- I need to tell my brother that his friends have been spreading rumors about him.
- I need to tell my boss that I am having some problems with my job.

(Questions continued on back)

Step 3—Next, you need to apply the rules from above and write down how you plan on approaching the communication situation, and specifically how you will say what you need to say.

FOLLOW-UP—

1. Assess how each communication situation went; discussing if it went the way you planned, what you could have done differently, and what you have learned from this experience.

2. Discuss the experience overall with your classmates and compare notes.

GROUP ACTIVITY #1
What Are They Communicating?

PURPOSE—

To assess the various interpretations that we have about what people are communicating.

PROCEDURE—

You will find this activity similar to the group activity #2 in the perception chapter. In chapter 3 you were simply looking at what you perceived immediately when you looked at the picture. For this activity you will be looking deeper at the photos and assessing what you believe the people are communicating.

Complete this activity in pairs or small groups.

For each photo, write down what you think the people are verbally and/or nonverbally communicating. Consider the four areas of our nonverbal behaviors: communicating your identity, exemplifying your personality, creating your persona, and expressing your mood. When writing your response, try to be as specific as possible.

(1) _____   (2) _____   (3) _____

(Continued on back)

(4) _____

(5) _____

(6) _____

(7) _____

(8) _____

(9) _____

(10) _____

FOLLOW-UP—

1. Discuss how you came to the conclusion about what they were communicating.

2. Share your assessments with other groups.

Name: _____ Date: _____

GROUP ACTIVITY #2

Semantic Reactions

(From *Communicate!, Sixth Edition* by Communication Research Associates.
Copyright © 1998 by Kendall/Hunt Publishing Company. Reprinted by permission.)

PURPOSE—

To examine your own semantic reactions to terms and enable you to see how each of us experiences semantic noise.

PROCEDURE—

Following is a list of 20 terms. Beside each term place a checkmark which corresponds to your **immediate** reaction to that word according to the scale indicated. Remember that the intent of the activity is to allow you to examine your semantic reactions, so be as honest in marking your reaction as you can. Your immediate reaction is usually the most reliable.

Reaction	Highly Positive +2	Slightly Positive +1	Neutral or No Reaction 0	Slightly Negative -1	Highly Negative -2
1. patriotism					
2. breast					
3. pusillanimous					
4. love					
5. communism					
6. Caucasian					
7. Mexican					
8. bureaucracy					
9. speech					
10. friendship					
11. chauvinist					
12. fox					
13. intercourse					
14. cancer					
15. exacerbate					
16. gay					
17. cum laude					
18. seersucker					
19. chicano					
20. whitey					
21.					
22.					
23.					

Now that you have completed the list, you will have a chance to compare your reactions with another member of the class and discuss the following questions:

1. How do you react to the various words?

2. Why do you react as you do? On what is your reaction based?

3. How can reaction to words (semantic reactions) affect communication?

4. With respect to semantic reactions, what suggestions could you make to improve communication?

5. What variables—i.e., sex, race, religion, income, age—influence your responses?

CROSSWORD PUZZLE
Reviewing the Terms

ACROSS

7. actual words that we communicate

9. how people use and structure their time

10. gesturing to control the conversation

11. symbols for objects, events, and feelings

12. the fluctuation in our vocal tones

13. anything we communicate, intentional or unintentional, without using words

DOWN

1. the feeling we associate with a particular word

2. what is attached to words and exists within the person who is perceiving the words

3. gesturing the "OK" sign

4. gesturing to relieve tension

5. gesturing to add meaning to your verbal message

6. the dictionary definition of a word

8. gesturing to express your mood

CHAPTER QUIZ
Reviewing the Chapter

1. Nonverbal communication has great usefulness in helping the listener(s) interpret your verbal messages through your:
(a) gesturing (b) voice inflections (c) body language (d) all of the above
(e) only a and c.

2. Nonverbal communication constitutes at least how much _____ of our total communication?
(a) 10% (b) 20% (c) 50% (d) 60% (e) none of the above.

3. Which of the following is gesturing to relieve tension:
(a) illustrator (b) regulator (c) emblem (d) affect display (e) adaptor.

4. The most significant nonverbal behavior can often _____ the spoken word.
(a) substitute for (b) carry (c) contradict (d) both a and c (e) none of the above.

5. In proxemics, the zone that everyone shares is:
(a) intimate (b) personal (c) social (d) public.

6. Which nonverbal behavior is an example of expressing your identity?
(a) touch (b) your height (c) your hair (d) your body scent (e) only c and d.

7. Which of the following is gesturing to express your mood?
(a) illustrator (b) regulator (c) emblem (d) affect display (e) adaptor.

8. In proxemics, the zone that a parent/child share is:
(a) intimate (b) personal (c) social (d) public.

9. Which nonverbal behavior is an example of exemplifying your personality?
(a) touch (b) your height (c) your hair (d) your body scent (e) only c and d.

10. Nonverbal communication can most easily communicate the following:
(a) You are in favor of capital punishment (b) You think marijuana should be legalized (c) You are bored (d) You voted for a tax increase (e) none of the above.

11. In proxemics, the zone that you share with people you are having an interpersonal conversation with is:
(a) intimate (b) personal (c) social (d) public.

12. Which nonverbal behavior is an example of expressing your mood?
(a) silence (b) your height (c) your hair (d) your body scent (e) only c and d.

13. Which of the following is gesturing to add meaning to your verbal message?
(a) illustrator (b) regulator (c) emblem (d) affect display (e) adaptor.

14. Paralanguage is nonverbal.
(a) true (b) false.

15. Sign Language is nonverbal.
    (a) true (b) false.

16. Which of the following is an example of how your pupils communicate?
    (a) Your pupils enlarge when you are interested in someone (b) Your pupils
    enlarge when you are happy (c) Your pupils get smaller when you are lying to
    someone (d) only a and c (e) none of them.

CHAPTER 5

UNDERSTANDING THE SELF

KEY TERMS

Physiological needs

Role

Role conflict

Safety needs

Self-actualization

Self-concept

Self-esteem

Self-esteem needs

Self-fulfilling
prophecy

Social comparison
theory

Social needs

True self

CHAPTER OBJECTIVES

1. Understand the difference between the roles that you play and your true self.

2. Describe the five levels of Maslow's Hierarchy of Needs.

3. Recognize how the self-fulfilling prophecy works.

4. Determine how to create a healthy self-concept.

5. Understand how to become self-aware, and practice positive self-talk

6. Practice skills for improving the self.

I looked in the mirror, I wanted to look away. Intrapersonally communicate—please, it couldn't be necessary! I was in my "birthday suit." Ok, I'll say it—I was naked. Why is that so hard to say to myself? Why is it even harder to look in the mirror? I know what I want to see. I want to see a beauty queen, who is longing to find peace in the world (I know—I'm an idealist). I'm afraid I'll see a woman who is showing her age in unflattering ways; one who's faced many challenges and lost a quite a few; one who has raised a few children and hopes they are finding their places in the world; and finally, one who is now desperately seeking peace within her true self. My roles have changed. I don't need to run my children here and there, no more fundraisers, no more rushing out the door. No more. A few friends have passed away—how do I make new friends at my age? And then there is my husband, he decided he needed to find himself, and he moved out. I wasn't expecting that; we have roles to play, people expect things from us, our children admired our relationship, and now what am I supposed to do?

It's time to look in the mirror (though now this intrapersonal communication stuff is becoming easier than the idea of looking in that mirror). Tears roll down my face and I haven't even looked yet. "Why is this so hard?" I scream. I check to ensure the bathroom door is locked and then I remember. Nobody else lives here anymore. I'm alone.

Ok, I am officially procrastinating. I need to look at myself; I need to find my true self. I slowly turn toward the mirror. I see the curve of my hips. I see the arch of my back. Tears are flowing uncontrollably. I pause. I am now standing face front. I wipe my eyes. I fight the urge to look away. I stand there. It's deadly silent. I look down at the reflection of my toes. "Not bad—cute polish," I tell myself. I slowly work my way up. "Coulda' shaved my legs first," I giggled. I get to my stomach. I begin to appreciate all that I have been through. I begin to appreciate my curves and marks of survival. They have served me well. I smile and stand tall.

I am a beauty queen. I am at peace with myself. "Isn't that where peace in the world should begin, anyway?" I ponder. If I want to find my true self, shouldn't it begin with finding peace within me? If I want anyone to find me beautiful, shouldn't I find myself beautiful first? If I need to redefine the roles that I play, I need to figure out me, without the roles. If I want anyone to understand me, I must first understand my true self.

UNDERSTANDING THE DIFFERENCES

There are many roles that we play in our lives. **Roles** are the parts that we are expected to play in our lives, which in turn govern our behavior. However, the roles we play are only a part of who we are. The **true self** is what is at the core of who you are when your roles are stripped away. Don't get me wrong; roles are important to how we define ourselves, especially when someone tosses out the line, "Tell me about yourself."

The roles we play should be an expression of the things that we value, that we care about, and that we need. We—as individuals—are so much more than our roles. As you begin to find your true self, you need to consider the answers to the following questions:

1. Do you want to be successful?
2. Do you want to know yourself?
3. Do you want to love yourself?
4. Do you want to feel powerful?
5. Do you want to express your needs and wants to others?
6. Are you willing to make sacrifices to better understand yourself?
7. Are you afraid of understanding yourself?
8. Are you willing to develop healthy relationships and let go of the unhealthy ones?
9. Are you willing to let go of feeling like a victim?
10. Are you willing to examine the messages you send to yourself and to others?
11. Are you willing to admit that you are not always right?
12. Are you willing to be more positive and let go of negativity?
13. Are you worth it?

When we strip away our roles we find the true answers to the questions above. The development of your true self begins developing during the first year of life. For a young person the roles are changing and not yet understood; therefore, they are challenged to figure out "who they are." I know you have heard a teenager tell you, "I know who I am." (Only to come back twenty or thirty years later and tell you that he did not have a clue about who he was.) As we get older, we fall into the roles that we create and the ones that are created for us. See figure 5.1 to see an example of the multiple roles we play at any given time. As many of you know, life can get very stressful. Therefore, we handle the roles that we need to and tend to ourselves "when there is time." After you read the next section on roles, I challenge you to try out the individual activity #1 about separating your roles from your true self. The results may surprise you.

> "Sometimes a role can be an insight to your true self, but your true self doesn't necessarily define a role."
>
> —Ashley Kolp

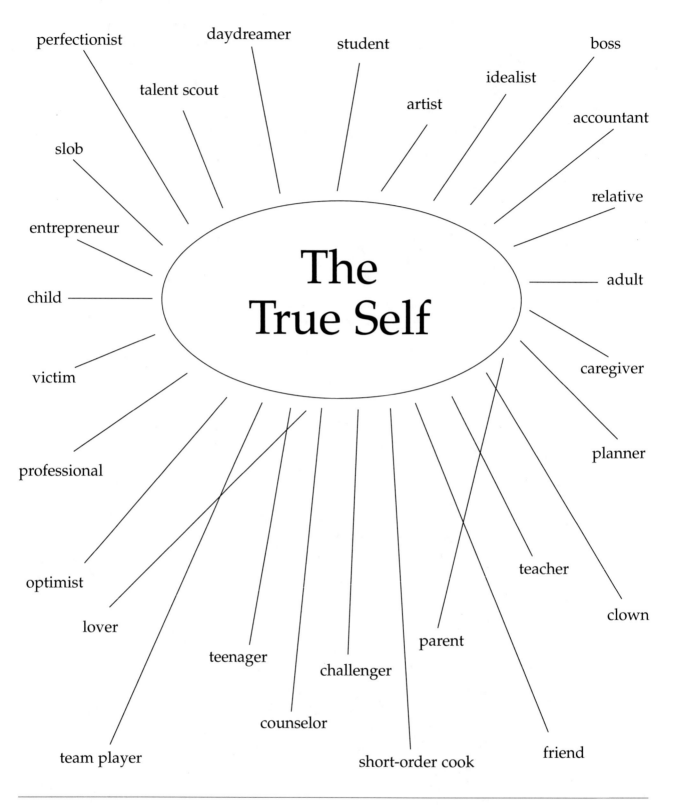

FIGURE 5.1.
Understanding the Roles We Play

UNDERSTANDING YOUR ROLES AND THEIR EXPECTATIONS

Sarah Trenholm and Arthur Jensen, in their book *Interpersonal Communication* tell us, "We know several things about roles: (1) They are learned, (2) they are general, (3) they affect our identities, and (4) most of us play multiple roles." Let's examine those four ideas about roles.

Roles are learned. We learn from our parents, teachers, friends, enemies, strangers, and so on. We learn how to behave in the grocery store, in the mall, in church, in school, and so on. We learn from making a lot of "mis-takes." Do you remember when your mom said, "Be quiet, we are in church." It is then you learned "When I am playing the role of a church member, I am to be quiet." However, how many children only need to be told once? It takes time to learn our roles, and many will challenge "the rules of the roles" throughout the learning process.

Roles are general rules for behavior. Yep—you get to figure out the specific behaviors for yourself. Everyone around you will tell you how you should behave in a given situation; however, people cannot tell you everything. As you are growing up you learn how to behave as a spouse. You learn that you are to be faithful, be patient, pay your bills on time, etc. However, nobody can teach you everything. For example, what if you don't have money to pay your bills? What if the other person isn't faithful? What if you have run out of patience? There is still a lot that you have to figure out, which is what leads to finding your true self.

Roles affect your identity. When a role is new (i.e., being a freshman or starting a new job) you are acutely aware of the awkwardness and newness of the role. However, as you spend time in the role it becomes a part of your identity. In other words, you have figured out the "other" rules that weren't explained to you in the beginning. To take it one step further, after spending enough time in a role, your true self becomes a direct reflection of that role. Imagine this—you have been a police officer for 20 years. You live the life of a police officer, both on and off duty, and you have firmly committed to that single role. What happens when the role is taken away from you, either because you are let go from the department or you choose to retire? This is why it is essential for us to have multiple roles and for us to understand who we are without our roles.

Roles come in multiple forms. We play many roles at one time—friend, sister, wife, volunteer, coach, colleague, party goer, neighbor, community member. As you become more comfortable in your various roles, it isn't as stressful to go from one role to another. However, if your roles pull you in opposite directions, you will experience **role conflict.** Your boss may tell you that you need to be at an important meeting, at the same time that your son tells you that you need to be at his play recital, while to complicate the situation one more time, your sister tells you that you need to attend a wedding with her. Role conflicts can also happen within the same role. For example, you have given your notice at one job to take a similar job with a few more perks. You want to end things on a positive note with the job you are leaving, so you work diligently to create a good situation for the new person. However, you want to impress the people at your new job and want to make yourself available to them. According to Trenholm and Jensen, "Resolving (role conflicts) is no easy matter; it may ultimately lead to painful choices."

> "Everyone has faults. In order to overcome your own faults, you first have to admit that you have them."
>
> —Felicia Jackson

MASLOW'S HIERARCHY OF NEEDS

It is very likely that you have read about or will read about Maslow and his Hierarchy of Needs theory in a psychology and sociology textbook. Maslow's research has been very important to understanding human behavior and human needs. As you read this section, consider why it is important to understand Maslow's Hierarchy of Needs in an interpersonal communication textbook.

We will first examine the five levels to the Hierarchy of Needs. Next, we will look specifically at level five, self-actualization, including the ways that one self-actualizes, and the four behaviors of someone who is self-actualized. See figure 5.2 for a visual representation of the hierarchy.

Level 1—Physiological Needs

Physiological needs are the most basic human needs that one must have in order to survive. Some examples of your most basic needs are air, food, water, and shelter. Many of you may not think about this level of need; however, there are many people around the world who spend most of their lives trying to fulfill this most basic level. If you have ever needed money for food, or experienced homelessness, then you know what it is like to not have this need met. Finally, as you read through the next levels of the hierarchy, I want you to imagine how you would meet the higher levels, if you are constantly trying to meet this basic level of need. Is it possible?

Level 2—Safety Needs

Your **safety needs** are creating and fulfilling a focus on predictability and familiarity in your life. Some examples of safety needs are feeling free from pain and disaster, or eliminating the fear of having your home or car broken into, or finally feeling comfortable with being able to pay your bills and having some financial security in your life (I can't wait to experience what that feels like).

You may find that your safety needs are challenged throughout your life experiences. For example, when you move out of your parent's home and have to fend for yourself, and when you get your first job, change jobs, or retire from your job.

Feeling safe in one's life and even in one's own skin is challenging for many people. Whether it is past or present experiences or a psychological disorder, feeling safe is not always a natural phenomenon. Dr. Stan J. Katz and Aimee E. Liu, in their book *Success Trap*, state "The rate of emotional depression over the last two generations has multiplied *tenfold*." People try so hard to rush up the ladder of success that they forget to put themselves first. Your financial consultant will tell you to pay yourself first and your psychologist will tell you

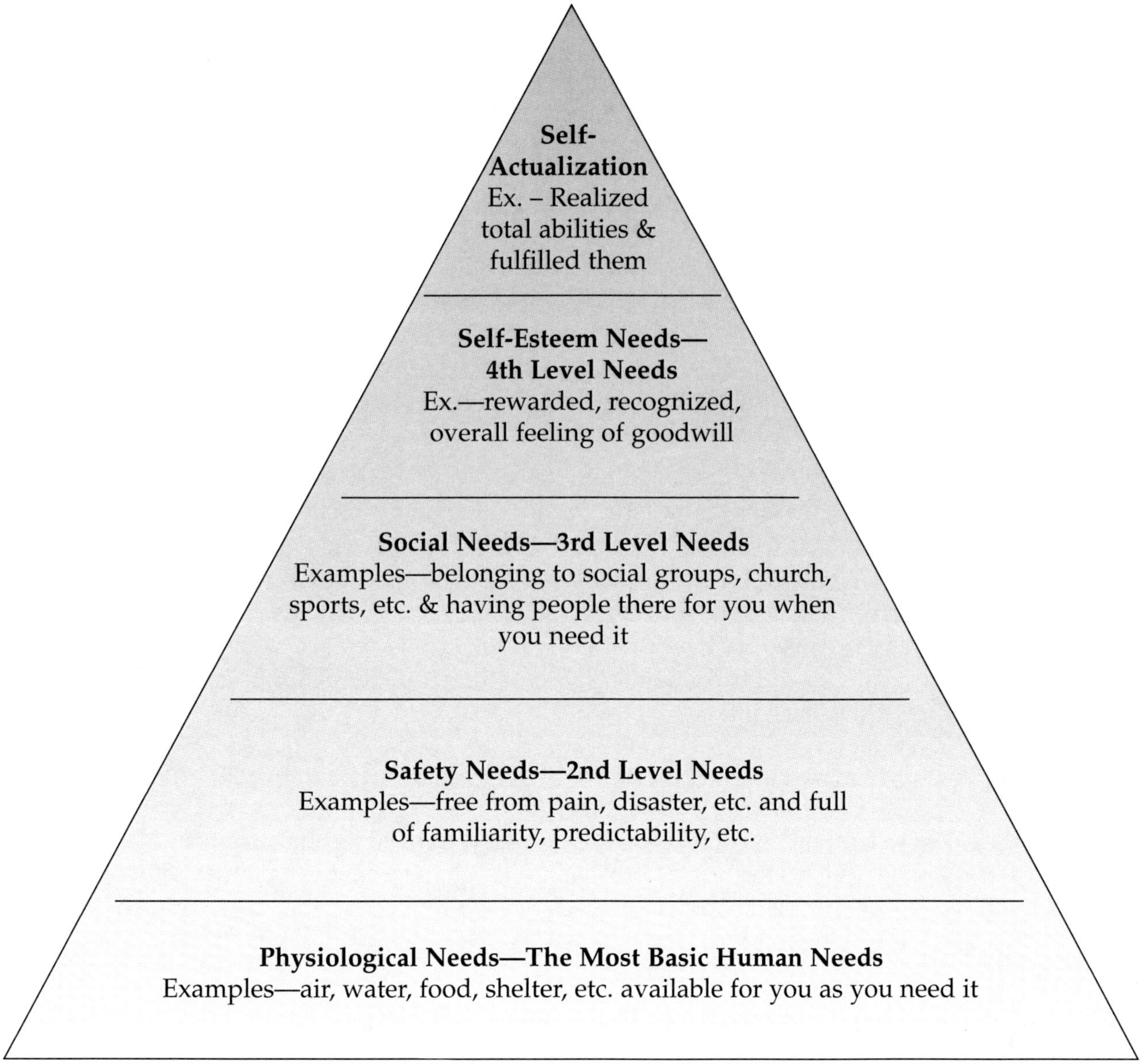

Self-
Actualization
Ex. – Realized
total abilities &
fulfilled them

Self-Esteem Needs—
4th Level Needs
Ex.—rewarded, recognized,
overall feeling of goodwill

Social Needs—3rd Level Needs
Examples—belonging to social groups, church,
sports, etc. & having people there for you when
you need it

Safety Needs—2nd Level Needs
Examples—free from pain, disaster, etc. and full
of familiarity, predictability, etc.

Physiological Needs—The Most Basic Human Needs
Examples—air, water, food, shelter, etc. available for you as you need it

The Essentials of Maslow's Hierarchy:

(1) The next level in the hierarchy can not be *fulfilled* until the lower level(s) are *fulfilled*.
(2) You can be working on fulfilling several levels of hierarchy at a time.
(3) As you climb the hierarchy, you can fall down to a lower level, even to the lowest level.

FIGURE 5.2
Maslow's Hierarchy of Needs

to take time for yourself, but do we listen? Katz and Liu remind us: "We are setting ourselves up for failure by targeting stratospheric goals while rejecting the social and emotional safety nets that could save us when we fall back to earth."

According to Abraham Maslow, in his paper entitled "Theory of Human Motivation," "If both the physiological and the safety needs are fairly well gratified, then there will emerge the love and affection and belongingness needs. . . ." It is up to you to determine what "fairly well gratified" means to you, because each level of this hierarchy has a significant amount of perception.

Level 3—Social Needs

Social needs include feeling that you belong and that people care for you. Some examples of your social needs are feeling like you belong to perhaps a church group, or a baseball team, or a volunteer organization; or to have friends whom you can rely on and who appreciate you.

For many fulfilling their social needs comes naturally as they are growing up; you have groups at school, and after-school sports, and you are typically surrounded by your family and/or your friends' families. Similar to safety needs, the challenge in meeting your social needs usually will come when you graduate from high school and then again when you graduate from college. It comes when you move away, if you get divorced, and when you retire.

Besides the examples I just mentioned, when do you believe social needs are difficult to meet? Consider people you know who do not have many friends, or people who are not involved in recreational activities? How do they fulfill their social needs? Consider those who are faced with depression, severe anxiety, phobias, chronic negativity, or an unsupportive or unavailable family. Finally, consider other cultures where collectivism is the predominant way of thinking. How can we help each other fulfill our social needs? Since social needs are, in essence, learning to and becoming social with those in your community and in your family, how can we help each other?

Level 4—Self-Esteem Needs

Maslow concluded that "satisfaction of the **self-esteem need** [author emphasis] leads to feelings of self-confidence, worth, strength, capability and adequacy of being useful and necessary in the world. But the thwarting of these needs produces feelings of inferiority, of weakness and of helplessness."

According to Camryn Manheim, in her book *Wake Up, I'm Fat*, "We all have our demons and our flaws, and unfortunately we let them define us. For most of my life I hated myself because I was fat. I let a single characteristic, which I perceived as highly negative, overshadow everything else about me. Sadly, I'll bet that sounds familiar to a lot of you. Hating ourselves just seems to come too easily. For me, it didn't matter that I was a loyal friend, an advocate for justice, kind to animals, a team player in volleyball, a good neighbor. It didn't matter that I always remembered birthdays. It didn't even matter that I was a nice person. All of that was obliterated by a blinding self-hate."

Matthew McKay, Ph.D., in his book *Self Esteem*, tells us, "The essence of self-esteem is compassion for yourself. When you have compassion for yourself, you understand and accept yourself. If you make a mistake, you forgive yourself. You have reasonable expectations of yourself. You set attainable goals. You tend to see yourself as basically good."

Many people struggle with a low self-esteem for several reasons, whether you had a challenging upbringing or an abusive childhood, or you faced rape or incest, or you simply have not figured out who you are. It is not easy to feel good about yourself if you listen to the negative messages from your family, friends, enemies, and the media, or the negative messages you send yourself. Fulfilling this level requires many of the qualities you will read about in self-actualization. It requires honesty, trust, and most importantly an ability to be assertive and stand up for yourself, recognizing that you are valuable, worthy, and worth an applause.

Level 5—Self-Actualization

In Abraham Maslow's book *The Farther Reaches of Human Nature*, he discusses why he began studying the idea of "self-actualization." As a student he wanted to understand more about a couple of his professors whom he adored; he wanted to understand what drove them and what made them so passionate about their work, their students, and their lives.

It is important to know that many great theories you will study during your college career have come from experiences in a researcher's life. When a researcher is intrigued by something (or someone), she then becomes driven to pursue the idea, research it, understand it, prove it, and draw conclusions from it. If you find something that intrigues you and want to pursue the idea, then check out Appendix C—The Team Research Project— and try to develop a theory of your own (or with a few of your classmates).

To that end, what did Maslow learn about those professors whom he admired? He learned a lot about how people self-actualize and why they self-actualize. **Self-actualization** is the realization of one's abilities and potentials. Self-actualization is an ongoing process. According to Maslow, self-actualized people, without exception, are involved in a cause outside of themselves. They work on something they love and that they are devoted to throughout their lives. Eleanor Roosevelt, Henry David Thoreau, Thomas Jefferson, Abraham Lincoln, and Aldia Stevenson are examples of people whom Maslow considered, through his studies, as self-actualized people.

Here are six ways in which one self-actualizes, according to Maslow:

1. One who can experience life fully, without limitations brought on by others.
2. One who makes choices in her life that will enable her to grow and move forward.
3. One who allows his true self to emerge and develop, and who finds his own voice in the world.
4. One who takes responsibility for her thoughts, feelings, actions, and values.
5. One who "dares" to truly, genuinely, and openly listen to others.
6. One who recognizes her potentials at any given time.

Self-actualization comes in one's adult life. Children typically do not self-actualize because they are beginning to create and develop their true identity (or true self). In a video recording entitled *Maslow and Self-Actualization*, Maslow is interviewed about four areas of one's self-actualized behaviors. The four areas of self-actualized behaviors are honesty, awareness, freedom, and trust.

"You can't be happy with others if you are not happy with yourself. It is important to know who you are and what you want."

—Vickie Rockwell

Behavior number one—honesty

- Being genuinely honest with yourself and being honest with others
- Having a pure, honest love for yourself and others. This includes not only romantic love, but also adoration and mutual respect for others
- Being able to look within for answers
- Being able to admit your mistakes

Behavior number two—awareness

- Being aware of how you intrapersonally, interpersonally, and extrapersonally communicate
- Lacking in preconceived notions of what should be or what ought to be in a given situation, and being open to new perceptions
- Being aware and being able to appreciate everything around you
- Being aware of what is right and wrong, and not allowing others to pressure you into doing what is wrong or immoral

Behavior number three—freedom

- Feeling free to be yourself and willing to be spontaneous
- Feeling free from others' opinions and limitations
- Feeling free to find answers and solutions in creative ways
- Being able to be alone and being able to look forward to that time alone

Behavior number four—trust

- Being able to trust your intuition
- Being willing to trust yourself, even if your decision is unpopular
- Being able to trust the world
- Trusting the process of discovering yourself, your life path, goals, and dreams; and being able to be patient throughout that process

SELF-FULFILLING PROPHECY

The **self-fulfilling prophecy** is simply if you think it, if you feel it, if you say it, then it will happen. Lynn Grabhorn, in her book *Excuse Me, Your Life is Waiting* tells us, "We get what we get by the way we feel, not by trying to slug things into place or control our minds. Every car accident, job promotion, great or lousy lover, full or empty bank account comes to us by the most elemental law of physics: like attracts like."

With all of this talk about self-actualization, I hope some of you are saying to yourself, "I want it! I want to self-actualize." The self-fulfilling prophecy is the first step. You have to think positively about what you want, you have to feel the success of what you want, you have to begin the journey, and you must get rid of the negativity. There will be people along the way who will try to take your positive mind-set and strong energy away from you—but don't let them!

When Kendall-Hunt Publishing first approached me about writing this book, a hundred million negative thoughts ran through my mind. Even today, as I write chapter 5 and am halfway home, the negativity still creeps up. The question is, what does one do with that negativity? Here's what I do. I acknowledge it. Yep, I acknowledge it. I try to understand why I am feeling negative, where that negativity comes from, and what purpose it serves. The first two answers take some real thought, and a true understanding of my self. But the final question—what purpose does it serve—is a no-brainer. It doesn't serve any purpose, except to hold me down, and frankly, I prefer moving forward.

Now it is your turn, when negativity creeps up on you, figure out—

1. Why are you feeling negative?
2. Where does the negativity come from?
3. What purpose does it serve?

After you have answered those three questions, let the negativity go and work on a positive self-fulfilling prophecy.

HOLD ON—I am not trying to say this process is easy. The process of letting go of negativity is not easy. I have had a lot of practice. I can recall an incident many years ago that remains a powerful turning point in my life. My newborn son and I were living in low-income housing, a.k.a. "the projects", and I was getting ready to head to Black Hawk Community College to start my summer school classes. As I was putting my baby in my run-down, rust pit, beat-up, driver-side-door-held-closed-by-a-hanger Toyota Celica GT (which I bought for $300), I said hello to a neighbor. It was bug spray day, so the housing authority had just sprayed all of the apartments for roaches, and my neighbor was sweeping a huge pile of roaches out of her apartment. As I was leaving, she said to me, "Why are you going to school? Why don't you just stay home with your baby, enjoy the summer, and let public aid pay for you?" I shook my head and left for school. It would have been easier to stay home, but easy was not the option I wanted my son to experience.

With all of the negativity that surrounded me and the hoops I had to jump through to get help for school, to feed my son and I, and to pay my rent, it would have so easy to just throw my hands in the air and quit. However, I understood the self-fulfilling prophecy. I took a class early in my college career, the Napoleon Hill *PMA* (Positive Mental Attitude) *Science of Success* course. In this course I learned so much about how to remove negativity and replace it with positive action. I believed in my education, I wanted to be successful, I wanted to be the best example that I could for my son, and most importantly, I learned that I could be patient through the process. I am worth it.

CREATING YOUR HEALTHY SELF CONCEPT

A healthy self-concept is essential to fulfilling the five levels of Maslow's Hierarchy of Needs. The **self-concept** is the *total view* of how you see yourself. The self-concept is made up of how you want to see yourself, how you actually see yourself, and how you think the world sees you. This is a tall order, in which many elements influence the ideas we have about our self.

Richard Weaver, in his book *Understanding Interpersonal Communication*, tells us, "The part of your self-concept that evaluates your true self is **self-esteem**." In figure 5.3 you can see

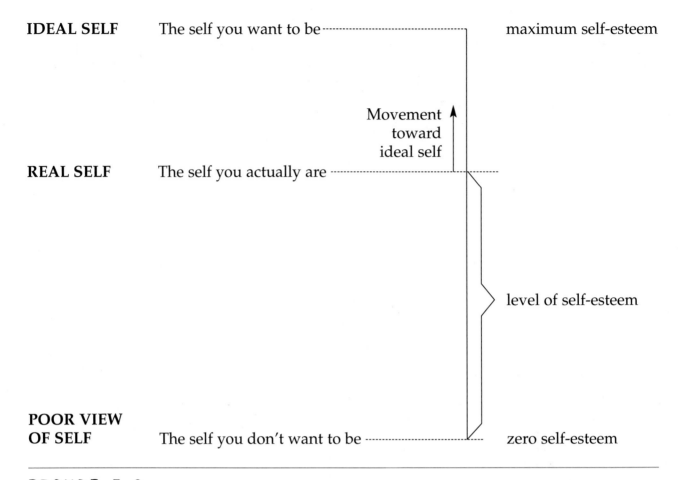

IDEAL SELF   The self you want to be ------------------------------   maximum self-esteem

Movement
toward
ideal self

REAL SELF   The self you actually are --------------------------

level of self-esteem

**POOR VIEW
OF SELF**   The self you don't want to be ----------------------------   zero self-esteem

FIGURE 5.3
The less distance between the ideal self and the real self, the higher the level of self-esteem.

Weaver's example of the relationship between the self-concept and self-esteem. The closer your real self (the way you actually see yourself) and your ideal self (the way you want to see your self) are, then the higher your self-esteem. It is important to understand that many people will use the terms self-concept and self-esteem interchangeably.

"A close relationship has been documented between low self-esteem and such problems as violence, alcoholism, drug abuse, eating disorders, school dropouts, teenage pregnancy, suicide, and low academic achievement," according to Robert Reasoner's article entitled "The True Meaning of Self-Esteem," on the National Association for Self-Esteem website.

"Individuals with defensive or low self-esteem typically focus on trying to prove themselves or impress others," according to Reasoner. He continues by telling us, "They frequently blame others for their shortcomings rather than take responsibility for their actions."

Though blaming others or playing a victim role is sometimes easier to do than taking responsibility for our behaviors, especially when we are young, it is important to understand that we learn those behaviors from everyone around us. The **social-comparison theory** tells us that the self-concept is developed, in part, by how we compare ourselves to others. We compare ourselves to everyone around us, whether we know them or not, whether they are actors in a movie or strangers on a reality television show. From our parents, we decide that we either want to be exactly like them or do things differently from what they did as parents.

"Nothing, but nothing, can shred a girl's self-esteem as easily as our families can," according to Susan Jane Gilman in her book *Kiss my Tiara.*

It important to know that if you want to understand yourself or develop your healthy self-concept, you must do two things: (1) become self-aware, and (2) practice positive self-talk. You can do it, if you are ready for great things in your life.

In closing, it is time to pause and reflect on what you have read. Consider the following questions and write down some notes in the space provided:

1. What didn't you know about the things you have read so far?

2. What surprised you the most about what you have read so far?

3. With what you've read so far, what don't you understand?

4. Is there anything you don't agree with, or is there anything you need more information about?

WHAT KIDS (REALLY) NEED
HERE'S A QUESTION TO DROP IN THE CENTER OF THE BREAKFAST TABLE AND BREAK IN TWO: WHAT IF DAY CARE MAKES OUR CHILDREN SMARTER—AND MEANER?

By Nancy Gibbs

It is the season again for working parents to brace themselves and shudder as the latest study on child care lands in the headlines to stoke their quiet fears. But not just theirs. Last week's survey, funded by the National institutes of Health and the largest ever on the subject, had something awful for just about everyone.

The more hours children spend away from their mothers, researchers concluded, the more likely they are to be defiant, aggressive and disobedient by the time they get to kindergarten. Kids who are in child care more than 30 hours a week "scored higher on items like 'gets in lots of fights,' 'cruelty,' 'explosive behavior,' as well as 'talking too much,' 'argues a lot' and 'demands a lot of attention.' " said principal researcher Jay Belsky. It didn't matter if the children were black or white, rich or poor, male or female, and—most confounding—whether the care was provided by a traditional child-care center, a nanny, a grandmother, even Dad. Only Mom will do.

But just in case those stay-at-home moms found comfort in the choices and sacrifices they have made, the study also suggests that kids in strong child-care programs tend to develop better language and memory skills, are in certain respects better prepared for school. Would you take that trade, Mom and Dad?

The news refueled some ancient rivalries, revived the most basic questions about what price our children pay for the hours we work and the choices we make. Parents peered into the data looking for themselves, but clear distinctions were hard to find. So far, the unpublished study has offered us only two kinds of children: those raised at home by their mothers (about 1 in 4 children) and everyone else. Which begs the question that the researchers didn't even pretend to answer: Why would kids who are cared for by anyone other than Mom develop disruptive behaviors, and what should we do about it?

For that matter, should we even be worried at all? The researchers noted that almost all the "aggressive" toddlers were well within the range of normal behavior for four-year-olds. And what about that adjective, anyway? Is a vice not sometimes a form of virtue? Cruelty never is, but arguing back? Is that being defiant—or spunky and independent? "Demanding attention" could be a natural and healthy skill to develop if you are in a room with 16 other kids.

Some experts in the field argue that the problem is not child care but bad child care. Across the nation there is a numbing range in child-care quality, rules and regulations. Some states allow only six babies in one room, others allow 20. States require all different kinds of licensing and accreditation. Childcare workers get paid about $7 an hour on average, roughly the same as parking-lot attendants; no wonder good care is hard to find. "There is a crisis in this country," says Mary Kakareka, a child-care consultant in Rockville, Md. "Middle-class families pay a lot to get into bad centers—and then down the line, pay again to get their kids in special programs to help solve the problems."

But what constitutes good care, whether in the home or outside it? What is the healthiest way for children to spend their time, especially in the years before school soaks up most of the day? Many anxious parents, wanting the best for their children and willing to pay for it, fill their kids' days with oboe lessons and karate classes, their rooms with phonics tapes and smart toys. And yet if you ask the experts to name the most precious thing you can provide your child, they often cite things you cannot buy: time and attention, the appreciation that play is children's work. Maybe, as the study results suggest, mothers have a special gift for giving that kind of gentle company. But it's hard to believe they are the only ones who can, as anyone with a great baby sitter, grandmother, husband or day-care provider can tell you.

This is the challenge to busy parents, working long hours, strung out at home. What would it take to create an easy, quiet space where you can just hang out with your kids, read a story or make one up, build a fort, make something goopy together? If in the process your children grow secure in the knowledge that you will forgive them for whatever they break or spill or forget, if they learn to share because you are sharing, if they don't have to fight for your attention, those skills may serve them better in the adventure that is kindergarten than being able to distinguish the octagon from the hexagon or fuchsia from lilac. The best news about raising a super child is that the secret to doing it is not to try too hard.

QUESTIONS FOR DISCUSSION—

WHAT KIDS (REALLY) NEED

by Nancy Gibbs

1. What are your top 3 reactions to this article?

2. What's your response to the question asked in the subtitle "What if day care makes our children smarter—and meaner"?

(Questions continued on back)

3. If you were a child who was cared for by someone other than your parents, what type of care was it (in-home care, relative, or a center)? How did this influence the person you are today? If you had a parent who stayed at home, describe how that influenced the person who you are today.

4. If you could change anything about how your parents provided care for you (they stayed at home, had a relative help out, you went to a day care center, etc), how would you change it?

5. Other thoughts about the article?

SELF-ESTEEM: A TWO-EDGED SWORD

By Lou Marano

High self-esteem—that most American of psychic treasures—might not be all it's cracked up to be.

At least it's not an unalloyed benefit when contingent on factors other than one's intrinsic worth as a human being, a University of Michigan study shows.

"The pursuit of self-esteem is ultimately self-destructive and may be costly to others as well," said Jennifer Crocker, a psychologist at the university's Institute for Social Research. Her study of 642 college freshmen, published in the September issue of the Journal of Social Issues, indicates that trying to raise or preserve self-esteem—even by getting good grades—can lead to more interpersonal stress and conflict as well as higher levels of drug and alcohol use.

"The focus is not on high or low self-esteem, but rather on what people base their self-esteem and what affects their self-esteem," Crocker told United Press International in a telephone interview.

"We find that basing your self-esteem on external sources—like other people's approval and appearance—appears to be quite unhealthy, whereas basing your self-esteem more on such internal sources as being a virtuous person seems to have positive consequences for students," she said.

"We find that the more students base their self-esteem on academics, the more hours they report studying every week. However, they do not have higher grades, and they report a lot more academic-related hassles by the end of the freshman year.

They are telling us that they are experiencing a great deal of time pressure, conflicts with their professors and teaching assistants. They are not interested in their courses, and they're dissatisfied with their performance."

Crocker said that other studies have shown that the self-esteem of students who have a lot riding on grades fluctuates with their marks. This instability of self-esteem proved to be a good predictor of depression.

But isn't it true, Crocker was asked, that depressed people tend to need the approval of others more than those who are not depressed?

"It's not just that your initial level of depression predicts what you base your self-esteem on," she replied. "What you base your self-esteem on predicts increases in depression across the freshman year of college. You get more depressed if you base your self-esteem particularly on appearance."

The 642 students filled out questionnaires before they started college, at the end of their first semester and at the end of the second semester of their freshman year. One was the Rosenberg self-esteem inventory, which asks subjects to respond to such questions as: "I feel I'm a person of worth, at least on an equal basis with others." Or: "I often feel like a failure. I sometimes wish I could have more respect for myself."

On the basis of the Rosenberg inventory, she concluded that most of the students—like most Americans—have high levels of self-esteem.

Crocker said her team "measured daily hassles, drug and alcohol use, symptoms of eating disorders, measures of depression, how they spent their time."

The researchers then asked questions about seven bases of self-esteem. Roughly, they can be described as: virtue, religious faith, family support, approval of others, competition, academic competence and appearance.

Only 4 percent of students said none of the seven bases of self-esteem were important to them. A university news release said that this low figure suggests how common it is to base self-esteem on accomplishments, behaviors and qualities other than one's intrinsic value as a person. Crocker's team looked at how well the seven questions correlate with high or low self-esteem. "The correlations are very weak," she said, but approval of others and appearance have a stronger correlation with low self-esteem.

"So it seems like there's not a strong relationship between what people base their self-esteem on and their level—whether they're high or low," Crocker said. "But the more one bases self-esteem on such external factors as appearance, approval of others and—to some degree—outdoing others in competition, the lower one's self-esteem tends to be overall.

"Having low self-esteem predicts symptoms of eating disorders, but even controlling for that, basing one's self-esteem on appearance predicts anorexia or bulimia even more strongly," she told UPI.

QUESTIONS FOR DISCUSSION—

SELF-ESTEEM: A TWO-EDGED SWORD
by Lou Marano

1. What are your top 3 reactions to this article?

2. Look up Crocker's study and describe your reactions to her survey questions.

(Questions continued on back)

From Michelle Burch, *Interpersonal Communication: Building Your Foundations for Success.* Copyright © 2005 by Kendall/Hunt Publishing Company.

3. Do you agree that "the pursuit of self-esteem is self-destructive . . ." according to Crocker?

4. Do you agree that most people have a high self-esteem, according to Crocker's interpretation? Explain.

5. Other thoughts about the article?

INDIVIDUAL ACTIVITY #1
Analyzing the Roles You Play—Finding Your True Self

PURPOSE—

To visualize the roles that you play and/or are expected to play and to verbalize what you see as your true self.

PROCEDURE—

Using the diagram on the next page, at the end of each of line write down the various roles that you play and the roles that you are expected to play. Use figure 5.1 for a guide. In the center circle, write down phrases that represent your true self.

FOLLOW-UP—

Compare diagrams with your classmates. Discuss the similarities and the differences in your diagrams. Discuss the relationship between your true self and the roles you play.

(Continued on back)

Name: _____ Date: _____

INDIVIDUAL ACTIVITY #2
Fulfilling Your Hierarchy of Needs

PURPOSE—

To visualize how you are currently meeting your needs and compare that to how you want to be meeting your needs.

PROCEDURE—

Using the chart below, fill in the following areas to analyze how you are currently meeting your needs. Then create a plan to improve how your needs are being met. Be practical—and take a few risks.

	How you are currently meeting your needs?	How do you want to have your needs met?
Level 1 – Physiological Needs		
Level 2 – Safety Needs		
Level 3 – Social Needs		

(Continued on back)

From Michelle Burch, *Interpersonal Communication: Building Your Foundations for Success.* Copyright © 2005 by Kendall/Hunt Publishing Company.

	How you are currently meeting your needs?	How do you want to have your needs met?
Level 4 – Self-esteem Needs		
Level 5 – Self-actualization		

FOLLOW-UP—

Take this table and hang it up somewhere that you will see it daily. Review it and make a few improvements every day. You are worth it!

Name: _____ Date: _____

GROUP ACTIVITY #1
Understanding the Many Selves That Create You

PURPOSE—

To visualize and identify with items that we know, in order to verbalize who we can relate to and why.

PROCEDURE—

For each of the categories, check the item, animal, etc. that best describes you. Choose only one for each category. There is an "other" for each category; if you choose that option, write down what should go there to describe you. In the space next to each column, write down why you chose that particular item, animal, etc.

Animals	**Communications Media**
___ bear	___ book
___ deer	___ film
___ fox	___ fourth-class mail
___ lion	___ radio
___ monkey	___ special delivery
___ rabbit	___ telephone
___ turtle	___ television
___ panda	___ internet
___ other	___ other

(Continued on back)

Sports

___ auto racing

___ baseball

___ boxing

___ football

___ ice skating

___ soccer

___ tennis

___ track

___ other

Transportation

___ bicycle

___ jet plane

___ horse and buggy

___ motorcycle

___ Rolls-Royce

___ van

___ Corvette

___ other

Colors

___ black

___ blue

___ gray

___ pink

___ red

___ white

___ yellow

___ other

Music

___ rap

___ country

___ popular

___ jazz

___ folk

___ opera

___ rock

___ other

FOLLOW-UP—

Compare your list with your classmates. Be sure to ask each other why s/he chose the item, animal, etc. It will be interesting to see if your rationale or interpretations are similar or different, and why.

GROUP ACTIVITY #2
What if You Just Opened Up?

PURPOSE—

To experience what it would be like if people knew things about your true self, if you practiced more self-disclosure, and to understand what it is like to allow people into the areas of life that people generally keep to themselves.

**WARNING—This activity is challenging. It is not for everyone. It is only for the truly open-minded, who are willing to take a risk for the sake of learning about people, and for those who are willing to be vulnerable.

PROCEDURE—

You are to wear a sign with a message about something you don't normally tell people, as suggested in the list below. Here are a few options for executing this activity.

First, everyone could write down a phrase that represents something they keep hidden, and then have everyone anonymously put their phrases in a hat. The phrase you draw will be the phrase that you wear on your sign. With this option you have the opportunity to feel what it is like for one of your classmates to carry around that particular secret.

Second, everyone could choose a phrase from the list below and wear that phrase on your sign. You could put the phrases in a hat and have everyone draw one out or you could have everyone pick a phrase that they would like to use. With this option you could write down how you anticipate people will react to your sign. Then discuss your assumptions with what actually happened at the conclusion of the activity.

Finally, a third option would be to create a sign that genuinely reveals something you normally keep hidden. This is usually the most challenging option; however, it is my experience that it is the most rewarding, for reasons you will learn about during the activity.

A couple of rules:

1. You can't tell anyone why you have to wear the sign.
2. You can't reveal if the sign is true or false.
3. You have to wear the sign at all times.

(Continued on back)

4. You need to keep a journal of your emotions as you wear the sign. The journal will allow you to remember the range of emotions you felt, as each day your emotions will change.

5. As a class you should decide how long this activity should take place, suggested time frame is 2 to 7 days.

Some suggested phrases are:

I am stupid	I was raped
I was molested by someone I know	I am afraid of commitment
I was a shoplifter	I was in a gang
I think my family hates me	I was a runaway
I have a big ego	I am a nerd
I am afraid of love	I am addicted to sex
I am a loner	I want to die
I am lesbian/gay	I am prejudiced
I hate old people	I am a thief
I never ask for help	I am unhappy
I cannot read	I cannot write
I had a drinking problem	I smoked marijuana
I hate women/men	I am a mean person
I have a severe case of road rage	I don't want to have kids

FOLLOW-UP—

As a class discussion and/or in a minimum 2-page reaction paper, answer the following questions:

1. Summarize what the experience was like for you. Include the range of emotions you felt throughout the experience, thoughts only how you anticipated to feel, how you ended up feeling, and what you would do different if you had to complete the exercise again.

2. If the message on your sign was not true, did you begin to feel like the message on your sign was true? How did you feel about that?

3. If the message on your sign was true, what was it like to have other people see your secret? How did you feel about that?

4. What would it be like if people (even strangers) knew your secrets, if you could be more willing to tell them?

5. Are you more willing to self-disclose because of this activity?

6. What did you learn about yourself?

7. What did you learn about other people during this activity?

WORD SEARCH
Reviewing the Terms

```
Y L S W W Q Q P C Z U S W F R J D S P Y Z Y D N R
K C F E J D M S T N A U L X O K D G Y K Z R L V Q
S V E L L J P N V F Y E W X L E L B W F X O A L N
C D C H M F Q E E X S E T P E C N O C F L E S T S
V Y E X P A E T A E I G V N C I L X D U E H U L Z
I Z A E D O Y S U I X S L Y O T J O B M E T H P Z
Q K A U N N R R T A D A A H N O M M A F E N Y B H
W M Y K E L T P G E C A I M F Z X E N G M O A P K
O V L E H X A V G I E E X T L N A E Y A N S M E P
I W D B C U X I G N R M G M I T X T P O E I S G S
A S X W M W X O C E I Q N D C A L S I B T R L H J
R R P Y O E L T M O C L F E T U F E T J L A E D L
W K N L M O S I Y J S I L A E K N F L D C P S C N
C K I D I R O L E L W P S I W D R L K V G M N D I
Z Y V S Y U T Q F M P Q R T F W S E W F R O R X V
U S Y V F P V E M F W I G L Z L D S V U T C R W B
C H I X A A E Q K U N W Y I S L U C S H P L L L D
P G W C J E S D V L E G K I Z K E F H N A A E D U
S E L F A C T U A L I Z A T I O N E F B P I B K I
F N P L C E Z S L A R T Y T H Y M B U L L C H Y P
Z C R C N S L E L U X C X T E V H F D E E O D K R
O E W P X S Q O V D I B V S U D F V W Z U S D H W
Z G A J J O W V G G B B O P I H Y T I H F I X A X
P A E J V S D R V K F B T J E T H O V O T M A H A
R V Y Z B B N X S W S Q B V F C V B B I Y P G L W
```

Definitions for the terms in the word search:

1. the most basic human needs
2. parts that we are expected to play
3. roles that pull you in opposite directions
4. predictability and familiarity in your life
5. realization of one's abilities and potentials
6. the total view of how you see yourself
7. evaluates your true self
8. feelings of self-confidence, worth, strength, capability
9. if you think it, if you feel it, if you say it, then it will happen.
10. how we compare ourselves to others
11. feeling like you belong
12. the core of who you are

Name: _____ Date: _____

CHAPTER QUIZ
Reviewing the Chapter

TRUE OR FALSE

_____ 1. The first level of Maslow's Hierarchy of Needs is safety needs.

_____ 2. Roles are the parts that we are expected to play.

_____ 3. Roles do not affect your identity.

_____ 4. Roles come in multiple forms.

_____ 5. One can never self-actualize.

_____ 6. The self-fulfilling prophecy is when you think something is negative, then you will see it as something negative.

_____ 7. Honesty, trust, freedom, and being liked are the four areas of self-actualization.

_____ 8. Self-concept is what others think of you.

_____ 9. Self-esteem evaluates the self-concept.

_____ 10. Your true self is the person who you are at the core.

_____ 11. Roles are learned.

_____ 12. The fourth level of Maslow's Hierarchy of Needs is self-esteem needs.

_____ 13. Our roles guide our behavior.

_____ 14. Physiological needs are the most basic human need.

_____ 15. Self-actualization is an ongoing process.

CHAPTER 6

ALL ABOUT EMOTIONS

KEY TERMS

Debilitative emotions

Emotional liberation
    process

Emotions

Facilitative emotions

Fallacy of approval

Fallacy of catastrophic
    expectations

Fallacy of causation

Fallacy of helplessness

Fallacy of
    overgeneralization

Fallacy of perfection

Fallacy of should

CHAPTER OBJECTIVES

1. Understand the role emotions play in the communication process.

2. Describe emotions.

3. Understand the role of your emotions in your relationships.

4. Recognize the types of emotions.

5. Understand how to manage your emotions.

6. Identify social anxiety.

7. Understand how to improve your emotional expression.

8. Practice skills for improving your emotional development.

"I said I don't know what's wrong!"

"Please, don't yell at me."

"If you wouldn't make me so mad, I wouldn't have to yell at you!"

"I am not trying to make you mad. If you would just explain why you are feeling this way, maybe we can understand each other."

"I'll let you know when I figure it out. Right now you're just ticking me off!"

"Maybe we should try some counseling?"

"COUNSELING??!! I can't believe you would say that."

"I feel like we need help."

"Help? We don't need help. It's only our EMOTIONS!"

Have you ever had a conversation similar to this one? Have you ever been so mad that you couldn't think straight? Have you ever felt something that was physically painful, but you couldn't explain what you were feeling? If you answered yes to any of those questions, this chapter will be one that you will want to share with your friends and loved ones. Emotions are complicated, and they can have a great impact on your relationships, both positively and negatively. You will notice that throughout this chapter we will focus particularly on the negative aspects of our emotions. This is not to imply that you are filled with negative emotions. However, negative emotions are typically the ones that we need help understanding and expressing. To that end, in this chapter we will explore what emotions are, how they affect our relationships, what specific types of emotions there are; and how to understand our emotions; finally, we will look at how to improve our emotional expression.

WHAT ARE EMOTIONS?

Believe it or not, that is a big question; there are easily over a hundred definitions attempting to define what we experience daily in our lives—your emotions. Let's add one more to the big list of definitions. **Emotions** are a state of feeling something that can include physiological changes, psychological interpretations, and nonverbal reactions.

When we feel something, that is the *physiological change* our body is experiencing. Our bodies can react to our emotions; for example, it can be a cramp in your stomach if you are feeling "stressed"; it can be a twitch in your eye if you are feeling "nervous"; it can be sweat in your palms if you are feeling "anxious"; or it can be a dry mouth if you are feeling "apprehensive." Each word that I put in quotation marks is the emotion word that we may apply to a particular feeling, which is the *psychological interpretation*. The physiological change that you experience can have several interpretations. You may feel as though you have butterflies in your stomach and, depending on the situation, you will interpret that a few different ways. You may say that you are feeling "anxious" or "nervous" or "stressed" or even "excited." Two things to remember about what I have said thus far:

1. You do not always have a physiological change.
2. You cannot always interpret what you are feeling.

The final component to our definition of emotions includes our *nonverbal reactions.* We *do not* always react nonverbally to our emotions; however, when we do, the reaction can be substantial to the overall experience of emotions. As you are probably aware, men have been typically taught not to express their emotions; or if they do express their emotions, it is a sign of weakness. Here are the facts:

1. Learning to express your emotions effectively, regardless of your gender, is healthy for one's mental state and one's spirit.
2. Hiding your emotions can increase your stress levels, and can do a lot of damage to your relationships.
3. We can only teach the next generation how to handle their emotions if we learn how to handle and express our own emotions.

Nonverbal reactions can either positively or negatively affect your interpretation of an experience. In my public-speaking course, many students experience a variety of emotions. Their feelings may include sweaty palms, dry mouth, and a feeling of butterflies in their stomach; and how do they interpret those feelings?—as nervousness. Then they will continue to get worked up, or get more nervous, by nonverbally reacting to the feelings. They anxiously rub their hands, hold their stomach, and rub their lips together. Those nonverbal reactions tell the

brain that the situation is getting worse; and in turn, the students tell me that they are getting more nervous or that they can't give the speech. Can you relate to this? Here is the interesting part regarding this idea of how we react to our feelings—we can control how we interpret what the body is feeling.

Take another example: you see somebody cute walking toward you. You think to yourself—this person is nice looking, I'm single, and I want to get to know this person. As this person walks toward you, your palms get sweaty, your mouth gets dry, and you have butterflies in your stomach. Then you say to yourself, "I am so excited." There it is. You have psychologically controlled your interpretation of the feelings you are experiencing. I am not implying it is always that easy. However, if you can learn to make conscious choices about your interpretations and reactions, you will be one step closer to controlling them. Now, if only I could get my public-speaking students to say, "I get to give my speech next—I am so excited!" Knowing that many people fear public speaking more than death itself, it may be awhile before my students get excited about a speech. However, I'll keep trying anyway.

UNDERSTANDING THE ROLE OF YOUR EMOTIONS IN YOUR RELATIONSHIPS

Our emotions play a significant role in our relationships. I'm sure you have heard phrases like the following:

"She is so emotional."
"He never shows his emotions to me."
"She is always giving me mixed signals; I never know how she is feeling."
"He always loses his temper."

Typically we hear those phrases in our relationships when either of the following is happening—we are not clearly expressing our interpretation of what we are feeling, or we are not being consistent in how we react to our emotions. How you interpret and express your emotions can either encourage growth in your relationships or it can inhibit growth. Learning how to take responsibility for how you are feeling, and learning to express your emotions, are significant steps to improving all types of relationships.

In chapter 8 we will thoroughly examine how our relationships develop and deteriorate. This chapter will prepare you for chapter 8; because you are now going to learn how to interpret your emotions, how to manage your emotions more effectively, and finally, how to improve your emotional expression.

> "I have learned a lot about my emotions. I've learned that I should express them more to my friends and family. In the long run it will help me. If I let my emotions out sometimes I won't be as depressed or upset."
>
> —Sarah Pritchard

UNDERSTANDING AND MANAGING YOUR EMOTIONS

Lynn Grabhorn, in her book *Excuse Me, Your Life Is Waiting,* poses a few questions in the opening of her first chapter.

How do we get what we get in life? Why do some people seem to have it all while others suffer so? Why did that bozo bump into you on the freeway? Why did that little child have to die so young? How come that guy got promoted, and not you? Why can't everybody have prosperity, and joy, and security?

These are some great questions. I don't know if you will have answers to them by the end of the chapter; however, you will get a few steps closer. Grabhorn also reminds us that, "If you really think that things come to you by some stroke of good or bad luck, or by accident, or coincidence, or by knocking your brains out against some very unsympathetic stone walls, then get a grip."

Understanding and managing your emotions can be one of your biggest *intra*personal challenges. Emotions can feel powerful, controlling, unexplainable, and overwhelming. Learning some tools to manage your emotions includes learning the types of emotions we experience, learning the difference between facilitative and debilitative emotions, and learning how to separate observing an emotion from evaluating the emotional experience.

Researchers have been trying since the 1800s to identify how many emotions we experience, and guess what? We still don't know. The list of emotional words is at least much longer than the number of definitions for the word emotion. To begin to understand how many emotional words there are, table 6.1 will provide you with a short list.

"The benefits of strengthening our feelings vocabulary are evident not only in intimate relationships, but also in the professional world," according to Marshall Rosenberg in *Nonviolent Communication.* He also states, "In a world where we're often judged harshly for identifying and revealing our needs, doing so can be very frightening."

Primary & Mixed Emotions

Robert Plutchik developed an emotion wheel to identify what he calls our eight primary emotions (see figure 6.1). He tells us that all the rest of the emotions we experience are a

TABLE 6.1
Increase Your Emotion Vocabulary

Accept	Energetic	Lazy	Seductive
Afraid	Envy	Lively	Self-reliant
Aggravate	Exhilaration	Loathing	Sentimental
Angry	Fear	Lonely	Shame
Annoy	Fearful	Love	Shocked
Anxious	Fed up	Love-struck	Shy
Artistic	Flattered	Mad	Sick
Beaten	Foolish	Mean	Sincere
Bitter	Forlorn	Melancholy	Sinful
Calm	Friendly	Miserable	Sorrow
Cantankerous	Glad	Misunderstood	Stupid
Cautious	Glum	Neglected	Sullen
Cheerful	Grief	Optimist	Suicidal
Closed	Guilty	Out-of-control	Superior
Comfortable	Happy	Passionate	Support
Concern	Helpful	Patient	Surprise
Confident	Hopeful	Pessimistic	Tender
Confusion	Hopeless	Phony	Tensed
Content	Hostile	Pity	Terrified
Contented	Humiliation	Playful	Threatened
Crazy	Hurry	Pleasure	Timid
Creative	Hurt	Powerful	Tired
Curious	Hyper	Powerless	Trapped
Defeat	Immobilized	Pressured	Trust
Defensive	Impatient	Proud	Two-faced
Dependent	Inadequate	Puzzled	Ugly
Depressed	Incompetent	Regret	Uneasy
Deprived	Independent	Relief	Unsure
Desperate	Inferior	Repulsive	Upright
Despondent	Insecure	Resentful	Wacky
Detached	Interest	Restless	Weak
Disgust	Irritable	Restrain	Weary
Eager	Isolation	Ridiculous	Worry
Elated	Jealousy	Romantic	Zany
Embarrassment	Joyful	Sad	Zonked

FIGURE 6.1
Plutchik's Emotion Wheel

manifestation of our eight primary emotions. Our eight primary emotions, which are listed inside the circle of the emotion wheel, are:

Expectancy	Surprise
Joy	Sadness
Acceptance	Disgust
Fear	Anger

The emotions listed outside of the circle begin to explain how at least two primary emotions can create a mixed emotion. Don't confuse the term mixed emotions with feeling mixed or confused about something. The term mixed in this context means a feeling of more than one primary emotion. According to Plutchick, a few examples of mixed emotions include:

Anger + acceptance = dominance
Acceptance + fear = submission
Fear + disgust = shame
Expectancy + joy = courage
Joy + fear = guilt

Similarly to most theories, not everyone agrees with Plutchick's emotion wheel. Some believe there are more than eight primary emotions. Plutchick himself agrees that there is still much more research that needs to be done on the subject of emotions.

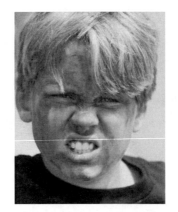

Many of the emotions we experience will either encourage or discourage the meeting of our needs. If we experience long-lasting feelings of acceptance, we will climb Maslow's Hierarchy of Needs. If we experience long-lasting feelings of anger, our growth in the hierarchy will be minimized.

As you know, emotions can have a wide range of intensity. The longer you experience an emotion, and the more types of emotions you experience, the more intense the emotion typically becomes. For example, feeling terrified in a haunted house during Halloween is pretty mild. You expect to feel terrified and typically you even hope for that feeling. However, if you continue to feel terrified the entire evening, long after leaving the haunted house, your emotion has become more intense. This shift in intensity can create more of a debilitative feeling. Let's examine facilitative versus debilitative emotions.

Facilitative vs. Debilitative Emotions

Most of the emotions listed in table 6.1 can be facilitative or debilitative emotions. **Facilitative emotions** are ones that encourage positive intrapersonal growth. For example, grieving over the loss of someone can be a facilitative emotion, because you are working through the process of accepting that a loved one is no longer with you, and you are preparing to move forward. Feeling depressed can also be facilitative because you may be working through sadness or loss. However, in both examples the emotion can become **debilitative** if they increase in *intensity* and *duration*. Both characteristics must be present for an emotion to become debilitative.

Debilitative emotions will begin to interfere with your daily activities. They can be so intense that you do not want to get out of bed or leave your house for long periods of time. Debilitative emotions also interfere with your relationships because you do not have control over what you are experiencing, and others typically do not know how to help you. Fortunately, in today's society there is a lot of help for debilitative emotions. First and foremost, we have a wide range of counseling services. We also have the ability to see our physician for drug therapy. Most people are encouraged to try counseling services first, then add drug therapy if needed.

Keep in mind that for both facilitative and debilitative emotions, your interpretation of the situation is essential. When you are in the middle of very intense emotions, it is hard to imagine that we have psychological control, but we do. How you interpret and react to your feelings is essential in maintaining facilitative emotions. This doesn't always come easy; however, if you are open to a new perspective and you are willing to change your interpretations, it is very possible for you to have healthier intrapersonal and interpersonal communication.

> "My emotions play a significant role in the way I perceive different situations. They can affect the way I interpret many aspects of my everyday life, the way I see myself, my environment, other people, and the messages I send and receive."
>
> —Raymond Boggs

Observation, Evaluation, & Expectation

Another task that we face daily is attempting to separate what we feel from what we experience and what we expect from others. We should be able to describe what we experience without evaluating it or saying what we expect to happen; however, this may be uncommon behavior for you. Look at the following examples and decide which one you are more likely to say:

- Observation with evaluation—"Stephanie is such a pain."
  Observation only—"I don't like it when Stephanie doesn't make it to our study groups on time."
  Evaluation and expectation—"Stephanie is unbelievable; I thought she was more responsible."

- Observation with evaluation—"Ingrid is so ugly."
  Observation only—"Ingrid is not appealing to me."
  Evaluation and expectation—"Ingrid got an ugly nose job; I can't believe she would spend her money on something like that."

- Observation with evaluation—"Steve hates me."
  Observation only—"Steve hasn't called me in three days."
  Evaluation and expectation—"Steve is avoiding me; I thought he was more mature."

Rosenberg tells us that we must learn the differences among:

1. What your emotions are,
2. What others are feeling, and
3. What we want others to feel.

When you learn to separate what you experience from what you feel and what you expect from others, you can begin to take responsibility for your own emotions. Ruth Ross, in her book *Prospering Woman,* tells us, "Only thought stands in the way of attaining what we want." Let's take that one step further and say that only thought and taking responsibility for that thought will stand in the way of attaining what we want.

Taking Responsibility for Your Emotions

How can your needs be met if you do not express them or if you express them to the wrong person? If you are the type of person who will vent to anyone who is listening, you need to improve the appropriateness of your emotional expression. It begins with taking responsibility for how you feel. Even when you don't like a feeling you are experiencing, you must attempt to figure out the answers to questions like the following:

1. What makes me feel the way I do?
2. Where does the feeling come from?
3. Is the feeling valid?
4. What do I want to do with the feeling?
5. Am I aware of whom I need to express this feeling toward?
6. If I express the feeling, am I ready to take responsibility for it?
7. Am I at a point where I can clearly express this feeling?

Take a moment to seriously consider those questions. Write the questions down in a place where you will see them whenever you are experiencing emotion.

 You are halfway done with this chapter; therefore, it is time to pause and reflect on what you have read. Consider the following questions and write down some notes in the space provided:

1. What didn't you know about the things you have read so far?

2. What surprised you the most about what you have read so far?

3. With what you've read so far, what don't you understand?

4. Is there anything you don't agree with, or is there anything you need more information about?

> "Emotions can greatly effect how we react to situations. Our emotions can get in the way of what we really want to do. Sometimes our emotions can make us blind to the reality of our surroundings."
>
> —Bryan Clark

SOCIAL ANXIETY

In general we have all felt anxious from time to time. Whether it's a job interview, the first day of class, a blind date, or heading home to visit the family, many people feel anxious in various

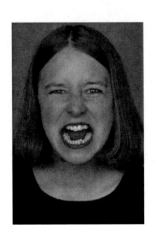 social situations. Feeling anxious in new, unfamiliar, or uncomfortable situations is normal; that would not be what is termed social anxiety. Actually feeling some anxiety is healthy; it gets your adrenaline going, it increases your overall awareness, and it typically increases your consciousness.

Mark Leary and Robin Kowalski in "Social Anxiety" cite the four situational domains where social anxiety occurs, as discussed in the *Journal of Anxiety Disorders*. The four domains include:

1. Public speaking and public interaction
2. Informal speaking and informal interacting
3. Assertiveness interactions
4. Observing others behave and interact

Similar to all emotions that we experience, the interpretation is in the mind of the person going through the experience. Therefore, the situation can be real or it can be imagined. Can you recall being concerned about how your friends felt about you, or if they would be your friend the next day? Have you ever assumed that others were talking about you?

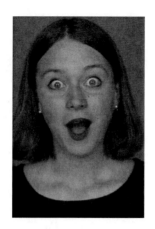

Leary and Kowalski tell us, "People have good reasons to be concerned with how others perceive them, and it is not unreasonable that they sometimes become worried about others' reactions. Social anxiety occurs when people become concerned about how they are being perceived and evaluated by others." They also state, "People may experience social anxiety even when they are alone if they worry about how others may regard them in an upcoming interaction. In fact, people may become anxious about social interactions that are entirely imagined rather than real."

When you become continuously concerned with how others feel about you and/or you become in a regular state of panic over whether or not they are evaluating you, there is cause to be concerned. Also, if these feelings begin to limit your ability to function throughout the day, there is cause to be concerned. It is important to recognize what is a normal reaction to a social situation and what is an extreme behavior. It is important to seek out help, whether you talk to your family physician or a counselor. There is nothing wrong with getting some help; you will do yourself and your relationships a big favor.

INCREASING YOUR EMOTIONAL EXPRESSION

OK, it is time—time for you to increase your emotional expression. If you already have healthy emotional expression, that is wonderful and you can consider this a review of what you already know. If you need a little help, I have a couple of questions for you. Are you ready to improve how you handle and how you express your emotions? Are you ready to have healthier relationships and less stress? Are you ready to take responsibility for your emotions? Great! Let's look at the fallacy's that impede us, how emotional intelligence works, and finally, how to work through the emotional liberation process.

Overcoming the Fallacies

The first step to increasing your emotional expression is overcoming any fallacies that you may hold. Fallacies are irrational beliefs that lead to conclusions that are illogical or unattainable. Ronald Alder, Lawrence Rosenfeld, and Russell Proctor, in *Interplay,* discuss seven potential fallacies that one may have. Those fallacies include the following:

- **Fallacy of causation.** This fallacy exists when someone believes that *anything* they do should not cause hurt or inconvenience to anyone else. The person who believes this fallacy always considers how their action will affect the other person, before they consider their own feelings. They go where others want them to go, rather than doing what would make them happy. They feel responsible for the feelings of others, rather than letting people take responsibility for their own feelings. They are hesitant to voice their own opinions, for fear it will hurt or negatively impact someone else.

- **Fallacy of should.** This fallacy exists when someone focuses on what *should* be rather than what *ought to* be, and they cannot accept the difference. This person typically complains about how things *should* be different, rather than how they *ought to* be different. It is to imply that there is some master plan out to change or alter what should be happening, as if to say that they do not have control over changing their perspective of any given situation.
- **Fallacy of overgeneralization.** This fallacy exists when someone takes one incident and draws conclusions about the entire person or the entire situation. They apply this fallacy to themselves, to others, and to every experience. For example, if this person fails one math test, they say, "I am so stupid at math." If someone doesn't hear them or hear them correctly, they say, "You never listen to what I have to say." These statements imply unqualified behavior; they take one instance and believe that it is absolute.
- **Fallacy of catastrophic expectations.** This fallacy exists when someone believes that if something bad or negative is going to happen, it will happen to them (similar to Murphy's Law). They believe that if they go somewhere, they or others will not enjoy themselves; they believe that if they try something new, they will fail at it; and they believe that if they try to tell others what they really think, it will make things worse or others will disregard it anyway.
- **Fallacy of helplessness.** This fallacy exists when someone believes that positive emotions and positive experiences are unattainable. They believe they are victims in life and that controlling the outcome of any situation is not possible. They may also believe that because of traits that cannot change (being a woman, being a minority, being a parent, etc), they do not have the ability to change their circumstances.
- **Fallacy of perfection.** This fallacy exists when someone believes they *have to* be perfect. They believe that they have to always communicate their ideas, thoughts, and feelings perfectly. They do not believe that it is OK to make mistakes, and they are extremely hard on themselves if they do make a mistake. You may see this fallacy with students who are extremely hard on themselves after a speech; you may see this from a student who will not accept anything lower than an A for a class; or you may see this from someone who pressures others to strive for perfection.
- **Fallacy of approval.** This final fallacy exists when someone believes that the approval from others is *essential* to their relationships. People who believe this fallacy will do whatever it takes to make sure that people like and accept them. They will abandon their own wants, needs, and desires to seek out the approval of others; they believe that if they do not win someone's approval, there is a problem in the relationship.

Getting One Step Closer to Emotional Intelligence

Wouldn't it be nice if you typically made decisions that your mind and heart agreed upon? Wouldn't it be great if you could be smart in life and in your relationships? Wouldn't it be wonderful if you could be willing to always approach situations with an open mind and a willingness to overcome the challenges you may face? The answer to those questions is YES and it is possible, with emotional intelligence.

Daniel Goleman, author of *Emotional Intelligence,* defines emotional intelligence as:

"abilities such as being able to motivate oneself and persist in the face of frustrations; to control impulse and delay gratification; to regulate one's moods and keep distress from swamping the ability to think; to empathize and to hope."

There are five basic components to emotional intelligence. They include:

1. Effectively handle your relationships.
2. Motivating yourself, removing the negative influences (internal or external).
3. Effectively manage and express your emotions.
4. Develop empathic behaviors.
5. Control impulses and be able to delay gratification.

Emotional intelligence is developed throughout our lifetime; however it begins early in our lives, as explained by Goleman:

The first opportunity for shaping the ingredients of emotional intelligence is in the earliest years, though these capacities continue to form throughout the school years. The emotional abilities children acquire in later life build on those of the earliest years.

He continues later to say:

Such emotional learning begins in life's earliest moments, and continues throughout childhood. All the small exchanges between parent and child have an emotional subtext, and in the repetition of these over years children form the core of their emotional outlook and capabilities. A little girl who finds a puzzle frustrating and asks her busy mother to help gets one message if the reply is the mother's clear pleasure at the request, and quite another if it's a curt "Don't bother me—I've got important work to do." When such encounters become typical of child and parent, they mold the child's emotional expectations about relationships, outlooks that will flavor her functioning in all realms of life, for better or worse.

It is essential to teach our children to be confident, curious, competent, and cooperative. It is also important to help them understand what it means to have self-control, to communicate effectively, and to be able to relate to others. All of those qualities incorporate the essentials of emotional intelligence.

Improving your Emotional Language

Many people have a very limited vocabulary when it comes to expressing how they feel about most anything. People typically have no more than twenty words to express anything and everything they are feeling.

There are four pronouns that I want you to become consciously aware of every time you use them. The pronouns are—**I, we, me, and you.** Taking responsibility for what you feel means taking responsibility for your emotional language. Increasing your use of "I" statements is essential for this process to work. However, before we go any further you need to be aware that people may view "I" statements as arrogant or self-centered. This is why I want you to also increase your use of "we" statements whenever it is appropriate. Here are a few examples:

- One way of expressing yourself—"You are so irritating."
  The more effective way—"When you forget to put the toilet seat down, I feel like you are not considering my feelings."

- One way of expressing yourself—"I hate it when you are late."
  The more effective way—"When we are supposed to leave at 7:00 p.m. and we do not leave until 7:30 p.m., I get upset because I do not like to be late."

- One way of expressing yourself—"That is ridiculous."
  The more effective way—"I do not like it when you tell me that you never get your way."

In short summary, two things you need to do to improve your emotional language are:

1. Increase your emotional vocabulary by using emotion words to ensure that you are effectively describing how you are feeling in any given situation.
2. Take responsibility for your emotional state. Remember that you cannot control how someone else feels; you can only be an example to yourself and others by controlling your emotions.

Reaching Emotional Liberation

It is time to find yourself at a point where you control your interpretation and your reaction to what you are feeling. You need to allow your emotions to be part of who you are, and not let them define who you are. If you can get to this point, you will find yourself one giant step closer to self-actualization in Maslow's hierarchy. You will also find lower levels of stress, and healthier relationships.

Rosenberg discusses a process of moving from *emotional slavery* to *emotional liberation*. The process is about taking responsibility for and expressing your needs. The process, in summary, looks like this:

Stage one—Emotional Slavery

In this stage we see ourselves as *needing* to be responsible for the way others feel; whether we are young and we learning about all of the feelings we can experience in any given day, or we are a parent trying to help our children through the experience. It is very easy for one to feel like a slave to their own emotions and the emotions of others.

Stage two—The Obnoxious Stage

Awareness begins here! In the obnoxious stage, we decide that we do not want to carry the burden of being responsible for how others feel. However, we are

still learning how to be "responsible to others in a way that is not emotionally enslaving." As we move through this process we are still learning how to let go of our own relentlessness, guilt, or fear about having our own needs and needing to express them.

Stage three—Emotional Liberation

All right, we have now come full circle. We know that we have needs, we know we can express them, we are learning effective ways of expressing those needs, and we know that meeting our needs should not come at the expense of others.

It is time to feel liberated from your emotions. It is time to learn how to appreciate and enjoy the emotions you experience, as well as, appreciating and enjoying the emotions that others go through. Emotional liberation is understanding that we all experience emotion. We experience all types of emotions, at all times of the day, sometimes for short periods and sometimes for long periods. It is a part of life; however, it should not control life.

In closing, I will leave you with this—the emotion of humor is essential to improving your experiences. It is a fact that you burn more calories during a one-minute belly laugh than you do during a twenty-minute walk. Therefore, laugh—laugh often—laugh out loud! Laughing is also contagious, so get your friends to laugh with you. Your body, your spirit, and your relationships will appreciate it, and remember that it's the perfect start on your journey of emotional expression.

 In closing, it is time to pause and reflect on what you have read. Consider the following questions and write down some notes in the space provided:

1. What didn't you know about the things you have read so far?

2. What surprised you the most about what you have read so far?

3. With what you've read so far, what don't you understand?

4. Is there anything you don't agree with, or is there anything you need more information about?

WHEN A BEST FRIEND BREAKS YOUR HEART

by Deborah Gregory

What Do You Do When You Find Out Your Girl Has Betrayed You?

I was 18 and a college freshman when Roni W.* and I met. She was 28 and had a master's degree, but was in a career crisis. She no longer wanted to teach, which is how she wound up working at the same dive bar I did. We were different in many ways, not the least of which was that my family background was fractured. When we met, I'd just aged out of foster care. Roni's family was stable and solidly upper-middle-class. But because we were both at a crossroads in our lives, we bonded on a deep emotional level, doing everything together that best friends do. We shopped, partied, cried and dreamed—and at alternating moments, we saved each other.

When I decided to leave school to make more money working full-time, it was Roni who pushed me not to, reminding me that getting a bachelor's degree had been my goal. With her encouragement, I reenrolled in school and completed my studies. And I still remember the night I stayed with her because she was too scared to be alone when she told her parasitic boyfriend he had to leave their apartment.

Over five years, we shared every aspect of our lives. But then Roni's life went in a new direction. While still working at the bar, she'd begun building a career as an advertising sales rep. Then she fell in love and became engaged. Eventually, we stopped speaking every day, and when we did talk her voice was distant. Roni was definitely too busy to see me as much as she had before. When I confronted her about it, she suggested I was imagining things.

By the time she wed, we weren't best friends anymore, although she claimed we were and said we'd be friends forever. It wasn't true. Roni moved to the West Coast and we lost touch. I was 23 by then, and the excruciating pain I felt at losing her friendship—which brought back all the losses I'd endured with my family—lasted for years and was worse than any pain I felt after breakups with men.

When a Friendship Falls Apart

Nothing prepares you for the day you realize a close friendship is over. Whether it's been suddenly destroyed by an act of betrayal or dies slowly of benign neglect, few life changes are as unforgettable and regrettable as learning that your main girl, whom you just knew you could count on, no longer has your back.

Often the hardest part is accepting it and moving on. There's no shortage of smart advice on how to recover when a love affair ends. But how do you process the pain when a best girl-friend breaks your heart? Who do you turn to for advice when your ace boon and number one confidante—who always had solutions for you—has now become the problem?

For women, the loss can be especially painful because we invest so much in our friendships. For Black women, our close bond with other women is deeply rooted in our history. "Our connection to one another was what it took to endure something as devastating as slavery," says Brenda Wade, Ph.D., a San Francisco psychologist. "Back then, even Black women who didn't know one another would offer help, food, care for our kids. Our lives depended on it."

Today, in a world rife with racism and sexism, the bond between Black women remains a critical source of support. Who knows our unique struggles better than another sister?

Still, even the most cherished friendships sometimes fail miserably. With Roni and me, I'm convinced that ours ended because, while I was integral to her "makeshift" life, I wasn't relevant once she settled down.

"Developmental issues are the main reason for friendship fallout," explains Marlene F. Watson, Ph.D., director of couples and family therapy at Drexel University in Philadelphia. "What you used to have in common changes. Maybe your girlfriend gets married, or she becomes a mother, so the two of you no longer socialize because she doesn't have time for that sort of thing anymore."

Cross the Fine Line: Lanette's Story

We often assume that a best friend is someone with whom we can discuss anything, only to discover that our honesty isn't appreciated. "Our expectations of each other—what we can handle, what we're willing to tolerate—can cause major misunderstandings," explains Watson. There must be a way for expectations to be mutually understood for a friendship to be successful. Without this understanding, Watson says, friends wind up reading from different "contracts" and unwittingly hurt each other.

In hindsight, Lanette Smith, 35, would have to agree. She lost her best friend, Candace, nine years ago because of a glitch in their contract. They were friends since college, and Lanette moved to Chicago—where

Candace lived—to begin her advertising career. By chance she found an apartment in the same building Mark, Candace's boyfriend, lived in. To Lanette's horror, she discovered one day that Mark was cheating on Candace. "I told her, and she was furious with me," Lanette recalls. Although Candace ended her relationship with Mark, she also immediately cut off her friendship with Lanette. "We haven't spoken since, but I felt I did the right thing," she admits.

And perhaps she did. But perhaps Candace was the type of person who didn't want to know—or didn't want to be told by her friend—how badly her man was treating her. Watson believes that such misunderstandings can be avoided. She thinks Lanette and Candace's friendship may have fared better if Lanette had found a non-threatening way to feel her friend out—like asking her girlfriend what she would like her to do if she ever saw her boyfriend kissing another woman—*before* telling her what she'd seen. It would have given Candace the opportunity to determine how she wanted to be treated in this kind of situation. Such candid conversations, while they may run counter to our socialization, are the foundation for a solid friendship, according to Watson. "Be clear about the terms of your friendship contract, and you'll be amazed at the problems you can avoid down the line," she advises.

Violating the Code: Theresa's Story

Sex with your girl's man is, of course, the ultimate betrayal, a sure way to destroy a friendship forever. Theresa Harris, a 32-year-old singer and mother, discovered this when her best friend, Faith, slept with her husband.

Theresa and Faith met in Atlanta eight years ago, when Theresa was working as a volunteer at a Christian university where her husband, Paul, a minister, led the school's choir. Faith was a student at the university and a choir member. Although Faith was four years younger than Theresa, they established a deep friendship. "I felt a real connection to her," remembers Theresa. "It was like having the younger sister I'd always wanted." The relationship was of particular significance to Theresa because the rest of her family lived in New York.

Over their close five-year relationship, Theresa treated Faith as if she were part of her family. "Her presence comforted me," Theresa recalls. "We shared everything—from clothes to secrets. I could talk with her about anything."

One day a woman in the church pulled Theresa aside and gave her the news that Paul was having an affair with Faith. Her whole world came undone. "I cannot describe the devastation I felt," she says. "I didn't see the betrayal coming at all. Not with my husband, not with her."

How could this happen? Experts lay some of the blame on a belief system in which women are taught to value men above all else. "If we buy into this system," says Watson, "then we'll go to any lengths to get a man—even if he happens to belong to someone else."

Many sisters also suffer from a scarcity mentality. "Time and time again we are told there aren't enough good Black men to go around," says Watson, "so we complete with one another but do ourselves a disservice in the process." She advises, "If you find yourself attracted to your friend's mate, don't put yourself in tricky situations, and definitely don't buy into the temptation, don't play around with him. In this game, there are no winners."

In Theresa's situation, there certainly weren't. Her life was completely shattered—as was her 7-year-old daughter's. Forced to uproot after she divorced Paul, Theresa eventually moved back to New York to try to rebuild a life for herself and her daughter. Paul and Faith's relationship ended, and both were ostracized from the church and the community.

Perhaps because we live in a society in which men are often expected to cheat, a part of Theresa felt even more betrayed by Faith than by her husband. "I expected her always to have my best interests at heart," she concludes sadly.

"So often we don't place a high enough value on our sisterfriends—that's one of the big mistakes Faith made," says psychologist Wade. "Don't underestimate or undermine the value of having close girlfriends. They're your best allies against the harsh forces in the world." When you lose your close friends, she warns, you lose a major part of you.

Disappearing Acts: Sarah's Story

Sarah and Priscilla met at a temp job ten years ago and became close friends despite certain differences: Sarah was a homebody; Priscilla liked to party. "But we enjoyed talking about spiritual things," Sarah remembers. "She made me feel needed and brought out a maternal instinct in me."

When Priscilla became pregnant, she asked Sarah to be godmother to her child, Lisa. Sarah readily accepted and took her duties very seriously, spending enormous amounts of time with Lisa—more time even than she did with Priscilla. "I really loved my goddaughter. It brought so much to my life, being there for both of them," she says.

When Lisa was 4, Priscilla fell on hard times and had nowhere to live. "I let them stay in my apartment for eight months and didn't think anything about it," Sarah recalls. During that time, Priscilla got her finances together and got her own apartment. She and Sarah remained close.

But three years later, Priscilla called one day out of nowhere and ended the friendship. She also severed Sarah's duties as godmother—without any explanation. Sarah was shocked; they'd never argued before. She begged Priscilla to tell her what had made her so angry. Priscilla refused, and even dismissed Sarah's concern about Lisa.

"I asked her, 'What lesson do you think this will teach her—that people will disappear from her life without any explanation?'" Priscilla was silent. "It was clear that she'd made up her mind, and it didn't matter what I said," Sarah recalls.

Since that conversation, the two haven't spoken. The hurt, for Sarah, is still palpable—as is the confusion. Sarah is left to speculate about why Priscilla cut her off. She often wonders if she'd spent too much time with Lisa and somehow Priscilla felt neglected. She'll never know and says it's unfair to have been dumped without being given a reason. But Sarah, her tone soft, also says, "If Priscilla called tomorrow, I'd tell her, 'I miss you' and embrace her."

Sarah and Priscilla's painful ending is a prime example of how poor communication can derail friendship. "Instead of discussing problems in a relationship, most of us simply cut the person off without saying anything because we're afraid of confrontation," says Watson. "We avoid conflict. We think it's better not to discuss touchy subjects, but that's not in the best interest of the other person."

When pushed, Sarah admits that she sensed Priscilla's frustration about the amount of time she spent with Lisa—and the lack of time it left for the two of them. But Sarah says that Priscilla never brought it up, so she didn't either.

It's also common for friendships to shift with major life changes. And sometimes it's fine when relationships end because you and your girlfriend no longer have much in common. "But sometimes we give up friends for no good reason and later regret it," warns Watson. Wade suggests calling a meeting with your friend, and "if necessary, ask someone who's objective to mediate." When you sit down to talk, advises Wade, "tell her what you're feeling, and give clear examples." She also says you must tell your friend—without attacking her—exactly what you need from her. If you find that, after you've tried to heal the friendship, the fracture is too deep, then "let the friendship go. This is especially true if violence, stealing, addiction or sexual betrayal are in the picture," Wade says.

But in the absence of extreme violations, if we must end a relationship with a sister, Wade says, do it with a measure of dignity and kindness. This lets both of you have closure and move on with one less gaping wound. And who deserves that more than Black women?

LEARNING TO LET GO

Psychologist Brenda Wade offers these suggestions on ways to heal. **GIVE YOURSELF PERMISSION TO CRY.** Look at your sisterfriend breakup like any other major loss. Let yourself grieve. Express your wounded feelings to trusted family and friends. Many of us keep our negative feelings to ourselves. Not dealing with them means they never really go away.

TALK THE TALK. Not with her—but with yourself. If you don't keep a journal, now is the time to start. Write down your feelings and unexpressed thoughts—the ones the breakup left you with and the ones you never told her about when you were friends. Or write her a letter—one you don't have to send. Describe the wonderful memories you have of her, ask for forgiveness for specific things you may have done wrong, and offer her your forgiveness. Or say nothing at all. If you can't say anything good, then at least resist the temptation to bad-mouth her. It only keeps negative energy circulating.

Name: _____ Date: _____

WHEN A BEST FRIEND BREAKS YOUR HEART
by Deborah Gregory

1. What are your top 3 reactions to this article?

2. Is the loss of friendships different for women from what it is for men? Explain your answer.

(Questions continued on back)

3. Are friendships different depending on your race? Explain your answer.

4. Pick one of the stories, Lanette, Theresa, or Sarah's story, and explain how someone from the story went through the emotional liberation process.

5. Other thoughts about the article?

ARTICLE FOR DISCUSSION—

AFTER GREAT PAIN
by Andrew Solomon

When I was little, my mother always told me that I had to be tough. "Terrible things will happen during your life," she said. "I hope they are few and far between. But you've got to be strong enough to endure them and make it through. You've got to be one of the survivors."

Last September 11 her words resonated hauntingly. Since then all of us have struggled through the disaster's aftermath. It has not been easy. People who previously suffered depression and anxiety disorders have relapsed; people who never had these complaints have felt their minds betraying them for the first time. The rate of substance abuse has increased significantly, and so have the rates of domestic violence and child abuse.

A friend's 5-year-old son asked her this summer whether the Empire State Building was now the tallest building in New York. She said that it was, and he said, "And if that falls, down, then what will be the tallest?" For many of us, the things we used to experience as permanent suddenly now seem conditional. What if all the skyscrapers fall down? What if America gets contaminated with radiation? What if we all die from drinking our water? Many of us have been dealing with both posttraumatic stress and what I'd call pretraumatic stress: anxiety about the terrible things we think might happen but that we cannot control. Such anxiety and fear are all ordinary responses to horror, but the fact that they are ordinary does not make them acceptable. They require attention and treatment. (It's ordinary that if you fall off a ladder you break your arm, but that doesn't mean the broken arm should be ignored.)

Even before the attacks, I had begun trying to understand what makes some people into survivors. Working on a book about depression for five years, I traveled around the world interviewing men and women who had been through experiences of great pain. What I found, often, was that the period following a devastation is rougher than the devastation itself—that surviving is not contingent on a single moment of strong will and spirit and strength but on a sustained state of mind, unremitting across time. "Inside, it took all our energy just to have food and warmth," a prison camp survivor in Russia explained to me. "When we came home again, that energy was freed up to search for meaning in our lives. It was then that we had to prove ourselves strong against death, by immersing our minds in the hidden strands of light that penetrated our darkness."

The many impressive people with whom I spoke during this research talked about looking closely at the horror they'd been through and about turning their back on it. In China I met an artist who lived for two years during the Cultural Revolution in a flooded basement jail where he had no dry place to sleep and almost no food. He managed to secure 66 pieces of paper from the supply kept for forced written "confessions," which he stitched into his padded coat, and during his imprisonment he covered them with almost-microscopic writing. He did not want to write about what was happening to him, about the terrible void into which he'd been cast. Instead he wrote out, during long sleepless nights, imaginary philosophical dialogues with great figures from history, including Tolstoy and Leonardo da Vinci. "By day I was a prisoner," he explained to me. "By night I was a prince."

A man I met from Rwanda insisted that one survives by looking forward. He told me how Western aid workers had tried to help people after the genocide by getting them to talk about what had happened, to be open and honest about their experiences. "And when people had finished these sessions of honesty," he told me bitterly, "those who had endured the most awful suffering would go kill themselves. It was awful. We soon put a stop to that: Looking at what had happened was the worst possible way to make yourself live afterward."

A woman who had survived the Khmer Rouge in Cambodia spoke to me of forgetting as the first step toward recovery, and she described how she filled the heads of other victims with distractions to obliterate some small piece of "what they would never entirely forget." She devoted herself unstintingly to the care of others who were needier than herself, eventually founding both an orphanage and a center for depressed women. This is how she saved, and continues to save, herself.

I talked to Inuit in Greenland who had been pulled by their dogs out of broken ice floes during winter hunting. "The only way to stay a hunter," one said to me, "was to go back to where I'd nearly died, as soon as possible, and to go without incident across that same place. To get the sound of the breaking ice and the penetration of that fierce water out of my head." Here the strength of a new reality had to subsume the agony of memory.

At the end of my journey, I found myself torn between the two schools of wisdom: the one that said you had to think hard about what you'd been through and the one that said you had to get away from the terrible realities you'd endured. I began to understand that, though people would tell me half their personal equation, there is actually always a balance to be struck between the remembering and forgetting. You can't simply hide from the facts. Feelings that aren't acknowledged, that aren't felt, are dangerous explosions waiting to happen. Feelings that are reexperienced too vividly, however, implode and are just as deadly. We've now moved beyond the old therapy idea that emotional repression is unhealthy and that you have to work through what's happened by delving deeply into all your feelings. If your feelings are too awful, it's best to keep them as much as possible at bay.

A year after the terror of September 11, the loss we suffered—like the personal loss of a single person you have loved—is something we have to integrate into ourselves, not something we can transcend and put behind us. Even if you think you have adjusted to the changed reality that follows a catastrophe, you may find yourself being regularly reshocked by the same episode. Eventually, you realize that there is no adjusting to something so profoundly grim, that the disastrous losses are perpetual losses, that you will never return to the innocence that predated them.

Once we've balanced the remembering and forgetting, we need to concentrate on controlling what we can control and to try to let go of the things we can't affect. A very limited part of our experience in the world is subject to our control, but we can make physical order in our own homes and we can accomplish goals in our work. We can avoid giving in to depression by availing ourselves of medications and psychotherapy. We can improve on how well we relate to the people around us. We can make deliberate, conscious lists of priorities. We can be nicer.

Helping people in greater need also gives us a feeling of control and purpose we might not otherwise be able to achieve, and is almost always an illuminating experience; I heard of its healing properties in every one of the exotic locations I visited. When you believe that you cannot stitch your own heart back together, go to work on the hearts of other people; there is no surer way to repair yourself than to repair them.

Perhaps the most difficult part of recovery is squeezing good out of the horror. Since we're stuck with September 11, we should try to learn from it. We should live more fully in the present tense because we have been reminded how fragile our lives really are. We should remember those many cell-phone calls from the buildings and planes that were about to go down, and how much that repetitive cliché of three words meant to all the people who heard "I love you" before the final moment. We can become a nation more conscious of our own good fortune.

The best antidote to pain is happiness, even if it is someday to be defeated by another sadness, in turn to be enlivened by another joy, and on in an endless cycle. The Italian political theorist Antonio Gramsci said that social reformers should have pessimism of the intellect and optimism of the will. This means that one must have the intellectual ability to see how bad things are and the emotional ability to look forward with hope. It's a hard combination to sustain, but if you can do it, you can change your world.

Name: _____ Date: _____

AFTER GREAT PAIN

by Andrew Solomon

1. What are your top 3 reactions to this article?

2. Explain some of the qualities it takes to be a survivor.

(Questions continued on back)

3. What happens when you don't face and deal with your emotions?

4. Describe how you felt about 9/11. How have you dealt with your emotions?

5. Other thoughts about the article?

Name: _____ Date: _____

INDIVIDUAL ACTIVITY #1
Emotions on the Internet

PURPOSE—

To examine how emotions are expressed on the Internet.

PROCEDURE—

Participate in three types of Internet discussions for at least a week. Types of discussions can be political, romantic, educational, special interest, etc. The key is to vary the types of discussions that you participate in during the week.

Explain your experience of listening to people communicate in the various chat rooms. Most importantly, discuss the emotions you experience and the emotions you feel others are experiencing. Consider the following: Identify specific types of emotions, including facilitative/debilitative emotions; how you think people are taking responsibility for their emotions; and how are you more emotionally aware because of this experience.

Discussion #1:

Type of Discussion Board: _____

Average number of people involved in the discussion: _____

Evaluation:

(Questions continued on back)

Discussion #2:

Type of Discussion Board: _____

Average number of people involved in the discussion: _____

Evaluation:

Discussion #3:

Type of Discussion Board: _____

Average number of people involved in the discussion: _____

Evaluation:

Follow-Up—

1. You can either have a classroom or online discussion about your results.

2. You can write a short paper explaining your experience.

Name: _____ Date: _____

INDIVIDUAL ACTIVITY #2
Exploring Your Emotions

PURPOSE—

To explore your emotions, how you handle them, and how you express them.

PROCEDURE—

Start this activity at the beginning of a week. Throughout the week write down, in the chart below, how you are feeling each day. To help, I suggest writing down how you feel first thing in the morning, at midday, and in the evening. Think about the words you use to express your feelings/emotions before you write them down (refer to table 6.1 on page 206 for assistance). Finally, write down the cause of that emotion.

Day of the Week & Time of Day	Emotions (physiological change, psychological interpretation, nonverbal reaction)	Cause/Reason for the emotion
Sunday—Morning		
Midday		
Evening		
Monday—Morning		

(Questions continued on back)

Day of the Week & Time of Day	Emotions (physiological change, psychological interpretation, nonverbal reaction)	Cause/Reason for the emotion
Midday		
Evening		
Tuesday—Morning		
Midday		
Evening		
Wednesday—Morning		
Midday		
Evening		
Thursday—Morning		
Midday		
Evening		

(Continued)

Day of the Week & Time of Day	Emotions (physiological change, psychological interpretation, nonverbal reaction)	Cause/Reason for the emotion
Friday—Morning		
Midday		
Evening		
Saturday—Morning		
Midday		
Evening		

FOLLOW-UP—

Write down your responses to the following questions.

1. How did it feel to think about the "word" you used to express your emotions?

2. Looking back, how do you feel about the words you chose to express your emotions?

3. Looking back, how do you feel about what you wrote down as the cause/reason for the emotion?

4. Looking back, what would you change about what you wrote down in any of the columns?

From Michelle Burch, *Interpersonal Communication: Building Your Foundations for Success.* Copyright © 2005 by Kendall/Hunt Publishing Company.

Name: _____ Date: _____

GROUP ACTIVITY #1
Emotions from Other Perspectives

PURPOSE—

To watch how others handle their emotions by comparing animals, children, and adults.

PROCEDURE—

1. Create small groups of 4-6 people.

2. As a group, choose one situation from the following list:

   (1) Animals in a zoo

   (2) Animals in a shelter

   (3) Animals in a home

   (4) Animals in a pet store

   As a group, choose one situation from the following list:

   (1) Children in a daycare

   (2) Children in a home

   (3) Children on a playground

   (4) Children in a classroom

3. Using the animal situation you have chosen, discuss in your group how you expect the animals to express their emotions. In the space provided, write down your hypothesis.

4. Using the child situation you have chosen, discuss in your group how you expect the children to express their emotions. In the space provided, write down your hypothesis.

(Questions continued on back)

5. Next, go and watch how animals express their emotions. In the space provided, describe the emotions that you perceive and how the animals express the particular emotions.

6. Now, go and watch how children express their emotions. In the space provided, describe the emotions that you perceive and how the children express the particular emotions.

7. Finally, compare the differences between animals and children. Compare the types of emotions you watched in the two groups and discuss the differences and the similarities. Also, discuss your hypothesis. Did both groups meet your expectations?

8. For further exploration—your instructor could have you write a paper on your experiences. You could compare animals, children, and what you know about how adults express their emotions. Discuss the difference and similarities between animals, children, and adults.

FOLLOW-UP—

1. As a class, discuss what you now understand about how others express their emotions.

2. Discuss the difference and similarities between animals and children.

3. Discuss how this relates to adults and what we can learn from animals and children. Are they more expressive or less expressive? Do adults have a larger emotional range?

Name: _____ Date: _____

GROUP ACTIVITY #2
Working through the Emotional Liberation Process

PURPOSE—

To assess your ability to be free from the limitations of your emotions.

PROCEDURE—

First, create small groups.

Second, in your small groups review Rosenberg's emotional liberation process.

Third, have everyone pick a relationship where they feel they can apply the emotional liberation process.

Fourth, discuss each person's relationship and help each other write down their assessment of how they can go or have gone through the process. Write your responses in your individual textbooks.

Summary of the Relationship:

Stage one—Description of emotional slavery.

Describe some examples of how you feel like a slave to someone else's emotional needs.

(Questions continued on back)

Stage two—Description of going through the obnoxious stage.

Consider what you have felt in the past or what you anticipate feeling throughout this stage.

Stage three—Emotional liberation.

Describe how you have gotten to this point or what you can do to get yourself to this point. Consider how this will affect you and the relationship.

FOLLOW-UP—

1. As a class share the emotions you experienced as you went through this activity.

2. Share any interesting things you learned about one another.

Name: _____ Date: _____

CROSSWORD PUZZLE
Reviewing the Terms

ACROSS

2. emotions that have increased in intensity and duration

4. emotions that encourage positive intrapersonal growth

7. a state of feeling something that can include physiological changes, psychological interpretations, and nonverbal reactions

8. a fallacy exists when someone believes that the approval from others is essential to their relationships

9. a fallacy exists when someone believes that if something bad or negative is going to happen, it will happen to them

10. a fallacy exists when someone takes one incident and draws conclusions about the entire person or the entire situation

DOWN

1. a fallacy exists when someone believes they have to be a perfect communicator

3. a fallacy exists when someone believes that anything they do should not cause hurt or inconvenience to anyone else

5. a fallacy exists when someone focuses on what *should* be rather than what *ought to* be, and they cannot accept the difference

6. a fallacy exists when someone believes that positive emotions and positive experiences are unattainable

CHAPTER QUIZ
Reviewing the Chapter

Name: _____ Date: _____

TRUE OR FALSE

_____ 1. Emotions can include physiological changes.

_____ 2. Emotions always include a nonverbal reaction.

_____ 3. Mixed emotions explain a state of feeling confused.

_____ 4. Debilitative emotions can be intense or long-lasting.

_____ 5. The fallacy of causation exists when someone believes that positive emotions and positive experiences are unattainable.

_____ 6. The fallacy of perfection exists when someone believes they have to be a perfect communicator.

_____ 7. The fallacy of approval exists when someone believes that approval from others is essential to their relationships.

_____ 8. The fallacy of should exists when someone believes that anything they do should not cause hurt or inconvenience to anyone else.

_____ 9. The fallacy of helplessness exists when someone focuses on what *should* be rather than what *ought to* be, and they cannot accept the difference.

_____ 10. The fallacy of overgeneralization exists when someone takes one incident and draws conclusions about the entire person or the entire situation.

_____ 11. The fallacy of catastrophic expectations exists when someone believes that if something bad or negative is going to happen, it will happen to them.

_____ 12. Emotional intelligence is having a high I.Q.

_____ 13. Using "I" statements can sometimes be perceived as self-centered.

_____ 14. Emotional liberation means that we know our needs should not come at the expense of others.

_____ 15. Social anxiety is feeling anxious from time to time.

U N I T   I I I

BEING SUCCESSFUL—
COMMUNICATING
IN RELATIONSHIPS

Chapter 7—Developing Decision Making Skills and Values

Chapter 8—Developing Healthy Relationships

Chapter 9—Conflict and Power

CHAPTER 7

DEVELOPING DECISION MAKING SKILLS AND VALUES

KEY TERMS

Attitudes

Behaviors

Beliefs

Central beliefs

Decision making

Derived beliefs

Instrumental values

Shared beliefs

Surface beliefs

Terminal values

Values

CHAPTER OBJECTIVES

1. Understand how we create our values.

2. Understand the types of values we hold.

3. Identify the values model.

4. Recognize where your values come from.

5. Describe the decision making process.

6. Identify what hinders our ability to make effective decisions.

7. Practice skills for improving your decision making skills.

8. Practice skills for understanding your values.

Boy Scouts oath:
> *On my honor I will do my best*
> *To do my duty to God and my country and to obey the Scout Law;*
> *To help other people at all times;*
> *To keep myself physically strong, mentally awake, and morally straight.*

Scout Law says that all scouts should be:
> *Trustworthy, loyal, helpful, friendly, courteous, kind, obedient, cheerful, thrifty, brave, clean, and reverent*

Sholin Karate Club pledge:
> *I pledge to honor those who are honorable,*
> *Respect those who are respectable,*
> *Tolerate those who are neither honorable nor respectable, and*
> *I pledge to ask no others to tolerate me.*

Clark State Community College guiding principles:
> *We believe in the power of education to change people's lives. Toward that end, we:*
> * place learners first
> * aspire to be innovative, accepting inherent risks
> * seek to improve continuously

- act as good stewards of the resources with which we are entrusted
- connect with the diverse communities we serve
- create synergy through partnerships
- trust, respect and care for those with whom we work and serve
- celebrate the creativity, diversity and accomplishments of our college community.

United States Pledge of Allegiance:
I pledge allegiance to the flag,
Of the United States of America,
And to the republic for which it stands,
One nation, under God, indivisible,
With liberty and justice for all.

The preceding examples of pledges, oaths, guiding principles, and so on, begin to briefly show what we, as a community, as a state, and as a nation, teach others to value, both indirectly and directly. Take a moment to examine the words on the paper, evaluate what values you can learn from those words, and add your own pledges and mottos that you have learned along the way. Jot your ideas down; this could make for a good discussion, either online or in the classroom.

UNDERSTANDING VALUES

Values are long-enduring beliefs that we hold. Values are extremely *resistant to change* because of how long they have been with you and your experiences in the past. Your values dictate your beliefs, attitudes, and behaviors, as we will discuss shortly when examining the values model. Values take *time to develop;* the keys to truly understanding your values are patience and time. Values are *not always easy to express;* we are not always able to verbalize what we value or where a value came from. Finally, values are *subjective,* just like your perception is your reality; your values are your own. Though many people may be able to say they value the same thing you do; it does not mean they understand or express a value the same way you do.

"Once a value is internalized it becomes, consciously or unconsciously, a standard of criterion for guiding action, for developing and maintaining attitudes toward relevant objects and situations, for justifying one's own and other's actions and attitudes, for morally judging self and others, and for comparing self with others," according to Milton Rokeach in *Beliefs, Attitudes, and Values.*

There are two types of values: terminal and instrumental values. Table 7.1 provides examples of these two values. Theorist Milton Rokeach explains terminal and instrumental values in his book *The Nature of Human Values.*

Terminal values are modes of conduct or how you believe you should behave in any given situation. Rokeach tells us that terminal values can be either personal or social, otherwise explained as intra- or interpersonal. For example, you may value forgiveness. Therefore, you believe that you should talk to yourself about issues you are dealing with; and in turn, you then talk to the other person about forgiveness. In this example the instrumental value is forgiveness and the terminal value is the way you behaved in the situation to create peace with yourself and with the other person.

TABLE 7.1
Terminal & Instrumental Values

Terminal & Instrumental Value Examples as described by Milton Rokeach	
Terminal Values **(your beliefs)**	**Instrumental Values** **(your attitudes & behaviors)**
A world at peace	Able minded
Beauty	Ambitious
Comfortable living	Clean
Dressing for success	Courteous
Free from debt	Creative
Financially secure	Friendly
God-fearing	Giving
Healthy eating	Helpful
Loved by others	Honest
Loving children and family	Independent
Peaceful living	Logical
Recognized by others	Loving
Respected by others	Open minded
Satisfying spiritual life	Polite
Successful career	Respectable
True and honest friends	Responsible

Instrumental values are end-state of existence or how you express yourself through your attitudes and behaviors. Rokeach also tells us that instrumental values can be either moral or competence values, otherwise explained as your attitudes or behaviors. Typically you learn what your instrumental values are through your family members, friends, and mentors. We learn from others either a value we want to hold or we learn what we do not want to value; either way we learn about our instrumental values. Instrumental values can be honesty, respectfulness, responsible, and so on.

Understanding terminal and instrumental values will become clearer as we look at the values model. You will begin to see how everything—your beliefs, attitudes, and behaviors—are a reflection of either terminal or instrumental values, or lack thereof.

THE VALUES MODEL

The values model is a visual representation that shows how our values, beliefs, attitudes, and behaviors link together, as shown in figure 7.1.

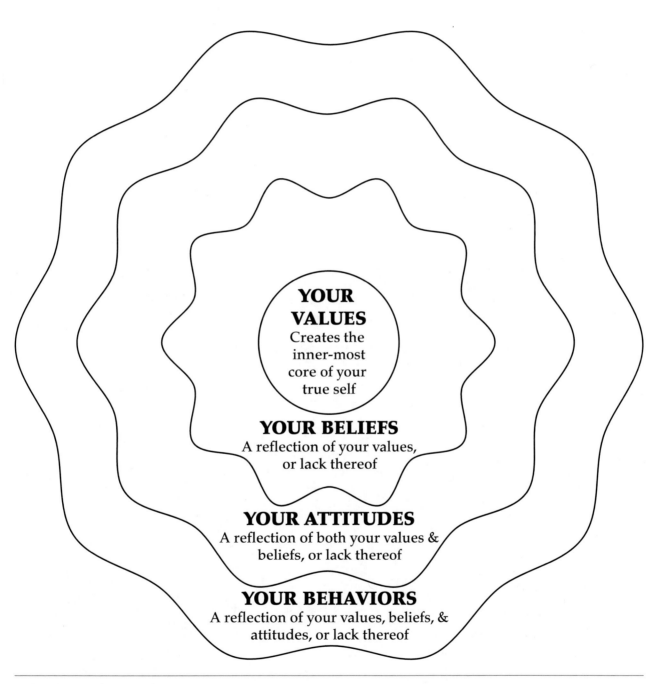

FIGURE 7.1
The Ripple Effect values model.

My friend Sonja once told me, when speaking of her family, "We don't live in a mansion, but we have values." A common misconception is that to have values means that you have what others expect you have (family, friends, society). Some think that they have to have money, fame, success, and so on, to express their values; this is a total myth. If you look at table 7.1, you do not even see those words on the table. Money, fame, and success are important to some people; however, most people would trade all of that in for a healthy family, successful relationships, and overall happiness.

Values, as stated earlier, are long-enduring beliefs that one holds. Values are at the core of who you are, and we spend most of our lives trying to figure out what we value and what we do not. Some of you can come up with a "laundry list" of what you do not value because you may have had a lot of negative examples in your past; others of you can come up with your healthy values because you have had wonderful examples in your life. In either case, just as you learn who you are from others, you learn what you value (or don't value) from others.

Before we go on to the next area of the values model, it is important to learn one more thing about values. Values represent what you desire and how you think things *should be*—values are not always a reflection of what *is*. To further understand, let's look at this example: You believe in equality among all people, regardless of gender, race, culture, age, or sexual orientation (equality is your terminal value). Therefore, you are polite, encouraging, loving, supportive, and so on. (Those are examples of your instrumental values.) As you know, equality still does not exist in our society; in other words, equality is what you value as something we should have, but it is not a reflection of how things are today.

Beliefs are a reflection of *what is* today. **Beliefs** are the conclusions that you come to because of what you value. Here are a few examples of the relationship between what you value and how it is reflected in a belief statement:

Value	Belief Statement
Education	"I will have my bachelor's degree this year"
Beauty	"I think Monica is an attractive woman."
Honesty	"I know my doctor will clearly tell me what is going on with my illness."
Fairness	"My professor is tough, but at least he treats everyone the same."
Respect	"My parents always knock before they come in to my room."

Beliefs work on several levels. Gerald Wilson, in *Let's Talk It Over,* describes beliefs as central, shared, derived, and surface beliefs. Let's examine the different levels of our beliefs:

- **Central beliefs** are the beliefs that are closest to what you value, and in turn, the most difficult to change. We typically do not share our central beliefs with others, since they are so close to what we value. Central beliefs can consist of your fears, your desires, your dreams, etc.

- **Shared beliefs** come from what we experience and what we discuss or share in our interpersonal relationships. The term **shared** is important here because these are the beliefs that we develop based on the conclusions we have drawn from our relationships.
- **Derived beliefs** are what we learn from others, either directly or indirectly. There are some beliefs that we hold simply because we have learned from other people to believe something. We may not even be conscious of where a specific belief comes from or why we think the way we do; until something (a stimulus) alerts us to a particular belief. Derived beliefs come not only from your friends and family; they also come from strangers, colleagues, the media, etc.
- **Surface beliefs** are the most flexible beliefs we hold and the easiest to change. Surface beliefs are basically the choices that you make every day. For example, why do you sit where you do in class? Typically because you believe you will be comfortable. Why do you order a particular dish at a restaurant? Typically because you believe it will be tasty, healthy, and/or satisfying. These preferences probably will not have any substantial impact on other beliefs; this is why they are called surface beliefs.

The next circle in the values model includes our attitudes. **Attitudes** are the way we react to any given experience or person. Attitudes are a direct reflection of what we do or do not believe in. If we lack conviction from our beliefs (meaning there is not a value to support it); then our attitudes have inconsistencies. For example, if you believe in monogamous relationships; yet you flirt with someone you find attractive while in another relationship, then your attitude has inconsistencies. Your belief about monogamous relationships does not have a value to support it.

Our attitudes are formed from our *past experiences* and *future expectations*. Our past experiences create our beliefs and values; we then express how we feel about people, topics, experiences, and so on, through our attitudes. Our attitudes typically *express our convictions, biases, and prejudices.* Many times we are not even consciously aware of our biases and prejudices until someone else makes us aware. Attitudes can range in *intensity* and *complexity.* Attitudes can create *direction* for your values and create *priorities* about the areas of your experiences that should be, or are, important to you.

The final ring in the values model includes our behaviors. **Behaviors** are the way we act out our values, beliefs, and attitudes: our hopes, dreams, fears, desires, convictions, biases, prejudices, and so on. Our behaviors are what others first see about us, creating the first impression. Therefore, people begin to conclude, to make assumptions, about what you value, based on how you behave. When you then say that you value something, and your attitudes and behaviors directly show something else, people then make further conclusions about your values. For example, if you tell someone that you think honesty is important, or something that you value, and then you do something that is misleading or dishonest, people begin to conclude that not only do you not value honesty but there are probably other things you say you value when in actuality you do not.

> "My values will change as I grow older. I'm 18 and I will be 19 next week. Most of the stuff I believe in is from what my family has taught me, but as I go through everyday life my values will change."
> —Tiffany Harvey

 You are halfway done with this chapter; therefore, it is time to pause and reflect on what you have read. Consider the following questions and write down some notes in the space provided:

1. What didn't you know about the things you have read so far?

2. What surprised you the most about what you have read so far?

3. With what you've read so far, what don't you understand?

4. Is there anything you don't agree with, or is there anything you need more information about?

WHERE DO YOUR VALUES COME FROM?

Learning what we should and should not do in various situations,
Learning what is acceptable and what is not acceptable,
Learning what it means to have good manners,
Learning what is respectful and what is not,
Learning what cleanliness is and why it is important.

The list above includes examples of values you may have learned—but where did they come from? Where do you learn how to behave in various types of situations? Where did you learn to like some foods and avoid others? Where did you learn how to greet or meet someone new? When did you decide that having a fulfilling career is a good thing, and when did you change your mind and decide you just want to stay at home, if you ever did? When did you decide that you want to live in a word of peace? When did you become a Democrat, Republican, or an Independent? These are important questions you should examine as you assess your values. Values come from a variety of experiences and people, including:

Books	Media (film, commercials, etc.)
Colleagues	Politicians
Culture	Religious leaders
Education Level	School bullies
Economic status	Social circles/groups/interests
Family	Strangers
Friendships	Supervisors
Love interests	Teachers

Use this list to assess your values, where they come from, and how you feel about your values in the first individual activity. Much of what you need to do includes making a few

> "No matter who you are, you have your own values. It is good to have your own values. You should never let someone try to change your values. They are what make you who you are and they are very important in your life."
>
> —Sarah Pritchard

decisions. We will examine one more aspect of values; then it is time to learn how decision making should work to be effective.

TESTING AND CHANGING YOUR VALUES

"The task of maintaining objectivity while exploring yourself is like trying to walk a straight line through a forest. You inevitably keep bumping into things. All you can do is continue trying for the general direction. As you test long-held rules of living, you may find yourself inadvertently acting in ways that promote the likelihood of a negative, catastrophic outcome," according to Matthew McKay and Patrick Fanning in *Prisoners of Belief.*

McKay and Fanning present a very important perspective about freeing yourself from values you are ready to change. Change of any kind is not always easy; however, change is an inevitable part of life. We need to accept change and embrace what we can learn from it. Changing or re-evaluating our values, especially ones that we do not know where they come from, is essential to personal growth and maturity.

Testing your values requires *assertiveness* because your family and friends will test you throughout the process. Our family and friends typically have a hard time going through change with us. If it is ultimately a change for the better, they applaud us after it happens, but they question us during the actual changing process.

Here is an example about how my family tested my decision to re-examine my values. I value education (I hope that is not too big of a shock for most of you) and I can recall when I made the decision to continue college, to work on my graduate studies. My family questioned my decision because I was a single mother with a child who needed me to "get a job." Here's the conflict—I agreed with them; I valued my education, but I also valued money, stability, and working. My family was focused on the latter; however, I was re-examining (or testing) my values. How much did I really value education? Was it just enough to get a job or was there more to it? Did I want a career, or just a job? Did I want to find a career that I would enjoy going to every single day, even the tough days? Did I want to make more financial sacrifices simply so I could be happy? The answer to all of those questions is—yes, absolutely and positively, yes! I needed to find a career that made me happy. I knew that—for me—if I could find a career that satisfied me, then I could be a better woman, a better friend, a better sister, and yes, a much better mom. I tested my values and I have not regretted it. And guess what? My family came along and they could not be more proud.

Through the example I just shared you learned that testing your values requires *effective decision making.* I can guarantee that you will need to make several decisions along the way and you cannot rely on others to make your decisions for you. It is your life and it will be your responsibility to live with your decisions, so why not make them yourself? Making decisions about your values is a significant part of the process of testing your values. The next section of this chapter, and the activities at the end of this chapter, will assist you in this process.

DECISION MAKING

We make decisions from the moment we decide to get out of bed (or hit the snooze a couple of times) and throughout the day and evening. Most of the decisions that you make happen unconsciously. Your challenge for the final section of this chapter is to turn the unconscious process into a conscious process. I want you to begin developing an acute awareness of the decisions you make throughout the day and why you make those decisions. You may be surprised at how many decisions to which you cannot answer the why question.

There are several "decision-making processes" and every one of them basically says the same thing. Some of the processes have two to four steps, and some of them have five to seven steps. The process that I really like is David A. Welch's nine-step decision-making process in his book *Decisions, Decisions*. His process is thorough, and you can apply it to several types of decisions, from small ones to large ones. I also like that the process includes assessing your values and evaluating your decisions; these are two important components to the overall learning process. The nine-step process is described as the following:

1. **Identify your objective.** Determining the goal or the purpose of the decision is the first and essential step. Even a simple decision should have a purpose that is *valid*. Hitting the snooze button on your alarm clock is a decision. However, what is the purpose and is it valid? I am assuming you are saying to yourself, "I'm tired; that's why I hit the snooze button." Yep, that is the purpose—but is it valid? What about the responsibilities you are ignoring because you need to get out of bed? What about the implications because of the decision you made? The validity of the decision must be addressed.

2. **Do a preliminary survey of your options.** You do this unconsciously; now try writing down your options. Keep it simple, though; you don't need to spend a lot of time in this step. Simply allow your intuition to work here and decide what the obvious options are for the decision. This will help you to focus through the next few steps in the process.

3. **Identify the implicated values.** Yes, all decisions should be a direct reflection of your values and your beliefs—from running a yellow light in an intersection, or choosing to stop; from choosing to go to work, or calling in sick; from choosing to go out with your friends, or staying home and studying for a big exam. Decisions need to reflect your values, as we discussed in the section on the values model.

4. **Assess the importance of the decision.** When I was making a decision to go to graduate school or getting a job, that was a very important decision. Obviously not all decisions are as important, and some are more important. However, even the small decisions can have great importance. Someone asks you a simple yes or no question—important or not? It can be. The question could be, "Could you please move your car?" Or it could be "Will you come home with me tonight?" We may answer each question with minimal hesitation; however, either question has the potential for tremendous implications.

5. **Budget your time and energy.** Yes, time management is an essential part of this process. A decision is only going to be successful if it is made in a timely manner. If it takes too much time, the decision may not be necessary anymore. Again, I can hear you talking to

me saying, "If I waste my time, I may not have to make the decision." Again you are right; however, is *that* the best decision? Is it right, is it ethical, is it responsible to delay making the decision? Are you trying to force someone else into making the decision for you? Maybe that is the lesson you need to learn during the decision-making process.

6. **Choose a decision-making strategy.** Strategies include creating your plan of action and figuring out how you will accomplish the task. Strategies are typically a reflection of your personality. In other words, you already have tendencies and preferences toward how you like to accomplish your tasks. This step is merely recognizing what those steps should be, and assessing how effective your current strategies are for making decisions.

7. **Identify your options.** Now it is time to take your list from step two and re-evaluate your options. Some of you have created a list of pros and cons before when making a decision; this is a similar idea, only you are now a more effective decision maker. You need to create a list of all of your options—do not limit yourself. Allow yourself to write down every single possibility, and do not evaluate any of them. You can also write down what others think your options are; this will be helpful, because on a subconscious level you have been listening to what others have to say about your decision. Again, it is essential not to evaluate your options; allow yourself to brainstorm all of the possibilities.

8. **Evaluate your options.** OK, now you can evaluate your options. Why is it important to separate the process? Good question. It is important because you need to give yourself the opportunity to remove any and all of the limitations that you put on yourself. Those limitations could include not listening to your intuition, or ignoring someone else's suggestion because you do not like the person who suggested it. When you evaluate your options, remember to consider seriously why you like an idea and why you do not like an idea. The why questions are the key to your success.

9. **Make your choice—on time, on budget.** Yes—it is time to actually make the decision. The two important ideas for this step are to (1) ensure that the decision has been made within a reasonable time frame, and (2) ensure the decision has not had or will not have a negative impact on your budget. The decision ultimately has to be yours, and even more so, it needs to feel like it is your decision. The decision itself is the learning step; allow the decision to be your teacher. Reflect on what you have learned during the process, and then come back to the decision a month or a year later and reflect on what you have learned.

The final aspect of the decision-making process is to not be too hard on yourself if the decision ends up going wrong or not as you planned. **All** decisions are beneficial, if they are capable of teaching you a lesson. Sometimes we have to learn the hard way or learn through "bad" decisions. However, if you allow a "bad" decision to stop you in the future, then it truly was a bad decision. Decisions are *never* bad, *if* they can teach you a healthy lesson. Be assertive—make decisions—and you will see yourself grow and mature in ways that you may not have ever thought possible.

Finally, you need to recognize that the first few times you use the nine steps to make effective decisions you may find yourself feeling emotionally and intellectually drained. It takes a lot of energy to move decision making from the unconscious to the conscious mind. However, when you become aware of the process that you go through, you are more likely to identify your strengths and your limitations. Welch tells us:

The first few times you use them [the nine steps] to help you make an important and difficult decision, you will find that they force you to think of a number of things that, in the ordinary course of events, probably would not break the surface of your subconscious, and which have the potential to disturb you. They may make you think explicitly about the things you value, about the kind of person you are, and about the kind of person you would like to become. They may force into the open the stark conflicts you feel (say) between your desires and your moral sensibilities.

In closing, it is time to pause and reflect on what you have read. Consider the following questions and write down some notes in the space provided:

1. What didn't you know about the things you have read so far?

2. What surprised you the most about what you have read so far?

3. With what you've read so far, what don't you understand?

4. Is there anything you don't agree with, or is there anything you need more information about?

My World Now:
Life in a Nursing Home, from the Inside

By Anna Mae Halgrim Seaver

This is my world now. It's all I have left. You see, I'm old. And I'm not as healthy as I used to be. I'm not necessarily happy with it but I accept it. Occasionally, a member of my family will stop in to see me. He or she will bring me some flowers or a little present, maybe a set of slippers—I've got 8 pair. We'll visit for awhile and then they will return to the outside world and I'll be alone again.

Oh, there are other people here in the nursing home. Residents, we're called. The majority are about my age. I'm 84. Many are in wheelchairs. The lucky ones are passing through—a broken hip, a diseased heart, something has brought them here for rehabilitation. When they're well they'll be going home.

Most of us are aware of our plight—some are not. Varying stages of Alzheimer's have robbed several of their mental capacities. We listen to endlessly repeated stories and questions. We meet them anew daily, hourly or more often. We smile and nod gracefully each time we hear a retelling. They seldom listen to my stories, so I've stopped trying.

The help here is basically pretty good, although there's a large turnover. Just when I get comfortable with someone he or she moves on to another job. I understand that. This is not the best job to have.

I don't much like some of the physical things that happen to us. I don't care much for a diaper. I seem to have lost the control acquired so diligently as a child. The difference is that I'm aware and embarrassed but I can't do anything about it. I've had 3 children and I know it isn't pleasant to clean another's diaper. My husband used to wear a gas mask when he changed the kids. I wish I had one now.

Why do you think the staff insists on talking baby talk when speaking to me? I understand English. I have a degree in music and am a certified teacher. Now I hear a lot of words that end in "y." Is this how my kids felt? My hearing aid works fine. There is little need for anyone to position their face directly in front of mine and raise their voice with those "y" words. Sometimes it takes longer for a meaning to sink in; sometimes my mind wanders when I am bored. But there's no need to shout.

I tried once or twice to make my feelings known. I even shouted once. That gained me a reputation of being "crotchety." Imagine me, crotchety. My children never heard me raise my voice. I surprised myself. After I've asked for help more than a dozen times and received nothing more than a dozen condescending smiles and a "Yes, deary, I'm working on it," something begins to break. That time I wanted to be taken to a bathroom.

I'd love to go out for a meal, to travel again. I'd love to go to my own church, sing with my own choir. I'd love to visit my friends. Most of them are gone now or else they are in different "homes" of their children's choosing. I'd love to play a good

---

game of bridge but no one here seems to concentrate very well.

My children put me here for my own good. They said they would be able to visit me frequently. But they have their own lives to lead. That sounds normal. I don't want to be a burden. They know that. But I would like to see them more. One of them is here in town. He visits as much as he can.

Something else I've learned to accept is loss of privacy. Quite often I'll close my door when my roommate—imagine having a roommate at my age—is in the TV room. I do appreciate some time to myself and believe that I have earned at least that courtesy. As I sit thinking or writing, one of the aides invariably opens the door unannounced and walks in as if I'm not there. Sometimes she even opens my drawers and begins rummaging around. Am I invisible? Have I lost my right to respect and dignity? What would happen if the roles were reversed? I am still a human being. I would like to be treated as one.

The meals are not what I would choose for myself. We get variety but we don't get a choice. I am one of the fortunate ones who can still handle utensils. I remember eating off such cheap utensils in the Great Depression. I worked hard so I would not have to ever use them again. But here I am.

Did you ever sit in a wheelchair over an extended period of time? It's not comfortable. The seat squeezes you into the middle and applies constant pressure on your hips. The armrests are too narrow and my arms slip off. I am luckier than some. Others are strapped into their chairs and abandoned in front of the TV. Captive prisoners of daytime television; soap operas, talk shows and commercials.

One of the residents died today. He was a loner who, at one time, started a business and developed a multimillion-dollar company. His children moved him here when he could no longer control his bowels. He didn't talk to most of us. He often snapped at the aides as though they were his employees. But he just gave up; willed his own demise. The staff has made up his room and another man has moved in.

A typical day. Awakened by the woman in the next bed wheezing—a former chain smoker with asthma. Call an aide to wash me and place me in my wheelchair to wait for breakfast. Only 67 minutes until breakfast. I'll wait. Breakfast in the dining area. Most of the residents are in wheelchairs. Others use canes or walkers. Some sit and wonder what they are waiting for. First meal of the day. Only 3 hours and 26 minutes until lunch. Maybe I'll sit around and wait for it. What is today? One day blends into the next until day and date mean nothing.

Let's watch a little TV. Oprah and Phil and Geraldo and who cares if some transvestite is having trouble picking a color-coordinated wardrobe from his husband's girlfriend's mother's collection. Lunch. Can't wait. Dried something with puréed peas and coconut pudding. No wonder I'm losing weight.

Back to my semiprivate room for a little semiprivacy or a nap. I do need my beauty rest, company may come today. What is today, again? The afternoon drags into early evening. This used to be my favorite time of the day. Things would wind down. I would kick off my shoes. Put my feet up on the coffee table. Pop open a bottle of Chablis and enjoy the fruits of my day's labor with my husband. He's gone. So is my health. *This* is my world.

Note: Seaver, who lived in Wauwatosa, Wis., died in March. Her son found these notes in her room after her death.

Name: _____ Date: _____

MY WORLD NOW:
LIFE IN A NURSING HOME, FROM THE INSIDE
By Anna Mae Halgrim Seaver

1. What are your top 3 reactions to this article?

2. Why is this article important to discuss in the values and decision-making chapter?

(Questions continued on back)

3. What does this article tell you about American values of today?

4. What you do believe are some of the author's primary values that have been impacted or affected by living in the nursing home?

5. Other thoughts about the article?

No Wedding? No Ring? No Problem
More and More Americans Opt for Cohabitation

by Jay Tolson

Before 1970, it was called "living in sin" or "shacking up," and it was illegal in every state of the union. Why then, many social scientists are beginning to ask, has America's 30-year rise in unmarried cohabitation remained a shadow issue in the family-values debate? "Unlike divorce or unwed childbearing, the trend toward cohabitation has inspired virtually no public comment or criticism," note David Popenoe and Barbara Dafoe Whitehead, co-directors of Rutgers University's National Marriage Project. University of Michigan sociologist Pamela J. Smock, whose survey of recent research will appear in the *Annual Review of Sociology* to be published this summer, finds that most Americans are still unaware of the extent or significance of cohabitation, even though more than half of today's newlyweds live together before tying the knot, compared with about 10 percent in 1965.

Scholars are quick to point out that the United States is still a long way from Sweden, where unmarried couples—who have all the rights, benefits, and obligations of married partners—make up about 30 percent of couples sharing households. In America, by contrast, cohabitating couples make up only about 7 percent of the total. And for most of those 4 million couples, living together is a transitory business: 55 percent marry and 40 percent end the relationship within five years. "In this country," says University of Chicago sociologist Linda J. Waite, coauthor of the forthcoming *Case for Marriage*, "it's still mostly up or out."

What Smock has found is that the proportion for whom it's "out" of the union is on the rise. In addition, more and more unmarried women who become pregnant choose to cohabit rather than marry, which means that living together is increasingly a substitute for marriage, particularly, notes Smock, among African-Americans.

One of the biggest revelations of the new research is how many cohabiting arrangements involve children. "About one half of previously married cohabiters and 35 percent of never-married cohabitors have children in the household," Smock reports. She adds that almost 40 percent of all supposedly single-parent families are really two-parent cohabiting families. Unfortunately, that doesn't mean that kids in these households fare as well as kids with two married parents. "The non-parent partner . . . has no explicit legal, financial, supervisory, or custodial rights or responsibilities regarding the child of his partner," notes Linda Waite in the winter issue of *The Responsive Community*. Studies cited by Popenoe and Whitehead suggest there is also a greater risk of physical or sexual abuse in those situations.

Few romantic notions about cohabitational bliss withstand close scrutiny. While there is a little more sex between unmarried cohabitors than between married couples (one more act per month), there's almost more cheating by both partners. Then, too, there's more domestic violence and a higher incidence of depression.

But since living together is still mainly a stage in courtship for the majority of marriagebound Americans, the critical question is how the experience affects the subsequent union. Here the evidence is slightly mixed. According to most research, couples who live together—with the possible exception of those who move in already planning to wed—tend to have rockier marriages and greater risk of divorce. Why this is so is hard to say. It could be that people who cohabit are less traditional in their ideas and less reluctant to divorce. But it's also possible that the experience itself has an effect. "We need to do more qualitative research," says Smock, "and talk to people in their 20s . . . to find out why they are doing what they are doing."

Old rules. Some of the scholars who are studying the phenomenon—including Popenoe and Whitehead—are also taking sides, urging young adults to reject the argument that cohabitation is good preparation for marriage. Other researchers are taking aim at the economic disincentives to marriage, including the marriage penalty in the tax code and restrictions on Medicaid, both of which often discourage less affluent cohabitors from tying the knot. There is even a movement to bring back an older form of courtship. Leon and Amy Kass co-teach a course at the University of Chicago described by the former as "a higher kind of sex education." Using their own recently published anthology, *Wing to Wing, Oar to Oar: Readings on Courting and Marrying*, they attempt "to train the hearts and minds by means of noble examples for romance leading to loving marriage."

Can such a quaint notion win over minds hardened by the "divorce revolution" of their parents' generation? Steven L. Nock, a University of Virginia researcher, is guardedly optimistic that durable marriages will make a comeback (and, in fact, since 1990, have been doing so), whether or not old courtship styles are restored. "My generation," says the 49-year-old sociologist, "was the first to confront equality of the sexes. As a result, many reacted to the changed rules by fleeing from marriage. I suspect that our children, who've grown up with gender equality as a given, will be less likely to flee marriage." That might not be the "horse and carriage" argument, but it makes some sense.

Name: _____ Date: _____

No Wedding, No Ring, No Problem
by Jay Tolson

1. What are your top 3 reactions to this article?

2. Why is this article important to discuss in the values and decision-making chapter?

(Questions continued on back)

3. What does this article tell you about American values of today?

4. Other thoughts about the article?

Name: _____ Date: _____

INDIVIDUAL ACTIVITY #1
Assessing Your Values

PURPOSE—

To explore what you currently value, where that value came from, and how you feel about your values.

PROCEDURE—

First, using the first two columns in the table below, write out your terminal and instrumental values.

Second, in the third column, write out where you believe the value came from.

Third, in the follow-up, reflect on how you feel about your current values, where they came from, and how you want to change or re-assess them.

Terminal Value	Instrumental Value	Where the Value Came From

(Questions continued on back)

Terminal Value	Instrumental Value	Where the Value Came From

FOLLOW-UP—

1. As stated earlier, examine the following:

    - How do you feel about your current values? Consider—do you understand them fully? Do you have the consistency among your values, beliefs, attitudes, and behaviors?

    - How do you feel about where you values came from?

    - What do you wish you could change about your values? What is your hesitation?

2. Consider comparing your values with the values of your classmates; be prepared to discuss them during a classroom discussion.

Name: _____ Date: _____

INDIVIDUAL ACTIVITY #2
Decision Making in Action through Observation

PURPOSE—

To utilize your observational skills and your increased knowledge of group dynamics that you may draw valid conclusions regarding a given group's effectiveness.

PROCEDURE—

1. Your assignment is to attend a meeting of a group—any group of your choice except family, close friends, job or a group of which you are already a member—observe the proceedings and respond to the questions below.

2. Some groups which have been observed in the past include: city and/or utility board meetings, Alcoholics and/or Parents Anonymous, religious conferences, Parent-Teacher Associations, Weight Watchers, Gay Awareness, therapy and/or sensitivity training groups, etc. It may be necessary to obtain advance permission to attend meetings of your target group. Check with a group representative regarding this.

3. Take the information you have received in class through lectures, textbook and participation and apply that information to answering the questions. Explain your answers! Devote at least one paragraph to each question so you may have sufficient space to reflect your thinking.

4. After submitting your written report, get into small groups and be prepared to:
    A. Relate your experiences and observations to other group members;
    B. Discuss whether you felt "competent" decisions were made;
    C. Identify those elements of group interaction that you think either contributed to or interfered with the participants' ability to resolve issues.

FOLLOW-UP—

1. What gathering did you observe? When/where did you observe?

(Questions continued on back)

---

2. Why do these particular meetings take place? That is, what kinds of decisions are being made? Are they related to therapy? commitment? learning? problem solving? communication? motivation? living skills? crisis/stress management, etc.?

3. How did communication flow? Did it go back and forth evenly, around in a circle, from a facilitator to participants and back to facilitator? Did any member try to dominate? Did the other members allow or block the behavior?

4. How were decisions formulated? Did the participants utilize the seven step Creative Problem Solving Process described in The Elements of the Decision Making Process article? Did they use a process developed by members? Was each individual allowed to use what ever methods s/he chose? How did the other members support or critique the efforts of one individual to decide something?

5. In your opinion, were "competent" decisions made? Why or why not?

GROUP ACTIVITY #1

Lost in a Lifeboat

PURPOSE—

To employ decision making techniques using values to guide your choices.

PROCEDURE—

Scenario: You are in the middle of a dream vacation you have been planning for the last five years, aboard a luxury cruise liner. Currently you are in the middle of the Pacific Ocean, and land is a nowhere in sight. As dusk approached, you hear the alert signal to abandon ship. Passengers pour onto the lifeboats, but many do not clear the ship before a massive fire erupts and kills hundreds, completely destroying everything on the ship. The remainder of the ship sinks. You made it into a lifeboat along with 15 other people; however, your lifeboat is only equipped to transport a maximum of 8 people. To make matters worse, you only have enough water for 10 people for three days, but the group decides to try to carry all 15 passengers. To plan ahead, the group decides that they must rank the persons from 1 to 15, with 1 being the most necessary person to stay and 15 being the first to go.

First, everyone has decided to figure out their own ranking. Therefore, with the "your deci-sion" column, create your ranking from 1 to 15, with 1 being the most necessary person to stay and 15 being the first to go.

Second, create small groups to create **one** group-decision ranking using the "group deci-sion" column to record your responses.

Directions: With the scenario above and the short descriptions of each person below, rank each person. Complete the task individually and then create one group ranking. As you are attempting to create one group ranking, remember the choices you have already made and remember what you value.

Your Decision	Group Ranking	
_____	_____	1. Priest, 25 yrs. old, male, no children
_____	_____	2. Electrical engineer, 43 yrs. old, female, single, 1 teenager
_____	_____	3. Olympic swimmer, 35 yrs. old, female, married, 3 young kids
_____	_____	4. Family doctor, 45 yrs. old, male, married, no children

(Questions continued on back)

From Michelle Burch, *Interpersonal Communication: Building Your Foundations for Success.* Copyright © 2005 by Kendall/Hunt Publishing Company.

Your Decision	Group Ranking	
_____	_____	5. Freelance artist, 62 yrs. old, male, single, 1 adult child
_____	_____	6. Navy captain, 71 yrs. old, female, widowed, 1 adult child
_____	_____	7. Nurse, 37 yrs. old, male, single, no children
_____	_____	8. Pregnant woman, 27 yrs. old, single, no children
_____	_____	9. Young man, 16 yrs. old, single, 1 child
_____	_____	10. Rabbi, 38 yrs. old, male, married, 2 young kids
_____	_____	11. Graduate student, 25 yrs. old, female, single, no children
_____	_____	12. Scientist, 36 yrs. old, female, single, no children
_____	_____	13. Young girl, 5 yrs. Old
_____	_____	14. Housewife, married, 6 children of various ages
_____	_____	15. Convicted ex-convict, male, single, 2 children

FOLLOW-UP—

1. How did you make your individual decisions? Are your values reflected in your decisions? If so, how?

2. If you were able to create one group ranking, how did your group accomplish that task?

3. How did you decide that you were willing to change your individual decisions to create a group ranking?

4. You have completed the group ranking; now, guess what? Remember that you are among the 15 passengers; however, thus far you have not been told which passenger you are. You are the person who the group has decided is the first to go or number 15. What do you do? Do you willingly commit suicide for the sake of the group or do you have the group go back and re-assess the ranking? How do you come to this decision?

From Michelle Burch, *Interpersonal Communication: Building Your Foundations for Success.* Copyright © 2005 by Kendall/Hunt Publishing Company.

Name: _____ Date: _____

GROUP ACTIVITY #2
What Affects Our Values?

PURPOSE—

To examine what areas of your life affect your values, both positively and negatively.

PROCEDURE—

First, create small groups.

Second, write down a specific value that all of you agree is something each of you value.

Third, write out what the group feels are the positive and negative consequences for each value. For consequences, consider—your mood, friends, family, job, culture, gender, age, etc.

Your value _____

Positive   Negative
Consequences   Consequences

Your value _____

Positive   Negative
Consequences   Consequences

(Questions continued on back)

Your value _____

        Positive   Negative

        Consequences   Consequences

Your value _____

        Positive   Negative

        Consequences   Consequences

FOLLOW-UP—

1. Discuss what you learned from examining the positive and negative areas of your values.

2. Were there any disagreements about the positive and negative areas of your values? Did you come to an agreement? Explain.

From Michelle Burch, *Interpersonal Communication: Building Your Foundations for Success.* Copyright © 2005 by Kendall/Hunt Publishing Company.

Name: _____ Date: _____

WORD SEARCH
Reviewing the Terms

```
B B S J X P R E S N V A L L E
W E O Z Q K S H A R E D A S C
I E H F M U W H B Q O T P A A
L M E A M U P Q D T N W L M F
X U P F V C F B P E V U T N R
S K K M J I E Y M R V J W M U
A H Y C Y L O U N M Q I G E S
V P R F I J R R I T F R Q S
H Z O E Z T L F S N A G R E Q
S Q F L S R T X Q A K U U P D
O S V N D W W V U L H L W D B
A G I L A R T N E C A P B C V
Q A H O C Y R G V S D R Z C
N H K K A T T I T U D E S G J
N B K W K O S Q G U Z H C H U
```

1. long-enduring beliefs that we hold
2. values that express how you believe you should behave in any given situation
3. values that allow you to express yourself through your attitudes and behaviors
4. the conclusions that you come to because of what you value
5. beliefs that are closest to what you value
6. beliefs that come from what we experience and what we discuss or share in our interpersonal relationships
7. beliefs that we learn from others, either directly or indirectly
8. beliefs that are the most flexible and the easiest to change
9. the way we react to any given experience or person
10. the way we act out our values, beliefs, and attitudes

Name: _____ Date: _____

CHAPTER QUIZ
Reviewing the Chapter

_____ 1. Values are:
(a) easy to change (b) easy to develop (c) easy to express (d) objective (e) none of the above.

_____ 2. Barriers to understanding values include:
(a) lack of accurate information (b) lack of pressure from peers and family
(c) feeling empowered (d) a lot of stability (e) none of the above.

_____ 3. Attitudes are a result of our behavior.
(a) true (b) false

_____ 4. Values are long-enduring ideas that serve as a basis for decision making, action, and judgment.
(a) true (b) false

_____ 5. Confusion frequently exists between what we are taught to believe as children and what we believe as adults.
(a) true (b) false

_____ 6. Parents and other authority figures have little to do with the values we create as adults.
(a) true (b) false

_____ 7. Values are a representation of what is today.
(a) true (b) false

_____ 8. Beliefs consist of the following levels:
(a) central (b) core (c) shared (d) derived (e) surface (f) only a, c, d, e
(g) only b, c, d, e

_____ 9. Which of the following beliefs are difficult to change?
(a) central (b) core (c) shared (d) derived (e) surface.

_____ 10. Our attitudes are formed from:
(a) past experiences (b) your behaviors (c) future expectations
(d) both a and c (e) both b and c.

_____ 11. Testing your values includes assertiveness and effective decision making.
(a) true (b) false

_____ 12. Values are important to the decision-making process.
(a) true (b) false

_____ 13. The decision-making process includes:
(a) assessing your mood (b) assessing what your neighbors think (c) assessing your values (d) assessing what your family thinks (e) none of the above.

CHAPTER 8

DEVELOPING HEALTHY RELATIONSHIPS

KEY TERMS

Affinity need

Avoiding stage

Blind self

Bonding stage

Circumscribing stage

Co-dependency

Control need

Dependency

Differentiating stage

Experimenting stage

Hidden self

Inclusion need

Initiating stage

Integrating stage

Intensifying stage

Interdependency

Johari Window

Open self

Respect need

Self-disclosure

Stagnating stage

Terminating stage

Unknown self

CHAPTER OBJECTIVES

1. Understand and analyze the four window panes of the Johari Window.

2. Understand the various types of relationships.

3. Recognize the rules of relationships.

4. Differentiate the three types of intimacy.

5. Understand how relationships develop, how they are maintained, and how they deteriorate.

6. Analyze the qualities of healthy relationships.

7. Practice skills for improving your relationships.

As the petals of the beautiful flower flutter to the grass she says to herself, "He loves me . . . he loves me not . . . he loves me . . . he loves me not." All the while she secretly prays to herself that the last petal follows exactly what her heart is screaming out. I remember pulling the petals off of several flowers in my childhood (OK, I may still pull a few petals but I won't publicly admit it). Relationships are so important, special, unique, and yes, each one has the potential to bring us great pain. We love relationships . . . we strongly dislike them . . . we love relationships . . . we can not live with out them . . .

VISUALIZING YOUR RELATIONSHIPS—JOHARI WINDOW

Everyone wants their relationships to be successful; however, few understand what it takes to have a healthy relationship, and even fewer still are willing to communicate with the other person about their wants, needs, and expectations for the relationship, for fear they may scare or turn off the other person. In order for you to begin on the path of healthy relationships (whether it is your brother, mother, grandparent, friend, or partner), you need to visualize how you perceive the current state of each relationship.

Joseph Luft and Harrington Ingham created the **Johari Window,** a diagram that allows you to examine the amount of self-disclosure in your relationship, (see figure 8.1 for an illustration). **Self-disclosure** is information that you share with others which is not readily known about

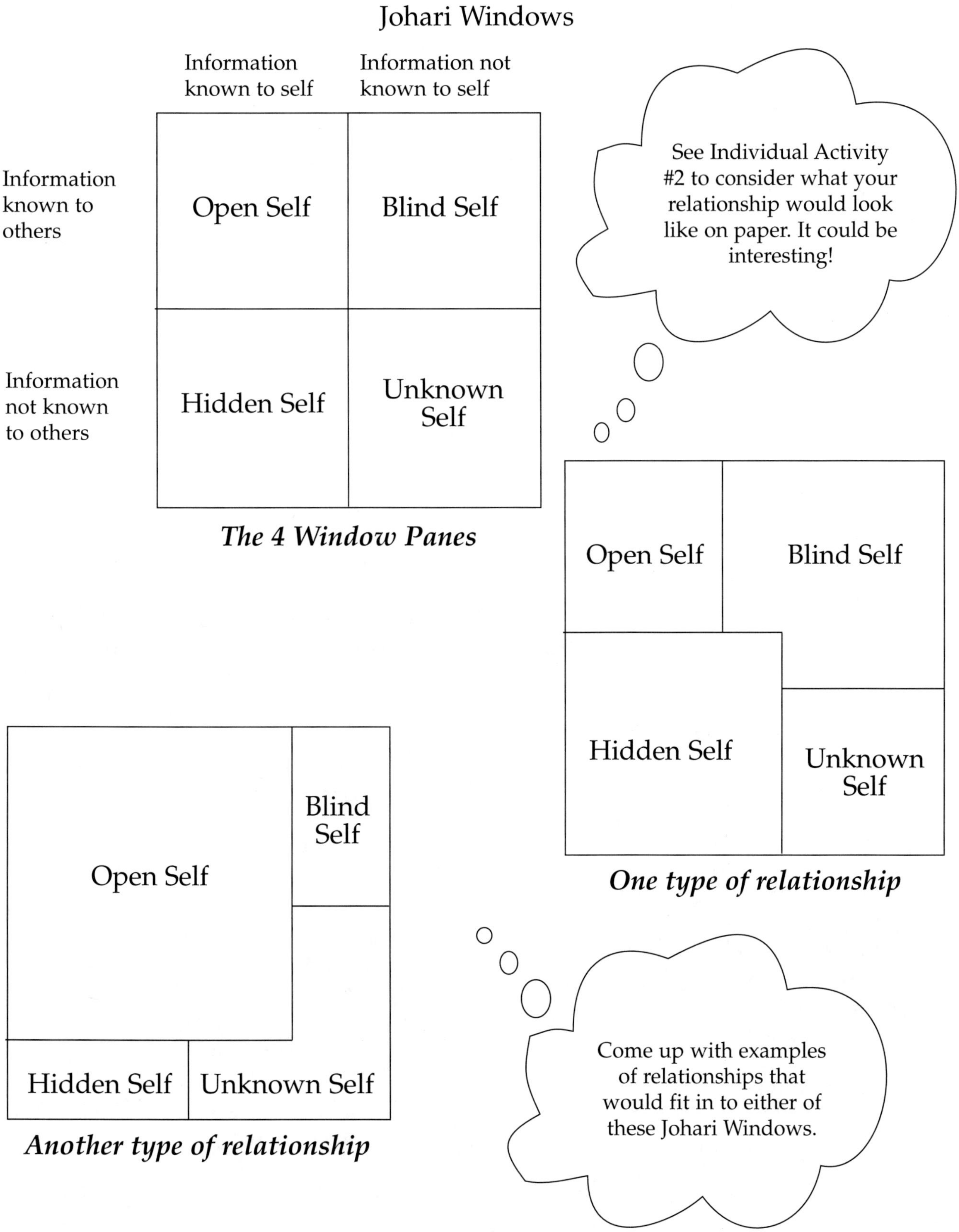

Johari Windows

Information known to self | **Information not known to self**

Information known to others

| Open Self | Blind Self |

Information not known to others

| Hidden Self | Unknown Self |

The 4 Window Panes

See Individual Activity #2 to consider what your relationship would look like on paper. It could be interesting!

Open Self | Blind Self

Hidden Self | Unknown Self

One type of relationship

Open Self | Blind Self

Hidden Self | Unknown Self

Another type of relationship

Come up with examples of relationships that would fit in to either of these Johari Windows.

FIGURE 8.1
Johari Window.

---

you. The Johari Window gives people a place to start when they are assessing how open they are in their relationships. There are four window panes to the Johari Window: the open self, the blind self, the hidden self, and the unknown self.

The **Open Self** is information that is freely communicated in the relationship. In other words, the open self is information that both people openly share with one another. In the beginning of a relationship this is typically basic information about your job, education, where you live, and so on. As the relationship progresses, the information can be things that you only share with the person in the relationship.

The **Blind Self** is information that the other person in the relationship knows about you; however, you do not know this about yourself. It may be that your mother thinks you are a selfish person, but you do not see yourself that way, or maybe, your boyfriend sees you as a beautiful woman, but you see yourself as an ugly person. Another example would be when your professor tells you that he thinks you have a lot of potential in his class, but you do not see that potential.

The **Hidden Self** is information about yourself that you do not want to share with the other person in the relationship. This could be a painful event in your past, a bad choice that you made, or feelings that you are having but do not want the other person to know about.

Finally, there is the **Unknown Self,** which is the area of the relationship that is yet to be determined. It does not matter how long you have been in a relationship—there will always be an area of the relationship that is unknown. Ask someone who was married to her spouse for thirty years and then out of the blue he asks for a divorce. Now, there may have been someone in his hidden self whom she was not aware of; however, may times the result (the divorce) was a part of the unknown self. Unfortunately—or fortunately depending on your perception—we cannot predict the future; therefore, there will always be the unknown.

STAGES OF RELATIONSHIPS

Now that we have visualized our relationships (if you have not done so, check out individual Activity number 2, which gives you an opportunity to create your own Johari Windows), it is time to look at the stages that relationships go through as we develop a new relationship, maintain a current relationship, and work through a relationship that is deteriorating.

Before I explain the specific stages of relationships, you can check out table 8.1 which summarizes Mark Knapp's Relational Maintenance model. There are many theories regarding the stages that relationships go through (Joseph A. Devito, Julie T. Wood, Steven and Susan Beebe, etc.); ask your instructor for more information about the various theories. For now we are going to examine Mark Knapp's model of relationship maintenance. There are a few basic ideas you should know as you explore the stages of relationships:

- People move forward through the stages of relationships.
- People move backward through the stages of relationships.
- People move within each stage.
- People generally understand what stage they are in, how they got there, and if they should be in that stage, though s/he may not share that information with the other person in the relationship.
- Everyone moves through the stages of a relationship at a different pace.
- Each relationship is unique.

TABLE 8.1
Relational Maintenance

Stages of Relationships	
The Stages	**Short summary of each stage**
(1) Initiating	• First day of class, initial encounters • Mainly nonverbal communication • Creating overall first impressions
(2) Experimenting	• Second day of class, later in the evening, or days/weeks later • A lot of small talk • Trying to determine if you like that person or want to get to know her more
(3) Intensifying	• Days, weeks, months, or even years later, depending on the people in the relationship • Self-disclosure begins here. • A relationship has begun (hopefully both have talked about it and are OK with it).
(4) Integrating	• The coupling stage • The couple has combined their social circles. • Use "we" statements all the time • There is a distorted perception of the relationship, i.e., "We are perfect together, we never fight."
(5) Bonding	• Publicly announcing that we are a couple • Cohabitate, marriage, have a child • The relationship has changed and now has to be maintained.
(6) Differentiating	• Relationship is too restricting. • Need some individual activities • Finding the differences in each other • Seeking their interdependence
(7) Circumscribing	• First stage of true deterioration • Many times this stage happens when there is a major event in the relationship—a new child, a death in the family, etc. • Avoiding intimacy and certain "hot" topics
(8) Stagnating	• The relationship is motionless, lacks activity • Couple is physically together, verbally silent • This can happen while parents are wrapped up in their children's lives, and they forget to work on their relationship.
(9) Avoiding	• The process of the end begins. • Couples find things to do—separately. • May even sleep in separate bedrooms
(10) Terminating	• The relationship has officially ended • Divorce, moving out, etc.

The relationship develops

The relationship deteriorates

> "I am in a good stage in my relationship with my boyfriend and now
> I kinda know how to keep it where it needs to be. There will be
> ups and downs but there is that in all relationships. We just have
> to learn to do the win-win thing when it happens."
>
> —Tiffany Harvey

THE COMING TOGETHER OF RELATIONSHIPS

Stage 1—Initiating. The **initiating stage** happens when you first begin to check someone out and decide if s/he is appealing to you. There is a lot of nonverbal communication going on here because you are assessing how someone is dressed, his hair, the color of his skin, his facial expressions, his posture, and his eye contact. The verbal communication is minimal here; it may be as simple as a "Hello" or a "Hey, how ya doing?"

Stage 2—Experimenting. Now the verbal communication truly begins. In the **experimenting stage** we are trying to find out if we have things in common and if this relationship is worth pursuing. Our conversation is impersonal, meaning that we are not necessarily self-disclosing anything. There is a lot of small talk that goes on in the experimenting stage; some have called this stage the "hallmark of small talk."

What does Mark Knapp say about the small talk that goes on in the experimenting stage? Here is just a little bit from his book *Interpersonal Communication and Human Relationships:*

- "It can be an audition for a future friendship or a way of increasing the scope of a current relationship."
- "It provides us a safe procedure for indicating who we are and how another can come to know us better (reduction of uncertainty)."
- "It allows us to maintain a sense of community with our fellow human beings."

Reviewing stages 1 & 2—How do we determine who we are attracted to?

- **Physical Attractiveness.** In case you didn't know, yes, it's true; sometimes we are just physical attracted to someone else. Ok, I am confident that you knew this already. A few things you should know about physical attractiveness:
    1. There is not one type of beauty. Beauty comes in all shapes, sizes, and attitudes.
    2. What one person sees as beautiful isn't necessarily what someone else sees as beauty. This should give us all hope! It should also give us all reason to stop being so judgmental. It is sad how quickly we judge a couple and may even say, "What do they see in each other?"
- **Social Attractiveness.** Sometimes we initiate a relationship with someone because we have similar social interests. It may be that two strangers are working on the same community service project and, to make the day more enjoyable, they begin making small talk as they work. It could be that when you attend a new church you naturally seek

out a friendly face in the crowd because you are attempting to be social. Small talk is the beginning of a new relationship and happens because you are trying to fit into a new situation and fulfill your social need (Maslow).

- **Task Attractiveness.** Finally, we sometimes find someone attractive because we have a task to complete and that person has the same goal. When you have a task to complete it is always nice to have people around you who have the same goal. You may find this a lot in classrooms as you are assigned a group for an upcoming group project. The people you may find "attractive" are the ones who are not slacking off, who are attending class regularly, and who are interested in the task being a success.

Stage 3—Intensifying. A change in the relationship has occurred and friendship begins in the **intensifying stage** of a relationship. Just as the name implies, areas of the relationship "intensify." You find yourself sitting closer to each other, holding hands, hugging, and so on. There may be increased physical intimacy here; however, that is not always the case. Some couples enjoy taking their time and may not be physically intimate until stage 5 of the relationship. Finally, a lot self-disclosure is happening in the relationship. If you are enjoying the relationship, then you want to strengthen it by sharing things yourself with your mate.

Stage 4—Integrating. Knapp tells us that in the **integrating stage,** "The relationship has now reached a point where the two individual personalities almost seem to fuse or coalesce, certainly more than at any previous stage."

Here are some of the "verbal and nonverbal manifestations" that you may see in the integrating stage of a relationship, according to Knapp:

- "Attitudes, opinions, interests, and tastes that clearly distinguish the pair from others are vigorously cultivated. . . ."
- "Social circles merge and others begin to treat the two individuals as a common package—one present, one letter, one invitation."
- "Similarities in manner, dress, and verbal behavior may also accentuate the oneness."
- "Sometimes common property is designated—'our song,' a joint bank account, or a co-authored book."
- "Empathic processes seem to peak, so that explanation and prediction of behavior are much easier."

Reviewing stages 3 & 4—How fast or slow should intimacy be happening in our relationship?

Intimacy should not be the goal of all relationships, even though there is more than one type of intimacy. When you are developing a new relationship, you should know that there are three types of intimacy. There isn't necessarily an order in which the types of intimacy are developed; however, far too many people think they have to connect on a physical level very early in a relationship. That is simply not the case, because what you may find out is that you *only* connect on a physical level; therefore, your relationship may lack breadth and depth, which is crucial for a healthy, long-lasting relationship. The three types of intimacy are:

- First, there is **intellectual intimacy,** which is where you connect with someone's intellect. This is when you find out that you enjoy communicating with one another, that you have similar interests or hobbies, or that you have always wanted to know more about something that the other person does.

- Next, there is **emotional intimacy,** when you are able to genuinely empathize with one another. This is when you are able to share your feelings or emotions with each other. You can cry, vent, or whatever you need to do and the other person will simply support you. S/he will not belittle you, criticize you, or pretend that you emotions do not count.
- Finally, there is **physical intimacy,** when you begin discovering each other physically and you begin to genuinely pay attention to and appreciate each other's bodies.

As you can see there is much more to intimacy than sex. *Intimacy begins with the connection you have with your inner self.* Then intimacy can be the connection you have with close friends, family, children, colleagues, neighbors, and yes, your animals. Intimacy is expressed through both verbal and nonverbal communication. However, it is important to remember that intimacy is not the goal of all relationships because, as you will learn or have learned through your own experiences, true intimacy requires a lot of effort.

TRY THIS OUT!

I have already said that intimacy begins with the connection you have with yourself. However, how often do you admire yourself? For this activity you need *complete privacy.* What I want you to do is, first, find a full-length mirror. Then you need to bare all—yep— take off all of your clothes. Keep the lights on and don't turn around! You need to find intimacy with yourself. Write down your reactions—be honest! Go back to the opening of chapter 5 and review the story; it may help you through this exercise.

1.

2.

3.

4.

5.

6.

Was this an easy exercise? Did it fill you with a great sense of joy? Did you smile as you admired yourself? Or were you in the majority? More than 60 percent of Americans do not like what they see when they are naked in front of a mirror. Yes, this exercise is tough for many. If the exercise wasn't tough for you, kudos to you! However, you need to understand and empathize with the people you have relationships with, because I bet that many of them don't feel the same way you do.

For the sake of critical listening, consider why I asked you do this activity. Write down your thoughts here and be ready to discuss them in class or online.

1.

2.

3.

> "In order for a relationship to be completely satisfying you have to make your desires known. If you expect the other person to read your mind, you will be unhappy."
>
> —Andonia Lynam

MAINTAINING THE RELATIONSHIP

Stage 5—Bonding. How quickly we got here—can you believe it? It is already time to maintain the relationship, though hopefully you have been thinking about how to maintain the relationship as it has developed. The **bonding stage** of the relationship is when the couple publicly announces their relationship to society. This can happen through a marriage or moving in together; for some, even having a baby can be their way of publicly announcing "we are together."

"Bonding usually marks an important turning point in relationships. Up to now the relationship may have developed at a steady pace: Experimenting gradually moved into intensifying and then into integrating. Now, however, there is a spurt of commitment. The public display and declaration of exclusivity make this a critical period in the relationship," according to Adler, Rosenfield, and Proctor in their book *Interplay*.

Stage 6—Differentiating. All of this coming together in a relationship can really make a person want to find his or her independence again—this is not necessarily a bad thing. The **differentiating stage** is where the two begin to find their individuality. The two don't need to do everything together anymore, and you may see an increase in conflict. Conflict often increases when the two are communicating about why they are feeling the need to express their individuality.

Reviewing the Maintenance Stages—How does this really work?

Many couples thrive through the changing stages of their relationship. They have learned to listen to their intuition, they understand that change is a necessary part of life, and they enjoy experiencing the change. However, this is not true for everyone. Some couples find one person becoming dependent on the other person, and some couples find codependency to be a problem in the relationship.

Dependency implies that there is a superior and subordinate relationship, where one person relies heavily upon the superior or is controlled by the superior. When there is this type of reliance, the relationship lacks balance and equality. In this type of relationship one is dependent on the other person for their acceptance, love, and approval; and without those three things the subordinate does not feel whole. With **codependency** there is mutual dependency on one another in the relationship. At first glance that does not sound so bad; it is a definite improvement over dependency. What codependency lacks is the independence or freedom in the relationship. Both partners depend on each other so much that they cannot make decisions on their own; they cannot do things independently, nor can they have their own friends.

"Codependent behaviors or habits are self-destructive, not only to themselves, but also to all their relationships. Most codependents have been so busy responding to other people's problems that they have not had time to identify, much less take care of their own problems," according to Velma Walker and Lynn Brokaw in their book *Becoming Aware*.

How do you know if you have dependent or codependent tendencies? Check out how you answer the following questions from Walker Brokaw:

1. "Have you become so absorbed in the other person's problems that you do not have time to identify or solve your own?"
2. "Do you care so deeply about other people that you have forgotten how to care for yourself?"
3. "Do you need to control events and people around you because you feel everything around and inside you is out of control?"
4. "Do you feel responsible for so much because the people around you feel responsible for so little?"

Is it possible to find a balance, where you depend on each other for growth, support, love, and so on; at the same time, how do you appreciate your individual uniqueness, enjoy having your own hobbies, enjoy spending time alone, and so on. It is possible, and it is called **interdependence.** When two people are in the bonding stage of the relationship, you see a lot of dependency. When they enter the differentiating stage, you see them searching for independence. When the two are maintaining a healthy relationship, you should see interdependence. There can be balance in the relationship—if you learn to communicate your wants, needs, and desires!

THE COMING APART OF RELATIONSHIPS

Stage 7—Circumscribing. The beginning of the end begins in the **circumscribing** (or constricting) **stage.** There are two major components to this stage: (1) minimal conversation and (2) lack of quality communication. At some point in time you may find this happen in a relationship; perhaps you get wrapped up in the very active lives of your children; maybe there has been a death in the family; maybe you cannot pinpoint the reason, but circumscribing is happening to your relationship. If both people recognize what is happening, and can communicate to each other, then they can move back to stages 5 and 6 with ease. However, some couples do not even realize what is happening until they have moved on to stage 8.

Stage 8—Stagnating. By definition, stagnant means without motion or activity. This is how to define the **stagnating stage,** which is a relationship that does not have any activity or growth. The couple continues with their normal routine and they have the same old conversations; however, they do not have any enthusiasm for one another and the joy of the relationship is gone.

"You might legitimately question why people would linger at this stage with so many apparent costs accumulating. Most don't. But when persons continue interacting at this stage they may be getting some rewards outside of the primary relationship, through increased attention at their work or in developing another relationship. They also avoid the pain of terminating the relationship, which they may anticipate will be stronger than the current pain. Others may have hope that they can still revive the relationship. Still others may spend time at this stage because of some perverse pleasures obtained in punishing the other person," according to Knapp.

> "Relationships vary greatly in their setting and situation. I don't think many people know what all needs to be put forth in a relationship. Some people are not sure what they need for relationships. I've learned through Mark Knapp's ten stages that a whole lot more is involved than I ever knew. I believe that these steps will enhance all of my relationships, old and new."
>
> —Nichol Righter

Reviewing stages 7 & 8—Is this relationship really doomed to end?

Some relationships are doomed to end right from the start. It could happen immediately following the initiating stage and soon after the intensifying stage, especially if you have moved through those stages at an accelerated speed. The most important lesson we can learn about relationships is: healthy relationships need time to develop, and maintenance takes effort.

"Things may seem to get worse in close relationships that continue over time because we don't realize that communication is inherently ambiguous and that conversational styles differ, so we expect to be understood if there is love. When misunderstandings inevitably arise, we attribute difficulties to failure: our own, or the other's, or a failure of love," according to Deborah Tannen in her book *That's Not What I Meant!*

She goes on to say, "Part of the reason this mutual aggravation of style differences is so disturbing is that we want so badly for communication to be perfect at home. Primary relationships have replaced religion, clan, and mere survival as the foundations of our lives, and many of us have come to see communication as the cornerstone of that foundation."

The bottom line: the relationship does not have to end if there is real, unquestionable love and commitment to the success of the relationship. Therapy is not a bad thing. Unfortunately, not everyone understands that going to a therapist is *not* a sign of weakness. Actually the opposite is true; seeking therapy to improve your relationship is a true sign of strength in character. If conflict is one of your biggest struggles in your relationship, then hold onto your hats because we will be discussing conflict and power in the next chapter.

Stage 9—Avoiding. The **avoiding stage** is where we close the channels of communication and work on indirectly terminating the relationship. There are a few basic qualities that summarize this stage: (1) minimal face-to-face contact, (2) a full run of excuses to be apart from one another, and (3) the end is extremely close. Relationships do not typically stay in this stage for a long time, unless they have invested a lot of time in developing the relationship. Terminating a relationship can be very tricky when you have shared financial responsibilities, living arrangements, and of course children. What we find in this stage is that the couple begins to develop strong relationships outside of their normal circle of friends. This happens because they may assume "change is inevitable; therefore, I might as well prepare myself."

Stage 10—Terminating. The **terminating stage** is an official end to the relationship. This could mean a divorce, moving out, or simply saying "it is over." Everyone ends their relationships differently.

"Characteristics of this stage include summary dialogues of where the relationship has gone and the desire to dissociate. The relationship may end with a cordial dinner, a note left on the kitchen table, a phone call, or a legal document stating the dissolution. Depending on each person's feelings, this terminating stage can be quite short or it may be drawn out over time, with bitter jabs at each other," according to Adler, Rosenfeld, and Proctor.

Not all relationships fit in this 10-stage model—some relationships jump around the stages all the time, some only go through stages 1 and 10, and so on. The hope is that you can see some of your past and current relationships. The hope is also that you have learned how to develop and maintain healthy relationships in the future.

 You are halfway done with this chapter; therefore, it is time to pause and reflect on what you have read. Consider the following questions and write down some notes in the space provided:

1. What didn't you know about the things you have read so far?

2. What surprised you the most about what you have read so far?

3. With what you've read so far, what don't you understand?

4. Is there anything you don't agree with, or is there anything you need more information about?

TYPES OF RELATIONSHIPS

We have looked at how relationships develop and deteriorate; now it is time to examine the various types of relationships that go through those stages. Similar to the many roles that we play, we also engage in a variety of relationships. From family relationships, friendships, romantic relationships, to online, professional, and mentoring relationships, we have many types of relational experiences during our lifetime. Each type of relationship has its own special qualities that give us unique opportunities to learn about who we are, what we expect, how we should communicate, and what we need from others.

Family relationships are the first type of relationships we experience; therefore, they are the most important relationships we will ever have. There are basically four types of family networks:

1. The nuclear or traditional family
2. The extended family
3. The blended family
4. The single-parent family

> "Relationships are much more complex than the average person would assume. There are many different aspects of each situation which determine what sort of relationship you have with someone. For example your eye contact, distance, and your perception on things; they all contribute to who you are and how you interact with someone else."
>
> —Enjoli Gates

"Families provide such basic necessities as shelter, warmth, and care. In addition, the family may also fulfill the following psychological functions: socialization, intellectual development, recreation, and emotional support," according to Sarah Trenholm and Arthur Jenson, in their book *Interpersonal Communication*, when discussing the internal functions of the family.

They also discuss the external functions of the family by saying, "The family serves the culture as much as it serves its individual members, in two primary ways: (1) passing cultural values to its younger members, and (2) accommodating cultural change."

Friendships, like family relationships, are important to the development of our character and of our social development. We begin learning about friendships very early in our childhood. I can recall my son Calvin's first real friendship: his name was Dax. There were acquaintances prior to Calvin's friendship with Dax; daycare is an amazing place for social development. However, it wasn't until kindergarten when my son and his new friend met. It gets even more interesting, when almost a month into the school year they realized that we also lived across the street from Dax. Things were never quite the same after they realized they were neighbors.

Friendships can provide us with a lot of wonderful attributes. Consider the following attributes:

- Enjoyment
- Acceptance
- Security
- Pleasure
- Assistance
- Trust
- Respect
- Pride

Romantic relationships should have the same attributes as friendships. The only difference is the breadth and depth of intimacy in the relationship, as you learned when we discussed Knapp's Relational Maintenance model.

"The love we feel for the person we choose to have a romantic relationship with is different from the love we feel for our friends or family. Even though statistics reveal that approximately 50 percent of all marriages in the United States end in divorce, when we enter into marriage we expect it to be permanent, and that expectation of permanence, at least in part, is what distinguishes a romantic relationship from other kinds of relationships," according to Gamble and Gamble.

Online relationships are unique because they can be a combination of so many types of relationships. You can create new friendships that develop into a romantic relationship or you can have a professional relationship that could easily be called a mentoring relationship. Finally, you can be reunited with a long-lost family member. There are so many advantages to developing relationships online. Can you consider some advantages? What are the disadvantages?

Professional relationships can happen in the form of networking, mentoring, or basic workplace relationships. We begin to learn the rules of professional and mentoring relationships when we begin our career as a student. We learn the rules (or expectations) from how our parents interact with the teacher, how the teacher interacts with other teachers and the principal, and how the teacher interacts with us.

In *The Interpersonal Communication Book,* Joseph Devito describes the mentoring relationship as providing "an ideal learning environment. It's usually a one-on-one relationship between expert and novice, a relationship that is supportive and trusting. There's a mutual and open sharing of information and thoughts about the job. The relationship enables the novice to try out new skills under the guidance of an expert, to ask questions, and to obtain the feedback so necessary in learning complex skills."

Finally, there is the networking relationship, which Devito describes as a "process that can be viewed as one of using other people to help you solve your problems, or at least offer insights that bear on your problem—for example, how to publish a manuscript, where to look for low-cost auto insurance, how to find an affordable apartment, or how to empty your cache."

HEALTHY QUALITIES OF A RELATIONSHIP

From your own life experiences and what you have read in this chapter, you probably can create your own list of healthy, and unhealthy, qualities of a relationship.

If you recall in chapter 5 we examined Maslow's Hierarchy of Needs, where level 3 (your social needs) focused on our need for relationships. Theorist William Schutz elaborated on Maslow's social needs and described three specific types of social needs for healthy interpersonal relationships. The three needs are the following:

1. We have the need for affinity, or affection, in a relationship. How much? Everyone is different. The **affinity need** relates to how much love we need to give and to receive. The "people pleaser" types are typically on the higher end of giving and receiving love. The "isolated" types are typically on the lower end. As you have learned by now, this is not always the case; many times it is our past experiences that dictate how high or low our need for affinity is, as you will also see with the other types of social needs.
2. The next type of social need is our need for control. The **control need** relates to the amount of influence and power that we desire in our relationships. Here is something interesting for you to ponder: the "people pleaser" types typical require a low amount of control. Take a moment to consider why that is, as you are reading. Next you will find that the "abuser" types (whether emotional, physical, or mental abuser) have a high need for control. You may find that every relationship is different for you. In some relationships, for example at work, you have a high need for control; however, in your intimate relationships you have a low need for control. That balance is good; however, it is even better to find balance in both relationships equally, rather than having extremes in each relationship.
3. Schutz's final type of social need is the need for inclusion. The **inclusion need** is our need to feel a part of various relationship or interest groups. The need to feel included is impor-

tant to the validation of our self-worth. As always, there are the extremes; there are those who enjoy spending every weekend at home or out and alone, then there are those who cannot stand the silence and need to be with people all the time.

Do you see the connection between these? There is—it is the need for balance. Each need is important, as long as it is in moderation. The need for affinity, control, and inclusion are all important; however, I am going to add one more need:

4. The need for respect. The **respect need** refers to the amount of regard that others show us and we show to others. This need fits into the esteem need on Maslow's Hierarchy. However, it is important enough to ensure that the respect need being met is our social need. The high end of the respect need is the type of person who makes all decisions based on the amount of respect that she will receive from others. The low end of the respect need is those who never consider how their decisions will affect others.

> "Relationships have many more steps than I once thought. After going over chapters in our book, I learned that in my previous relationships I moved from step one to step four way too fast which inevitably moved me to step ten. If I had taken my time going through the steps and thought more of what I was doing then maybe some of those failed relationships could have flourished."
> —Hollie Young

RULES IN OUR RELATIONSHIPS

Yes, there are rules that apply to relationships! Relationship rules are different for each culture. Rules in the American culture include things like:

- Respect each other's privacy. Privacy is healthy; it assists in maintaining the interdependency of the relationship.
- Ridiculing each other is unacceptable both in private and in public.
- Active listening regularly with each other is a must.
- Leftovers should always refer to food and not your friends. They were there before you had a man or woman in your life, and hopefully, they will be there until the end.
- Agree to disagree as much as needed.
- Help each other out as much as possible and show emotional support.
- Lust is one of the seven deadly sins; be aware of your weaknesses when it comes to giving in to sex too early in a relationship.

Now you are thinking to yourself, "When are these relationship rules developed? I have heard some of things on that list, and I even do some of that stuff, but I know them more as expectations and not as rules." This is very true. However, have you ever heard someone say, "I wish having a baby came with instructions" or "I wish I understood what she was expecting from me"? Believe it or not—we have the instructions and we have the opportunity to understand each other's expectations. The rules lie in our communication with others. When we communicate our expectations, they become the rules that govern the decisions we make in our relationships.

In closing, it is time to pause and reflect on what you have read. Consider the following questions and write down some notes in the space provided:

1. What didn't you know about the things you have read so far?

2. What surprised you the most about what you have read so far?

3. With what you've read so far, what don't you understand?

4. Is there anything you don't agree with, or is there anything you need more information about?

MARRIED AGAIN . . . WITH CHILDREN
HAPPY HOUSEHOLD, OR BRADY BUNCH GONE BAD?

by Wendy Swallow

I'm standing in front of a mirror at home in a lacy silk dress, wondering why someone my age would ever walk down an aisle. I do not look like a bride, not at age 46. Instead, I look like someone's mom and, in fact, I am. I'm the mom of those two teenagers behind me, dubiously eyeing this soft pink concoction.

"Aren't you supposed to wear white?" my younger son asks.

"White is for virgins," my older son says.

"Oh, jeez," says the other. "That's a problem."

That's me, the problem bride.

Since announcing my engagement, I've stumbled across a minefield of social commentary on remarriage. Many of my single friends are envious, seeing it as a fairy tale ending. Others look at the two sets of teenage boys we hope to merge into one happy household and shake their heads. Instead of a fantasy, it's the Brady Bunch gone bad. Indeed, roughly two out of three second marriages fail, and for families blending children, it's even higher. If someone told me I had cancer and those were my odds, I'd start writing my will.

But then there are our parents, who are elated—relieved actually—at the thought of getting us back inside this maddening, wonderful and mysteriously strong institution. Married again, with someone to watch out for us.

Charlie proposed during a thunderstorm, on the couch where we first smooched. For years I'd reveled in the identity of a scrappy single mom. Now I'm going to be a wife again. Someone cared for. Not scrappy, but indulged. This is both unsettling and attractive.

Our engagement is a secret at first from the kids, but the planning machine starts rolling anyway—Will I sell my house? Will we renovate Charlie's? What about schools?—and within weeks I sink into irritability.

Everything Charlie suggests makes me angry, and then I realize I'm mad at him for upsetting our lives. Months later my younger son will say, "He's a nice guy. Why did he ask you to marry him?" What he means, when I tease this apart, is that no nice person would do this to us—ask us to give up our home, our neighborhood, our life.

I try to explain this to Charlie: "I'm mad at you for wanting to marry me."

He looks at me, his worry lines deepening: "I'm trying to make you happy."

"I know," I say, "and it makes me mad as hell."

The night I tell my boys, they cry, they argue, they shake their heads. My younger son, citing his own deep distress, the chaos theory and how we've moved four times in nine years, finally says, "Why do we all have to live together?"

It's an interesting question.

The point of the chaos theory, he says, is that you can't really control things, even with good planning. He knows this from reading *Jurassic Park*. As much as I hate to admit it, I think he's on to something.

I lie awake at night, trying to plan meals and computer use and chores, and the image

---

of dinosaurs crashing around a kitchen feels appropriate. Charlie's family goes to bed late and sleeps in. We work on the Ben Franklin model: lights out at 10, up at 6:30. They are nutritionally pure, while our ice-cream habit recently morphed into a root-beer-float addiction.

"Don't you worry about the kids' teeth?" Charlie asks.

"Uh, yeah," I say, feeling defensive. "But don't you worry about your kids' sleep deprivation?"

We both fret about how to get four boys showered, breakfasted and out of the house before school. I have visions of towels assigned by color, matching toothbrushes and lockers in the kitchen, one for each boy. Charlie listens and says patiently, "We have to be careful with the kindergarten model. I think the boys will laugh at this."

Instead, the boys develop their own model for family harmony: Each kid gets a room of his own, equipped with a fridge, computer and TV. One son suggests a food allowance, "so we can go out and get our own meals."

"No," I tell them. "That's called college and you get to do that in a few years, but for now we're going to be a family. A family eats together and watches TV together."

"Okay," they say. "Who gets to hold the remote?"

At least they're trying.

It's March, a few months before the wedding, and we've taught the kids to play Murder in the Dark, a game that involves cards and a murderer and bumping around in blackout conditions. It draws attention away from that tricky question about the remote.

The renovation of Charlie's Victorian is underway, my house is on the market, and the school issue has been settled. Wedding plans are in place.

Things are moving along nicely—yet I'm depressed. For years I've had a sign in the kitchen that says "Ain't Nobody Happy If Mama Ain't Happy," and I believe that. My sons believe that. Now I'm afraid that I'm going to be unhappy, the one who cracks in all this testosterone-scented mess. We decide to see a psychiatrist.

"After all these years of counseling couples and of being married myself," he says, "I'm convinced that the single most important thing to making a marriage work is . . ." He pauses for dramatic effect. Charlie and I inch to the edge of our set.

"Communication?" I ask.

"Well, all that stuff is important, but what it comes down to is—the ability to tolerate the neuroses of the other."

We look at each other. Nobody said it was going to be easy.

Finally, within weeks of the wedding, I wander into a store that has dresses for me. Not too *jeune fille,* not too mother-of-the-bride. I find one that seems perfect for a garden wedding, a simple but elegant ivory linen sheath. It makes me happy. I find nice ties for the boys, order yellow boutonnieres. And when they all get dressed up and slick their hair back, they take my breath away.

Minutes before the service, a thunderstorm slices through the garden. Everybody dashes for the house, where we huddle for half an hour, listening to the rain. Soon it clears, and the birds start to sing. We go out into the garden, say our vows, promise the four children we'll build them a family life of tolerance and support, and—poof!—we are married.

I know it won't always be easy—that our children will test our commitment, each other, and us. That there will be days I trip over too many sneakers left in the hallway.

But I also believe in unexpected blessings. When we told the boys we were getting married, and most of them were so distraught, Charlie's older son called and said, "Hey, I think this is great." That night his call was what pulled me through. We will all have our moments, moments of doubt and of believing, but so does every family. What feels wonderful is that we get to create them together.

And if they fight over the remote? We'll just turn off the lights and plan Murder in the Dark.

Name: _____ Date: _____

QUESTIONS FOR DISCUSSION—

MARRIED AGAIN . . . WITH CHILDREN
by Wendy Swallow

1. What are your top 3 reactions to this article?

2. Describe the reaction of her boys. Why did they react the way they did? Do you think that is a typical reaction? Why/why not?

(Questions continued on back)

3. With everything you have learned from this textbook, what do you think this couple did well? What should they have done differently? Clearly explain your ideas.

4. Other thoughts about the article?

'BRING ME HOME A BLACK GIRL'
by Audrey Edwards

The first time I saw my stepson, Ugo, make a move on a girl, he was about 7, and so was she—dark-skinned little cutie standing at the jukebox in a Brooklyn family diner looking for a song to play. In a flash, Ugo was at her side, shy but bold at the same time. He pretended to be looking for a song, too, but he was mainly just looking at her, instantly in puppy love. "That's right," I said to him, fairly loudly and pointedly, "When it's time to get married, I want you to bring me home a girl just like that—a Black girl." The girl's parents, sitting at a table nearby, looked at me in surprise and then suddenly beamed. Ugo's father, sitting with me, just nodded and grinned.

"Bring me home a Black girl." It's one of those commandments Ugo has heard from me most of his life, right up there with "Don't do drugs," "Finish school" and "Use a condom." Over the years he has rolled his eyes, sighed in exasperation, muttered that I was racist or been mortified whenever I'd blurt out things like "Dark, light, shades in between—it don't matter to me as long as she's Black." But Ugo has also grown up to be very clear about what that edict really means: *Don't even think about marrying a White girl.*

I myself became clear about this—or clear about a mother's role in imparting to male children what's expected when it comes to marriage—when I interviewed the son of a Black magazine publisher ten years ago. The publisher had three sons and a Black wife who had made it clear to her boys that they were not to bring home any White girls. "We could have them as friends," the eldest son recalled, "but we were definitely not to marry them."

In all the grousing and hand wringing we do over brothers' marrying outside the race, it had never occurred to me that the issue might be addressed by something as simple and basic as child rearing. We tell our sons almost every day what we expect when it comes to their behavior, but we seldom, if ever, tell them what we expect when it comes to that most serious of decisions: choosing a partner. Oh, we may ask vague, cursory questions about the women they bring home: Can she cook? What work does she do? Who are her people? Bur rarely do we come right out and make the case for marrying Black. Truth be told, we're much more likely to make the case for marrying "light" or marrying someone with "good hair" so we can have "pretty grandbabies." Or we might argue, shouldn't people be allowed to marry whomever they want? Wasn't that one of the goals of integration?

If we were playing on an equal field, yes, we'd all be free to marry anyone. But the fact it, we're not. For Black women, one of the inequities on the current playing field has been the rate at which Black men are marrying outside the race. While most Black men still marry Black women, according to a joint survey by the U.S. Census Bureau and the Bureau of Labor Statistics, the number of Black men marrying White women has increased tenfold in the last 40 years, up from 25,000 in 1960 to 268,000 today. That's more than double the number of Black women who marry White men.

Where Black people are concerned, the increasing numbers of interracial unions could eventually lead to what sex therapist Gwendolyn Goldsby Grant, Ed.D., calls annihilation through integration, a weakening of the culture and economic resources of the Black community. So the question becomes, How do we ensure our cultural and economic survival as a people? One way is to start early and plainly telling our boys to marry Black girls. We need to put the emphasis on our boys because they are more likely than our girls to choose a White partner. Add to that the fact that men still take the lead when it comes to choosing a marriage partner, and it becomes obvious that molding our boys' attitudes is critical.

Of course, we may first have to get past what we think telling Black boys to marry Black means. "Somehow Black people are taught that to be ethnocentric is to be racist," says Grant. "But to want to be with people who share your values, religion and culture is very normal. It is not anti-anybody else."

Indeed, it seems almost anti-self to want to mate with someone from a culture that has historically denigrated, despised and oppressed you—and continues to do so. "People don't consciously say, 'I don't value myself, so I'm going to seek an image outside my culture,' but the choices you make reflect what you believe," Grant explains. "This is why images are so important. Our children must see themselves positively reflected in the world, and if they don't, they start valuing the dominant culture. And when you worship the dominant culture and pay no attention to your own, you're not making choices for your highest good. You're confused."

As Maxwell C. Manning, an assistant professor of social work at Howard University, points out, "If you look at strong cultures, like the Jews, you'll find they have a high rate of marrying within their group. That's how they remain strong." Manning, who says he would be surprised if his own 21-year-old son "walked in the door with a White woman," notes that when as a young man he dated several White women, his parents were very upset. "That told me I should never think about marrying White," he recalls.

"I really wanted to be connected to my community," he continues. "Carrying the name and the culture is so important, and I think that would have been more difficult had I married a White woman." The expectations of Manning's parents no doubt influenced his choosing a Black woman when it came time to marry, just as his expectations for his son may well lead him to choose a Black woman as his wife.

How parents communicate to their children the importance of marrying within the group will vary, whether it's an in-your-face admonishment like the kind I've always given my stepson, or simply letting your child know, as Manning's parents did, that you're not pleased when he dates White girls. What's most important, says manning, "is that we communicate to children what our values are. And one of the values should be to marry within the race to further our heritage and our culture."

But culture and heritage are only two factors in a complicated race equation. For me it's just as important that Ugo affirm the beauty and desirability of Black women by choosing to marry one. When he zeroed in on that little Black girl at the jukebox many years ago, he was displaying what I thought was natural—an instinctive attraction to someone who looked like him. But according to experts, by age 7, Black children have already been bombarded by media images that can negatively shape how they view themselves and the partners you'd think they would naturally be drawn to.

That's why it's so important that we constantly affirm our children, helping them to appreciate their own intelligence, beauty and strength. Whether it's in the artwork on your walls, the posters in your child's room or the books and magazines lying around the house, positive Black media images should be as integral a part of a Black child's life as the images coming in through television, videos and other media.

Fortunately for Ugo, his African grandmother and mother and his Afrocentric Black American father have all contributed to his being grounded in a strong Black identity. But that doesn't mean he hasn't also been shaped by seeing his two handsome Black male cousins have relationships and children with White women. So I try to be as relentless in countering the White-is-right images he's assaulted with as our society has been in perpetuating them.

Clearly, one of the most insistent images going is that White women are the most beautiful and therefore should be the most desired. If you buy into this notion, then Black women can never be fully prized— and this is the message we get every time a brother dates or married a woman who is not Black. Maybe we shouldn't take such behavior personally, but it's damn hard not to. Black women are more likely than women of any other race to remain without a partner. So when Black men marry out of the race, it not only further diminishes the number of brothers available to Black women, but it also undermines our very confidence as desirable women. I don't want this to be a message Ugo ever sends out. He knows that if he wants to keep Mommy Audrey happy, he will bring me home a Black girl.

This is the message senior marketing executive Valerie Williams has also given her 15-year-old son. "I tell him I want to have grandchildren who look like me," says Williams, who is frank on racial matters. "I don't want to be sitting around the dinner table at Thanksgiving feeling I have to bite my tongue." Nor does Williams think it's possible to escape issues of race and White supremacy in interracial unions, no matter how great the love may be. "I don't care what anybody says," she argues, "there's not a White person in America who doesn't feel superior to a former slave. Why would I want my son to marry someone who will probably always subconsciously feel she's better than him just because she's White?"

We often forget that relationships are also built on economic foundations and that Black-earned money leaves the community whenever a Black man married out of the race. This is what rankles whenever we see wealthy Black athletes, entertainers or CEOs of Fortune 500 companies choose to lay their riches at the feet of White women by marrying them. So I have not doubt what motivated the Black publisher's wife to insist all those years ago that her three sons never think about marrying out of the race. Her husband had spent half his life building a multimillion-dollar business, and she did not want the wealth he would leave to his sons to pass out of Black hands. The publisher's wife was very clear about that. And her sons all married beautiful Black women and gave her beautiful Black grandchildren who look like her and will keep the money where it should be—in the Black family. In the Black community.

Last spring, while touring with Ugo the predominantly White college he would attend in the fall, I felt a moment of panic. Too many of the White girls, it seemed, were grinning in his direction. He is 19 now, strapping, handsome and a magnet for women of other races who find Black men as irresistible as we do. "Ugo," I instinctively blurted out, clutching his arm. "Please. Bring me home—" "Don't worry," he interrupted, putting his arm around me with calm reassurance, "I will."

Name: _____ Date: _____

QUESTIONS FOR DISCUSSION—

BRING ME HOME A BLACK GIRL
by Audrey Edwards

1. What are your top 3 reactions to this article?

2. What do you think about the "commandment" that they placed on their son? Explain your answer.

(Questions continued on back)

3. The author tells us, "We often forget that relationships are also built on economic foundations and that Black-earned money leaves the community whenever a Black man marries out of the race." Explain your reaction to this notion.

4. Other thoughts about the article?

Name: _____ Date: _____

INDIVIDUAL ACTIVITY #1
Finding Out What Others Think about the Relationship

PURPOSE—

To examine how other people feel about a relationship that you are engaged in, and determine how much their opinions affect that relationship.

PROCEDURE—

Pick one relationship that you are currently in, where you would really like to know how your friends and family feel about it. Then use the chart below to ask your friends and family to rate how they perceive the relationship. Good luck—you may be surprised at the results!

You have a couple of options regarding how to fill out the chart. You can (1) photocopy the chart and give a copy to each person to fill out or (2) you can have each person put a mark in each appropriate box and then tally the marks.

Type of Behavior	Low Amount		Occasionally	All the Time	
	1	2	3	4	5
Respect to my partner					
My partner shows respect to me					
Affection to my partner					
My partner shows affection to me					
Controlling my partner's behavior					
My partner controls my behavior					
Respect my partner's privacy					
My partner respecting my privacy					
Listen to my partner					
My partner listens to me					
Allowing my partner to grow/learn					
My partner allows me to grow/learn					
Emotional support to my partner					
My partner shows me emotional support					
Conflict between my partner and me					
Communication between my partner and me					

From Michelle Burch, *Interpersonal Communication: Building Your Foundations for Success.* Copyright © 2005 by Kendall/Hunt Publishing Company.

FOLLOW-UP—

1. If your instructor wants you to turn this in for grading, see him or her for follow-up instructions.

2. It is essential for you to evaluate the responses from your friends and family. If you do not agree with them, it will be challenging for you not to get defensive. Remember what you have learned from this text and try understanding their perspective with an open mind. What were they trying to tell you? What was their motive? Are there any necessary changes needed in the relationship?

Name: _____ Date: _____

INDIVIDUAL ACTIVITY #2
Creating Johari Windows

PURPOSE—

To visualize two relationships using the Johari Window.

PROCEDURE—

Using two different relationships, create a Johari Window for each one. Each window should have an open self, a blind self, a hidden self, and an unknown self.

(Continued on back)

FOLLOW-UP—

When you look at the windows, consider the following questions:

1. Explain what in each of the two relationships makes up the windows that you have created?

2. How do you feel about the panes of the windows? Do you wish they were different? If so, how? If you are satisfied with how the panes of the window look, why?

Name: _____ Date: _____

GROUP ACTIVITY #1
Exploring How Relationships Develop & Deteriorate

PURPOSE—

To examine people whom you know in various types of relationships, and see how those relationships relate to Knapp's theory of Relational Maintenance.

PROCEDURE—

Step one—Pair up with someone in the class. Together you will interview the following people: a married couple who has been together for more than 20 years; an engaged couple; a widow; and a divorcee.

Step two—Together you and your partner need to develop questions that will help you understand how the relationships developed, how they maintained the relationship, and how it deteriorated. As you know, from what you read in this chapter, most relationships experience some form of deterioration. In your interview of the couples who are still together, try to find examples of challenges they have faced that could be considered relational deterioration, and how they worked through those challenges. Be sure to conduct the interviews with your partner so you both receive the same answers and you can both ask any necessary follow-up questions.

POTENTIAL QUESTIONS

(Continued on back)

From Michelle Burch, *Interpersonal Communication: Building Your Foundations for Success.* Copyright © 2005 by Kendall/Hunt Publishing Company.

Step three—Using the space provided, write examples (from the information you received in the interviews) of how each couple has gone through the various stages of relational development and relational deterioration. If they have jumped around in the stages, explain how that worked in the relationship. Your instructor may have you submit your interview notes.

Married couple for 20+ years

Engaged couple

Widow

Divorcee

FOLLOW-UP—

1. Following the interview, explain to the interviewees what the relational model is, what stages you believe they have experienced, and where they are in the relational model. Write down some of their reactions or comments.

2. As a class, discuss the experience, what you learned from the interviews, and if you were surprised by the answers from the interviewees.

Group Activity #2
Relationships in the Movies

Purpose—

To examine various relationships.

Procedure—

Step one—Watch one of the following suggested movies (or as a class choose another movie):

1) *Barber Shop*	2) *Bend it Like Beckham*
3) *Cast Away*	4) *Erin Brockovich*
5) *Remember the Titans*	6) *The Rookie*
6) *You've Got Mail*	8) *Mississippi Masala*

Step two—Prior to actually watching the movie, choose one or two relationships in the movie to examine for this activity. See the instructor for more information.

Step three—From what you learned in the chapter, as a class discuss the answers to the following questions:

1. Describe the types of relationship(s) that you examined.

2. Describe the qualities of the relationship(s).

3. Describe how the relationship(s) went through the stages in the relationship maintenance model.

4. Describe the spoken and unspoken rules of the relationship(s).

5. Describe the types of intimacy present in the relationship(s).

6. See your instructor for additional questions.

(Continued on back)

FOLLOW-UP—

As a class, discuss the following questions:

1. How can you relate to the relationship(s) that you examined? Discuss specific examples.

2. What relationships do you want to work on because of what you have learned (not only from this activity but from the chapter as a whole)? What specifically do you want to work on in those relationships?

WORD SEARCH
Reviewing the Terms

```
E  R  H  Q  W  L  Z  J  G  N  I  T  A  I  T  I  N  I  R  I
C  C  E  Z  C  V  F  A  O  D  G  U  U  C  M  B  E  G  E  N
G  U  Y  R  W  O  N  L  E  H  U  N  O  R  L  N  N  K  S  T
N  H  Y  L  U  Q  N  F  E  K  A  D  I  I  Q  I  M  H  P  E
I  P  Q  C  A  S  I  T  D  S  E  R  N  D  T  B  I  W  E  N
T  G  V  X  N  J  O  O  R  P  N  D  I  N  I  D  Z  D  C  S
A  N  X  E  G  E  A  L  E  O  S  W  E  W  D  O  I  M  T  I
R  I  D  J  N  Y  D  N  C  E  L  M  O  E  I  F  V  K  N  F
G  B  N  A  I  S  D  N  L  S  I  N  N  N  F  N  A  A  E  Y
E  I  G  K  D  E  E  F  E  R  I  S  E  E  K  A  D  J  E  I
T  R  E  C  N  E  D  N  E  P  E  D  R  E  T  N  I  O  D  N
N  C  D  C  O  Z  U  P  V  L  E  E  F  Y  D  G  U  N  W  G
I  S  Y  S  B  U  X  M  F  R  N  D  F  L  E  S  N  E  P  O
U  M  C  D  J  E  B  L  P  T  J  A  B  V  E  A  F  A  Q  D
L  U  I  N  C  L  U  S  I  O  N  N  E  E  D  S  Z  X  W  Q
K  C  Y  F  M  L  F  A  D  E  E  N  Y  T  I  N  I  F  F  A
O  R  G  T  V  H  T  E  R  M  I  N  A  T  I  N  G  P  N  I
S  I  Y  X  G  I  W  U  S  T  A  G  N  A  T  I  N  G  R  L
E  C  M  A  N  F  K  E  W  B  C  A  C  I  V  P  G  K  F  R
L  A  X  G  A  L  Y  Q  V  E  M  Z  Z  G  Y  A  W  V  S  J
```

1. information that you share with others which is not readily known about you

2. a diagram that allows you to examine the amount of self-disclosure in your relationship

3. information that is freely communicated in the relationship

4. information that the other person in the relationship knows about you; however, you do not know this about yourself

5. information about yourself that you do not want to share with the other person in the relationship

6. the area of the relationship that is yet to be determined

7. when you first begin to check someone out and decide if s/he is appealing to you

8. trying to find out if we have things in common and if this relationship is worth pursuing

9. a change in the relationship has occurred and friendship becomes closer

10. the relationship has now reached a point where the two individual personalities seem to fuse

11. the relationship is when the couple publicly announces their relationship to society

12. two people in the relationship begin to find their individuality

13. a superior and subordinate relationship

14. mutual dependency on one another in the relationship

15. dependency on each other for growth, support, love, etc.; at the same time, you appreciate you individual uniqueness, you enjoy having your own hobbies, you can spend time alone, etc.

16. the beginning of the end of the relationship

17. a relationship that does not have any activity or growth

18. we close the channels of communication in the relationship

19. an official end to the relationship

20. how much love we need to give and to receive

21. the amount of influence and power that we desire in our relationships

22. our need to feel a part of various relationship or interest groups

23. the amount of regard that others show us and we show to others

CHAPTER QUIZ
Reviewing the Chapter

_____ 1. When engaged in small talk, our relationship is probably in the _____ stage.
(a) experimenting (b) intensifying (c) integrating (d) differentiating (e) bonding

_____ 2. When a relationship begins to deteriorate, it is described as:
(a) experimenting (b) differentiating (c) avoiding (d) circumscribing

_____ 3. A stage in a relationship where two people begin to find their individuality.
(a) experimenting (b) differentiating (c) avoiding, (d) circumscribing

_____ 4. Effective ways to maintain or improve relationships would include ALL of the following EXCEPT:
(a) sharing feelings (b) listening (c) eating out (d) keeping a sense of humor, (e) none of the above

_____ 5. Information that others know about you, but you do not know about yourself is:
(a) blind self (b) hidden self (c) free self (d) unknown self or (e) none

_____ 6. Information that you know about yourself, but do not want to share with others is:
(a) blind self (b) hidden self (c) free self (d) unknown self (e) none

_____ 7. Information that both people know about each other is:
(a) blind self (b) hidden self (c) free self (d) unknown self (e) none

_____ 8. Intimacy is:
(a) emotional (b) physical (c) intellectual (d) A and B only (e) all of the above

_____ 9. Which need relates to how much love we need to give and to receive?
(a) affinity need (b) control need (c) inclusion need (d) respect need (e) none

_____ 10. Which need relates to the amount of influence and power that we desire in our relationships?
(a) affinity need (b) control need (c) inclusion need (d) respect need (e) none

_____ 11. Which need relates to our wanting to feel a part of various relationship or interest groups?
(a) affinity need (b) control need (c) inclusion need (d) respect need (e) none.

_____ 12. Which need refers to the amount of regard that others show us and we show to others?
(a) affinity need (b) control need (c) inclusion need (d) respect need (e) none

_____ 13. A type of relationship where there seems to be a superior and subordinate quality.
(a) dependency (b) codependency (c) interdependency or (d) none of those

_____ 14. A type of relationship where there is mutual dependency on one another:
(a) dependency (b) codependency (c) interdependency or (d) none of those

_____ 15. A stage in a relationship where it has now reached a point where the two individual personalities seem to fuse:
(a) initiating (b) experimenting (c) intensifying (d) integrating (e) bonding

_____ 16. A stage in a relationship where two people are trying to find out if they have things in common:
(a) initiating (b) experimenting (c) intensifying (d) integrating (e) bonding

_____ 17. A stage in a relationship where the couple publicly announces their relationship to society:
(a) initiating (b) bonding (c) intensifying (d) integrating (e) none of those

_____ 18. A stage in a relationship where a change has occurred and friendship becomes closer:
(a) initiating (b) experimenting (c) intensifying (d) integrating (e) bonding

CHAPTER 9

CONFLICT AND POWER

KEY TERMS

Accommodator

Avoider

Coercive power

Collaborator

Competitor

Compromiser

Conflict

Ego conflict

Expert power

Informational/
  persuasive power

Interpersonal conflict

Intrapersonal conflict

Legitimate power

Pseudo conflict

Referent power

Relational conflict

Resource conflict

Reward power

Value conflict

CHAPTER OBJECTIVES

1. Understand interpersonal and intrapersonal conflict.

2. Describe the fallacies of conflict.

3. Understand how our conflict styles affect our relationships.

4. Recognize the various types of social power.

5. Determine the costs vs. the benefits of using power.

6. Understand the games we play with power in our relationships.

7. Practice skills for improving your conflict techniques.

8. Practice skills for understanding power in relationships.

Student ideas about conflict and power:

- *"I hate conflict. I hate the way I feel physically sick when someone or myself has resorted to yelling, pointing fingers, or even avoiding one another. There is a deep place in the pit of my stomach where the truth lies; conflict is sure to bring it up and spill out of my mouth."*

  — Christina Warfe

- *"I don't like conflict because conflict leads to other things. I am not talking about good things. Conflict leads to violence."*

  —Kyle Wade

- *"Conflict affects everyone's life every day. I feel conflict is bad when people don't talk about it, but conflict is good when two people sit down and come to a resolution."*

  —Lindsey Grubbs

- *"I feel that conflict should not express power but it should compare ideas. Once power is executed, emotions, feelings, and pain come into effect."*

  —Armatine Travis

- *"I feel conflict is good for a relationship, as long as the conflict is discussed, aired out, and resolved. To harbor negative feelings over time will only eat away at yourself and your relationships."*

  —Marty Shaver

- *"I absolutely hate conflict. For me conflict never ends in a good way, it's always bad. My relationships always involve conflict and I do my best to avoid it."*

  —Andrea Lewis

- *"Conflict is good to have in your life. It teaches you how to express yourself in a good way in dealing with bad things that happen in life."*

  —Jerriline Williams

- *"I feel the power in conflict and relationships is often negative because people mostly tend to grow angry and discouraged with someone when it arrives."*

  —James Stephano Stanton

- *"I do not like conflict because it just causes lots of problems and drama. It causes people to get physically and/or emotionally hurt. I do like conflict because I am a police cadet and conflict is what keeps my job."*

  —Terry Griffith

- *"Conflict is the fastest and easiest way to see how people feel about a subject. Conflict is good."*

  —Jacqueline Bescoe

Everyone has an opinion about conflict, and most students look forward to this chapter because conflict is such a large part of all relationships. However, few truly have the patience to understand and genuinely work through their conflicts.

In this chapter we will define the different types of conflict, then examine the role that power plays in our conflict and how we use power to play games, which typically escalates the conflict. Next we will find our conflict styles, or the way we tend to handle a conflict. We will then look at healthy versus unhealthy perspectives about conflict. Finally, we will examine how to manage or resolve conflict in our relationships in a healthy way.

HOLD ON—before you get started, you should know that this chapter *may* challenge the way you currently look at conflict, the way you like to handle conflict, and/or the way you like to ignore conflict. It *will* challenge you to find the benefits of conflict in your relationships, and you *may* not like how the learning process feels. However, you *will* benefit from all that you learn in this chapter. Good luck and remember—your relationships are worth it!

WAIT—you need to do one more thing before you read any further. Turn to Individual Activity number 2 at the end of this chapter and write down how you currently feel about conflict. Then you will complete the activity when you finish this chapter.

> "Conflict with others can be one of the biggest barriers to getting anything done. This could be in work, school, or at home. When someone verbally attacks you, it may be conflict within them and not with you."
>
> —Bryan Clark

CONFLICT DEFINED

It's time, it is finally time, to begin the last chapter in this textbook—your last stop on your journey of self-discovery and how to communicate more effectively in all of your relationships. Appropriately so, since conflict is one of the biggest roadblocks a relationship will ever come upon, the last stop is a discussion about conflict. Let's examine conflict on three levels: the conflict we face in general, our intrapersonal conflict, and finally, our interpersonal conflict.

Conflict, in and of itself, is a mental, physical, emotional, and/or spiritual expression of a struggle between at least two people. Conflict can happen on a *physical* level; however, most of the time conflict is more verbal and more likely to happen on a mental and emotional level. It is true, however, that when there isn't a relationship, and the conflict is not interpersonal, it is more likely that a conflict will become physical. We are more likely to be in a physical confrontation with a stranger than we are with people we are close to. This is true because a physical conflict *will* damage the relationship; therefore, when there isn't a relationship, we may not show as much restraint.

Most of the time conflict is *mental* and it is communicated through our words and our *emotions.* Since we can become so overwhelmed with emotion during a conflict, many people associate the word "conflict" to an image of two people in a physical fight. As it was stated earlier, conflict typically does not happen on a physical level. The truth is that conflict happens most often through our words; and in turn, it is our words that will hurt another person more than a physical confrontation. Words will linger in our subconscious long after we have forgotten about a physical conflict. Adults spend thousands of dollars in therapy discussing the mental and emotional abuse they receive from their parents. As an adult or as a child, words stay with us for a long time.

The *expression* of conflict is what differentiates conflict, and interpersonal conflict, from intrapersonal conflict. The other person must be aware, directly or indirectly, of your negative feelings in order for there to be a conflict. Awareness can be direct with verbal language, and it is typically reinforced through our nonverbal communication, that is, your facial expressions, the tone of your voice, the crossing of your arms, and so on. However, someone may not understand why you are "upset" or "mad." Conflict is based on what you perceive to be happening with another person; however, what you think might be happening may not be the other person's reality. Only if the other person is aware that you are upset with him or her, through your verbal and/or your nonverbal communication, the expression is present and the conflict between the two people does exist.

The final component of conflict is *spiritual.* Have you ever had a conflict with someone and it affected the rest of your day? Of course you have, and when something negative happens, it produces more negative energy. Conflict is a "blow" or a feeling of being punched in our spirit, typically through someone's words. This is why people typically associate conflict with a physical confrontation. Our spirit is damaged or challenged for a short period, and sometimes longer, because of conflict. For example, when my son was in elementary school I realized that there was a correlation between our having an argument in the morning and his getting in trouble that day at school. It took me a little while, but I began to see that he only got in trouble at school on the days we had an argument in the morning. I already knew that I was affected by the argument, or my spirit was negative for at least the morning hours; unfortunately, it took me a while to see what was happening to him. The conflict damaged his normally upbeat and positive spirit for the short term. If I had not seen the pattern developing, it may have damaged his spirit for a much longer period. Could it be that children who regularly have bad days at school are facing conflict, directly or indirectly, in the home? Of course, and many studies have proven this to be true. Regular conflict will damage the spirit.

Examples of conflict:

- The cashier gives you back incorrect change, and he does not believe you when you tell him about what happened; therefore, you go to the manager about the situation.
- The person in the car in front of you is driving 20 m.p.h. in a 35 m.p.h. zone, and you are going to be late for work; therefore, you honk your horn and attempt to pass the person.
- You want to purchase a new car, and the salesperson is not willing to negotiate the price; therefore, you become disgruntled and try to talk to another salesperson.
- You have had too much to drink, and you think someone is "coming on" to your boyfriend; therefore, you confront the person about the situation.
- You are walking down the street and someone steals your purse; therefore, you begin yelling and screaming for help.

Moving along, let's look at **intrapersonal conflict,** which is an internal struggle over unresolved issues or contradicting issues. The conflict may or may not involve other people, as in the examples below. The conflict remains intrapersonal if the other person involved with the conflict is not aware of what you are dealing with internally.

Examples of intrapersonal conflicts:

- Unhappy or unsatisfying relationships where you have not discussed the issues with the other person in the relationship.
- Trying to stay on a diet, while dealing with the desire to overeat. Others may be aware you are on a diet; however, they cannot understand your internal struggle (in other words, your intrapersonal conflict).
- Unsatisfying job, which can lead to several things—You aren't able to pay your bills, you are bored by the job, or you are uncomfortable with your responsibilities.
- Negative feelings about the appointment you have in an hour with your physical fitness trainer.
- Torn between your list of priorities and responsibilities for the day, while wanting to meet your own needs.
- Inability to balance your financial budget or an inability to create a budget.
- Overwhelmed by goals and lack direction in achieving your goals.
- Surrounded by negative people/family.
- Decisions you want to make which you believe will not be supported by others.
- Feelings of depression; in other words you are faced with long-lasting feelings of sadness because of an internal struggle.
- Overall lack of focus or direction in your life leads to an internal struggle.

> "Conflict and power are areas where I learned a lot. I learned about how I deal with conflict. Sometimes I am an aggressor, but most of the time I am an accommodator."
>
> —Ty Frost

As you can see there are many examples of intrapersonal conflict. This is why it is essential to create time with your inner true self; if you do not deal with some of these unresolved issues, they will ultimately affect your self-esteem and your relationships. If you are ready, and want some help beginning the process of dealing with your intrapersonal conflicts, then you should check out Individual Activity number 1. Otherwise, let's examine one final type of conflict.

Interpersonal conflict is an expressed struggle (mental, physical, emotional, and/or spiritual) between at least two interdependent parties. The difference between conflict and interpersonal conflict is that in an interpersonal conflict a relationship, *interdependence,* currently exists.

Interpersonal conflict can happen in a several different forms and it can happen for several different reasons. Consider the following forms of conflict, and see if you can match them up with the examples that follow. Keep in mind that you can have more than one form of conflict going on at the same time.

1. **Pseudo conflict.** Pseudo or fake conflict is a conflict that exists about nothing. Have you ever been upset with someone and you don't know why? It could be that you were in a bad mood and took it out on someone else; in turn a pseudo conflict exists. If, however, the people involved in the pseudo conflict do not discuss what is going on, a real conflict may actually exist.
2. **Ego conflict.** An ego conflict is a conflict to protect your pride. Men are accused of having an ego conflict most often; however, women have just as many ego conflicts. Women are typically more indirect with their ego conflict. They may appear to reason out or talk through an issue, when they may in fact be simply trying to protect their ego.
3. **Resource conflict.** A resource conflict exists when there is a short or limited supply of readily available resources. The resources may be tangible or intangible, for example, love, time, money, food, supplies, and so on. A resource conflict may also involve a conflict over how to appropriately use the resources that are available.
4. **Value conflict.** A value conflict happens when at least two people disagree about what they see as valuable. It may be that an important decision needs to be made in the relationship (to get married, have children, etc.); it may be that a decision needs to be made about how to spend the evening (to go to the bar or to the movies, to stay out until 2 a.m. or until 11 p.m.). Regardless of the decision that needs to be made, in order to have value conflict the person is aware of what s/he values. Then in order for this to be an interpersonal conflict the person needs to be able to communicate (verbally or nonverbally) his or her values, not necessarily effectively (it is a conflict after all). If there isn't any communication, the value conflict remains intrapersonal.
5. **Relational conflict.** When people in a relationship disagree over what they want, need, or expect from each other, a relational conflict exists. There may not be any specific content issues that are involved; it may be that one's wants, needs, or expectations in the rela-

tionship are not being met. This is not a simple conflict; it may even feel like a pseudo conflict, until someone is able to identify why they are feeling upset. Many times we enter into a relationship, it may be a friendship, a romantic interest, or a superior-subordinate relationship; we come in to the relationship with a list of expectations.

Examples of interpersonal conflict:

- A married couple having a disagreement over how to pay this month's bills.
- Two children tugging on the same toy.
- Some friends debating where to spend their vacation.
- Two roommates trying to negotiate their individual space in a small apartment.
- Two people arguing over what to watch on television.
- A husband trying to control a wife's behavior.
- A boss beginning to flirt with an employee.
- Two sisters who share a bedroom having a conflict over how to clean their bedroom.
- A friend calling in the middle of the night and waking you up from a sound sleep.
- Letting your child borrow the car and she brings it back with an empty tank of gas.
- A child upset with his parents because they were late picking him up from school.
- A married couple arguing over a type of car to buy with the money they have to spend.

We have defined conflict, intrapersonal conflict, and interpersonal conflict; now we could take this one step further and examine extrapersonal conflict. I have this form of conflict—do you? For example, my plants and I have conflict regularly; they cry out for water and sometimes I ignore them for a while (I can be extremely busy and extremely lazy). I know—it's wrong—I feel guilty—I am sorry. However, I do deal with the conflict (before they die) by watering them; they are then happy and all is well.

My dog and I have extrapersonal conflict too. He wants me to get out of bed at 6:00 a.m. on a Saturday morning! Is he crazy? Doesn't he know that I need to sleep in on Saturday morning? Does he not realize the value of beauty rest? OK, OK this is obviously an example of an unresolved extrapersonal conflict between the two of us (if only my dog could talk to my therapist, this would all be resolved by now).

Moving right along. . . . You need to consider a few questions before you get into the heart of this chapter:

1. Why does conflict happen?
2. Who do you have conflict with most often?
3. What bothers you the most about conflict?
4. When do you feel most vulnerable in conflict?
5. What benefits can you see when conflict happens?

It is essential to understand the underlying reasons for conflict, if you want to learn to handle it more effectively. Are you ready to create a conflict-free zone? Unfortunately, here is the bad news (if you want to look at it that way): *conflict is inevitable.* That's right. No matter how hard we would like to create a conflict-free zone, you cannot; conflict will happen and does happen to all of us. Not only does conflict happen in our relationship, people will typically exert some power to assert themselves. Let's examine how power works in our relationships, and more specifically in conflict.

POWER IN CONFLICT AND RELATIONSHIPS

Power is everywhere and we are all influenced by the power of people around us. Before we look at the specific types of power that are used in relationships, there are a couple of things you need to know about power:

- **Power is perception.** One cannot have power unless the other person believes him or her to have it. Therefore, power has only the *potential* to influence others.
- **Power is a part of all relationships.** Simply because the relationship exists, there is the potential for power to be used.
- **Power is used in both verbal and nonverbal communication.** It may be the person's tone of voice that is persuasive, rather that the words being used.
- **Power needs balance.** It can be easy, and sometimes tempting, to abuse the power you have over someone else. However, an abuse of power *will* ultimately damage the relationship.
- **Power needs consistency.** If you do not use the power you have over someone else in a consistent manner, your power will diminish. For example, if a parent tells a child that he will be grounded if he is late, and then the parent does not ground the child, the child will very quickly learn that there will not be a punishment for being late (and yes, parents, I mean they will learn quickly).

Researchers John Raven and Bertran French developed the six bases of social power. In Raven and French's early work, they identified five bases for power—referent, legitimate, expert, reward, and coercive power. Later they recognized a need for a sixth type of power, the information/persuasive power. Let's examine the six bases of social power.

- **Referent Power** is when you have power over someone because s/he looks up to you, identifies with you, or wants to be like you. It may be that a younger brother looks up to his big brother, and he wants to someday be just like his older brother. Referent power may also be given to a mentor, or someone who is famous; it could be given to a teacher. Referent power typically happens on a conscious level; however, sometimes you are simply drawn to someone and you are not sure why until later in the relationship.
- **Legitimate Power** usually arises because of someone's job title, someone's position in the community, or someone's role in the family. Legitimate power is when you have power over someone else because of the justifiable position or role that you play. This may be a physician, doctor, mechanic, city council member, or parent.
- **Expert Power** comes about when someone is seen as an expert in a given field of study or holds knowledge about something where you do not possess it.
- **Reward Power** happens in all relationships. Reward power arises because you can control or create something that is valuable to the other person. The reward can be tangible or intangible. A few examples of rewards are a pay raise or a bonus from your boss, more hours at your job, your allowance from your parents, a night out with your girlfriend, an intimate evening with your husband, a good grade from your instructor, or a gift from your best friend. There are many more types of rewards that we can give

people; typically rewards come in the form of material goods, time, affection, security, or confirmation that the other person cares for you.

- **Coercive Power** also happens in all relationships and for the most part it is the opposite of reward power. Coercive power is the ability to administer punishment or remove/withdraw the reward. A majority of the time coercive power is associated with a threat or with force. If the person does not follow through with the threat or the force, then the perception of power will diminish.
- **Information/Persuasive Power** is the newest of Raven and French's bases of social power. Raven and French felt like they needed a type of power where one would have power simply because s/he has the ability to provide information or create a persuasive argument. It may be that your classmate asks you how you liked the new restaurant in town, and you are not a food expert, nor do you have the ability to reward or coerce them. You have simply eaten at the restaurant and you can provide the information that your classmate needs to make the decision.

Examples of how power is used:

- Your father as he tells you to clean your room.
- The local news as they show their perspective about what is going on in your area.
- Politicians as they do or do not create laws that will affect you.
- Police officers as they pull you over for speeding.
- The car mechanic as he tells you it will take about $850 to fix your car.
- The website that explains a process that you didn't understand.
- The professor as she tells you that your paper is due by 5:00 p.m. that day.
- The gas station as they raise their gas prices.
- Your wife as she provides the cooking because nobody else knows how to cook.

"Conflict is inevitable in all situations. Even if a person goes to extremes to avoid it, it will still arise. What most people do not realize, and I was one of them, is that not all conflict is bad."

—Megan Leffel

OH, THE GAMES WE PLAY WITH POWER AND CONFLICT

Yes, it is true—people use power to get what they want or to simply get their way about something. People also play games to escalate a conflict, and many times they don't even realize they are doing it. People simply play some of the games that follow out of habit or because they genuinely do not know any better. Of course, I am not naive, many times people use power and they are completely aware of what they are doing.

You may have heard of some of the games that follow. They may have been termed "crazymakers," "dirty fighting techniques," or simply "power games." Regardless of the names you may have heard them called, these are just of few of the games people play with each other. Before you read any further, answer these two questions: (1) Why do people play games with power or try to escalate a conflict? The game may be a habit we picked up from our family, from a past relationship, or from a friend; or it may be a way one adapted to manage her emotions; (2) How can we manage these games or end them? I suggest that you confront the person with what you think he is doing. Typically when you confront the behavior, the other person will either (1) pretend like she doesn't know what you are talking about or (2) he will begin talking about why he is doing it.

Here are a few power/conflict games:

- **The Over-Expressionist** is when someone acts shocked, surprised, expresses utter disbelief that you did or said something, when it is unnecessary. Typically someone uses their tone of voice to reinforce the expression. For example when someone says to you, *"What did you say to me?"* Or perhaps, *"I cannot believe you just said that to me."*
- **The Name Caller** is someone who calls another person a name, typically to assert power, which in turn begins or continues a conflict. You may hear a phrase like this, "I can't believe you are so *stupid.*" Or perhaps, "How can you date that *jerk?*"
- **The Obligator** is someone who creates an obligation or a commitment, typically out of guilt. This is a conscious game that people play when they say things like, "You owe me one." Or it may be, "I am paying all of this money for a college education, you need to show your appreciation."
- **The Interrupter** is one who will interrupt you when you are talking for one of two reasons. (1) to disrupt your train of thought, or (2) because that person believes that their thought is too important to wait. Someone may deliberately interrupt you or it may be an unconscious habit.
- **The Silent Treatment** is when you simply pretend the other person is not there or you did not hear him. You may give the person the "cold shoulder" or remain silent when the person addresses you.
- **The Blamer** is someone who will find someone else to blame for whatever may have happened. It could be a sister or a friend; however, it may also be society's fault or the church's fault for what happened. This person will find any one person or group of people to blame, and does not believe (consciously or unconsciously) that he needs to take responsibility.
- **The Joker** is someone who uses humor to deflect what she is truly feeling. This person refuses to take the conflict seriously; rather he jokes around and tries to make "light" of the situation.
- **The Armchair Psychiatrist,** AKA the Mind Reader, is someone who likes to analyze the situation, act like she knows exactly what is happening, and only focus on the other person. This person would rather be the therapist than handle his own problems.
- **The Kitchen Sink Fighter** is someone who does not deal with the conflict simply for what it is; rather, this person needs to bring up anything they have ever had a conflict about in their relationship.
- **The Back Stabber** is someone who pretends they agree with the resolution to the conflict. However, they in turn either don't follow through or tell other people a different story about what happened.

Those are some of the games we play in our relationships. I am sure you have found yourself and your friends in a few of the games listed. Remember, to move from playing the games to more effective conflict management techniques, you need to (1) be aware of what you are doing, and (2) make others aware of what they are doing.

 You are halfway done with this chapter; therefore, it is time to pause and reflect on what you have read. Consider the following questions and write down some notes in the space provided:

1. What didn't you know about the things you have read so far?

2. What surprised you the most about what you have read so far?

3. With what you've read so far, what don't you understand?

4. Is there anything you don't agree with, or is there anything you need more information about?

> "Conflict can be good (what a concept). I tend to avoid conflict because I don't want to hurt others; however, in doing that I'm hurting myself."
> —Hollie Young

FALLACIES OF CONFLICT

Before we examine conflict styles, let's demystify the four major fallacies, or myths, about conflict which contribute to conflict's negative reputation. They include the following:

- **Conflict can be avoided.** As stated earlier, conflict is inevitable and cannot be avoided no matter how hard you try. According to Beebe, Beebe, and Redmond, "It is a myth that we should view conflict as inherently unproductive and something to be avoided. It happens, even in the best of relationships."
- **Conflict always hurts a relationship.** Of course the key word here is "always." Conflict can hurt, damage, and even end a relationship. However, if we understand that the relationship is more important than whatever we are arguing about, we can learn to manage conflict effectively. When that happens, the conflict can only help the relationship become stronger and healthier.

- **Conflict is always bad.** There is definitely a lot of negative, unproductive conflict in the world. However, conflict has a lot of benefits and can help a relationship grow and work through some tough issues.
- **Conflict can always be resolved.** Unfortunately we cannot solve all conflicts, or see eye to eye all of the time; sometimes we have to learn to "agree to disagree" with each other. We need to understand that it is our uniqueness and differing opinions that make this country such a great place to live.

We have looked at many aspects of conflict and power in our relationships; however, there is still more to learn. If we want to have healthy, manageable conflict, we need to learn what our current conflict style is, and learn about more effective ways to manage conflict. With that in mind, let's examine our conflict styles.

CONFLICT STYLES

The conflict styles we will examine are adapted from Ralph Kilmann and Kenneth Thomas' work in the mid-1970s. Table 9.1 provides you with a summary of the positive and the negative sides of each conflict style. However, before we look at the details of each conflict style, we should examine the three biggest influences on your conflict style—gender, age, and culture.

- **Gender**—It is true that men and women express themselves differently. Anne Campbell, in her book *Men, Women, and Aggression*, examines how gender and aggression are interrelated. Here is a short excerpt from her book:

  > Women's aggression emerges from their inability to check the disruptive and frightening force of their own anger. For men, it is a legitimate means of assuming authority over the disruptive and frightening forces in the world around them. This difference in the way the sexes understand aggression drives a behavioral wedge between them, expressed in everything from their unique styles of fighting to the gross disparity in their rates of violent crime. In marriage, husbands' and wives' separate ways of reading aggression meet head-on in dangerous spirals of misunderstandings.

- **Age**—With age and experiences we have developed our style for managing conflict. Just like any habits that have developed over time, it may not be easy to change.
- **Culture**—Depending on your cultural background, you will approach conflict in a variety of ways. If you are a part of a high-context culture, you are more likely to have conflict over group or collective values. If you are a part of a low-context culture, you are more likely to have conflict over individual needs or values. Other cultural factors that will affect how conflict is expressed include: what type of verbal and physical abuse is accepted in the culture, and the appropriate ways to respond to conflict in your culture.

Why should you try to change your conflict style or try to handle conflict more effectively? Well, ultimately you have two choices: (1) You can let conflict get the best of you; you can even try to hide, run away, and fight conflict every step of the way; (2) You can decide if your relationship is worth the effort; and if the relationship isn't worth it, the question becomes "are you worth it?" Are you worth less stress, higher self-respect, and freedom

TABLE 9.1
Conflict Styles

Conflict Styles—The Good and the Bad		
Conflict Style	**The Negative Side**	**The Positive Side**
Avoider	• Acts like the conflict doesn't exist • Tries to change the subject • Will damage or end a relationship to avoid the conflict • Can be seen as weak or doesn't care about the relationship	• The conflict doesn't escalate • The parties have time to cool down • Recognizes that we don't need to have a conflict every time we don't agree
Accommodator	• Doesn't get their own needs met • The relationship may be damaged • Won't make a decision • Abandons individual goals • Can be seen as having a lack of power	• People pleaser • Friends are typically happy • Good in a superior/subordinate relationship
Competitor	• Always needs to win the conflict • Tends to intimidate others • Others can be afraid to speak up • The relationship may be damaged • Can easily escalate the issues	• Issues are brought out • If your goals are more important than the relationship, this can be useful
Compromiser	• Feels like you have to always give something up in order to resolve the conflict • Focuses more on resolving the issues and less on the individual needs • Lacks seeking out creative ways of resolution	• Conflict feels like it is resolved • Seems like you are reasonable • May not damage the relationship
Collaborator	• Can feel like a lot of work • May not feel like it is not worth the work • It may feel like one person is doing all of the creative thinking	• Conflict is resolved, without giving something up • Both people are happy • Because the conflict is dealt with, the relationship is typically improved and healthier • Encourages creative thinking to resolve the issues • Very beneficial in long-term relationships

TABLE 9.2.
Conflict Styles

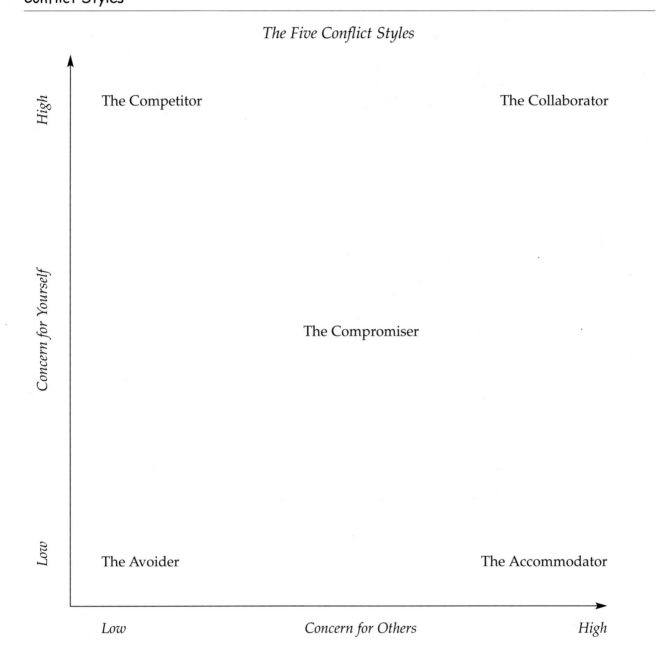

The Five Conflict Styles

from fear of conflict? The answers should be easy—you are worth it—everyone is worth it. Let's examine Kilmann and Thomas' five conflict styles (see also table 9.2):

1. **The Avoider.** An avoider is someone who chooses to avoid conflict at all costs. In the conflict model (table 9.2), this reflects both a low concern for yourself and for others. As we discussed earlier in the chapter, conflict is inevitable and no matter how much you want to avoid conflict, you should not. An avoider will deny that conflict exists, change the

subject to avoid discussing the conflict, make abstract remarks to downplay the conflict, or make jokes to avoid the conflict.

2. **The Accommodator.** An accommodator is someone who wants to please everyone, and it usually comes at the expense of his own needs. An accommodator will usually give up or give in to end the conflict; he will disengage himself from the conflict; she will deny her own needs; or he will express a genuine desire for harmony in the relationship.

3. **The Competitor.** A competitor is someone who wants to win the conflict, and protect the ego. A competitor is even willing consciously or unconsciously to end the relationship, if it comes to that point. A competitor will ask hostile questions to provoke the other person, will deny any responsibility to the conflict, will make offensive jokes, will reject any responsibility to the conflict, or will criticize the behaviors of the other person.

4. **The Compromiser.** A compromiser is someone who appears to be fair to both parties, provides a moderate amount of cooperativeness, and attempts to develop an acceptable resolution to the conflict. A compromiser genuinely wants to resolve the conflict, but is not willing to put the creative energy into resolving it. Therefore, a compromiser is willing to give something up in order to provide an immediate and quick resolution.

5. **The Collaborator.** On the conflict styles model, a collaborator has the highest regard for herself and for others. A collaborator provides as much cooperation as possible, as well as, assertiveness to resolving the conflict in the best way possible. Collaborators are descriptive in their communication; they seek disclosure from the other person and they seek criticism to improve the relationship through the conflict. A collaborator is supportive, willing to change, and flexible, and will accept responsibility for their actions.

"The power of discovery encourages us to explore solutions rather than spend excess energy on blame and justification," according to Thomas Crum in his book *The Magic of Conflict*. Thomas later goes on to say, "In creatively resolving those everyday fights at home or in the office, the willingness to understand the other side is essential."

Crum challenges us to look at all types of conflict from a creative perspective. We need to change the current reputation of conflict. We need to find the positive side of conflict and learn to focus on the benefits that conflict can provide us.

Henry Ford said, "Whether you think you can or you think you can't, you're right." Are you willing to say, "I can handle conflict more effectively"? If so, let's explore the final section of this chapter.

> "Conflicts are an inevitable part of relationships and should be dealt with in a prompt and appropriate manner. Talking out the problem and listening effectively are vital to resolving a conflict. Not all conflict is bad. Sometimes it can merely be a reality check to let the people in the relationship know they have differences that can be compromised. Conflict also brings about communication when it is dealt with, which is crucial to the relationship."
> —Jared Chamberlain

MOVING TOWARD COLLABORATION AND CONFLICT RESOLUTION

Tim Ursiny, in his book *The Coward's Guide to Conflict*, tells us:

> Honoring [the other person] can look exactly like giving in, but it is completely opposite in its impact on both the person being honored and the person doing the honoring. When I honor someone, I do the behavior because it pleases me to please the other person. But I do it without bitterness and regret. Rather, I am actually happy to let go of what I previously wanted because it gives me such joy to give the other person what she wants. When I honor, it is also a win-win situation because the other person gets what she wants and I get the complete pleasure of knowing that I was the one to give it.

That's a collaborator for you—always finding the positive perspective in any conflict situation. Table 9.3 provides us with a vocabulary list of terms to describe a collaborator, and in

TABLE 9.3.
Collaborator Terms

Terms That Describe a Collaborator
(and in turn a Competent Communicator—Are *YOU* ready to be ONE?)

Accessible	Example	Poised
Appropriately responsive	Expectations	Positive
Balanced	Fair	Prepared
Calm	Follow through	Problem solver
Committed	Friendly	Resourceful
Competent	Harness strength	Respectful
Composed	Healthy boundaries	Risk taker
Consistent	Identify weaknesses	Role model
Constructive	Integrity	Self-confident
Courageous	Knowledgeable	Sense of humor
Decisive	Lifelong learner	Teachable spirit
Dependable	Listener	Teacher
Effective communicator	Loyal	Thinker
Effective listener	Motivator	Timely
Enthusiastic	Passionate	Verbalizes feelings
Evaluative	People builder	Visionary

turn, a competent communicator. Take yourself back to the end of chapter 1 for a moment, where we briefly examined the qualities of a competent communicator. The list of competent communicator qualities looks very similar to the terms that describe a collaborator, because they are one in the same. A competent communicator must strive for collaboration whenever it is possible. OK—so how does it happen? If you are ready to move toward collaboration and conflict resolution, let's examine Marshall Rosenburg's four components of nonviolent communication.

In Rosenburg's book, *Nonviolent Communication: A Language of Compassion,* he describes the process of conflict resolution as a four-component process: observations, feelings, needs, and request. As we examine them, you should notice some similarities between this process and the perception-checking process and listening process, since conflict resolution does require both perception checking and listening. Let's look at each one:

1. **Observations**—The first step in resolving conflict requires an ability to articulate what you see without judgment. I think Crum would agree with this step, as he states in his book, "A powerful approach to promoting understanding in a conflict is to focus on asking questions and listening, rather than on giving answers or solutions."
   We must be honest with ourselves, ask questions that will promote communication, and genuinely listen to what the other person has to say before we move on to step number two.

2. **Feelings**—The next component in this process is to state how you feel when you see the action or hear the words. Again, focus on taking responsibility for your feelings, not allowing yourself to assume how the other person is feeling. Let the other person tell you how s/he is feeling.

3. **Needs**—The third step is to specifically and descriptively communicate what you need because of your feelings. Don't forget that the other person has needs, which are also important. However, you need to first examine what your needs are, especially if you do not know what you need. Take some time to figure them out. These steps do not have to happen all at the same time.

4. **Request**—Finally, you need to create a very specific request to resolve the conflict and improve the relationship. Together the two of you can develop creative solutions to your conflict and create the ultimate win-win situation.

The process will not be easy at first—I will promise you that one! Some will reject what you are doing and what you are saying. Some will get defensive, telling you that you sound controlling or snobbish. You will get all types of reactions, especially if people are used to you being an accommodator or a competitor. You may shock people. However, I challenge you to give people time to adjust. Don't stop trying to improve your communication skills and your conflict resolution tools. Give people a chance. If you let them in on what you are doing, you might be surprised. They may want to learn a few new ways to communicate too—remember, metacommunication is the best tool that you have in a relationship.

In closing, it is time to pause and reflect on what you have read. Consider the following questions and write down some notes in the space provided:

1. What didn't you know about the things you have read so far?

2. What surprised you the most about what you have read so far?

3. With what you've read so far, what don't you understand?

4. Is there anything you don't agree with, or is there anything you need more information about?

FROM CONFLICT TO COLLABORATION
by Greg Giesen

I'm often asked to perform a quick fix on two or more people who are not getting along. Usually, I'm summoned to help them work out their differences. As a conflict mediator, I am happy to help resolve disputes; however, I find that happy endings are rare. Often the conflicts that arise are symptomatic of bigger problems, system errors—things like poor leadership, dysfunctional work groups, inadequate performance management, and a lock of soft skills training and resources.

It is a mistake to limit the scope of conflict mediation to the immediate players in the dispute. You also need to look at the system. Without such an assessment, managers can easily get into the habit of treating the symptom while ignoring the problem.

Four Checkpoints

To assess the system factors that add to conflicts, I use four checkpoints:

Checkpoint 1: Is leadership being demonstrated? First check the leader to assess whether the conflict is a symptom of a bigger problem. Look for efforts made by the leader to address the conflict. Is the leader modeling effective conflict resolution skills? What has the leader done to create a supportive environment? Does the leader address conflicts? Is the leader held accountable for resolving conflicts? Are effective conflict resolution skills being practiced? If leaders are ineffective in handling conflict, are they are receiving any coaching or guidance?

Checkpoint 2: Do co-workers or team members foster a supportive environment for conflict resolution? Co-workers and team members (including those involved in the conflict) share responsibility for the interpersonal dynamics within their group. Look for group norms around conflict, who is impacted by the conflict, what isn't happening that needs to happen to resolve conflict, how the group sees the role of the leader, what guidance and support does the group need from the leader.

Checkpoint 3: Is there an accountability that supports teamwork and communication skills? Define appropriate behaviors. What gets reinforced is the behavior that gets exhibited. Are conflict resolution skills part of the criteria in performance reviews? Are core values reflected in the review process? Are team norms identified around conflict resolution and followed consistently? Is peer input part of the performance review process? Is the disciplinary process ever used for employees who exhibit poor communication or cooperation skills? The performance review process must reflect the desired skill sets required for effective conflict resolution. These include teaming skills, communication and problem-solving skills, collaborative and listening skills. Create accountability around these skills to foster effective communication and conflict resolution.

Checkpoint 4: Is the organization providing skill training and resources to maintain effective working relationships? It takes a

---

proactive philosophy when it comes to effective communication and conflict resolution skills. Proficiency in the soft skills area requires time, effort and practice. By helping their people to grow in these areas, managers can't empower them to resolve their own conflicts.

If any one of these four "checkpoints" are suspect, the conflicts that arise will likely be symptoms of a system error. If two or more of these are lacking, the system is faulty.

So, the next time there is a conflict, investigate whether or not the conflict is an isolated event or a system error. You might be surprised by what you find.

Creating Collaboration

The goal of collaboration is to achieve a desired outcome in the best way possible for all parties. Cooperation, synergy and teamwork can only be achieved if the parties pay as much attention to how they work together as they do to the work itself.

Before agreeing to collaborate, people must know the key elements: parity among participants, mutual goals, shared responsibility for participation and decision making, shared resources, shared accountability for outcomes, and mutual trust. Collaboration is a highly interdependent process that requires an upfront commitment to work within these elements from all participating entities before going forward.

The collaborative process involves creating guidelines for how people will work together. You might customize these seven items to fit your situation: 1) Bring the parties together; 2) define the scope of the project; 3) define success, expectations, or desired results; 4) discuss leadership, roles, responsibilities, support, ownership, control, communication, decision-making, time management, prioritization, disagreements, accountability, resources, milestones, rewards, recognition, and evaluation; 5) identify possible barriers to collaboration and problem solve around those; 6) identify components that may not need to be completed collaboratively; and 7) obtain a commitment to collaborate from each member to move forward under the guidelines.

Once people engage in the collaborative process, they are well on their way to achieving superior results. The process is not for everyone or for all situations that call for greater teamwork. It needs to be used with the right people, for the right reasons, and with the full support of management.

Name: _____ Date: _____

FROM CONFLICT TO COLLABORATION
by Greg Giesen

1. What are your top 3 reactions to this article?

2. Describe, in your own words, Giesen's four checkpoints.

(Questions continued on back)

3. Describe, in your own words, Giesen's collaborative process.

4. How does this article compare to what you read in the chapter? Explain.

5. Other thoughts about the article?

TIPS FOR SOLVING FAMILY COMMUNICATION PROBLEMS

by Sean Brotherson

Communication is how we solve problems, so it's important for family members to keep lines of communication open with each other. "If you are trying to solve a problem, you have to be attentive to whether people are prepared to problem solve rather than simply to debate, disagree or criticize," says Sean Brotherson, North Dakota State University Extension Service family science specialist. "In order to foster good family communication, it is important for each family member to feel their ideas will be heard and respected."

Brotherson has some suggestions for fostering open communication in your family:

- Listen with sensitivity and speak with respect for feelings when an issue is raised.
- Allow different family members to take the lead in discussing family concerns.
- Make sure that all family members have a chance to offer ideas.
- Avoid letting a discussion become a gripe session that distracts from clear communication.
- Focus on sharing feelings and making suggestions rather than finding a solution.

"If you're going to try to communicate about a problem and solve it, it's usually wise to prepare yourself ahead of time," notes Brotherson. "Make sure you're both going to talk at a time when both of you are ready. For example, you might have a rule that you avoid discussion of serious concerns late at night because you're both hungry, in a hurry or tired."

It may also be wise to have a clear idea of what you wish or need to discuss and avoid other topics. You may want to share your feelings about what is bothering you and why you would like to discuss it and find a solution.

"You also need to determine if you and the other person are emotionally ready to discuss the issue of concern," says Brotherson. "Sometimes you may be ready to discuss something but the other person may or may not be receptive. You need to ask yourself whether others are preoccupied, tired, defensive or really ready to talk about an issue. Some issues take time and patience to discuss or work through, so assess the level of willingness to discuss a concern and the pace at which it should move."

There are several ways to work through an issue according to Brotherson. He suggests brainstorming together to find ideas and solutions to a concern. Get a variety of ideas and put those ideas on paper before beginning to make judgments. "Then decide which suggestions are more possible or desirable, then drop the rest from the list. Also, talk about the possible outcomes for each choice and the best solution."

Working through an issue should involve the sharing of feelings in a healthy and respectful way. Exchange ideas or preferences. Give the other person "the floor" to speak while you listen, then trade off. From there, find a solution that family members can agree on or compromise to reach a decision. Then take steps to implement it.

Brotherson says it's a good idea, once the solution is implemented, to study the effects. "Set a time to follow up and evaluate the decision made and discuss how it is working."

Name: _____ Date: _____

QUESTIONS FOR DISCUSSION—

TIPS FOR SOLVING FAMILY COMMUNICATION PROBLEMS
by Sean Brotherson

1. What are your top 3 reactions to this article?

2. Which 2 of the "tips" do you agree with the most? Explain your answer.

(Questions continued on back)

3. Which 2 of the "tips" do you disagree with? Explain your answer.

4. Come up with 3 of your own tips to give to your family, to assist them in communicating more effectively.

5. Other thoughts about the article?

Adoption by Lesbian Couples
Is It in the Best Interests of the Child?

by Susan Golombok

The report of the American Academy of Pediatrics in February[1] supporting the introduction of legislation to allow the adoption by co-parents of children born to lesbian couples sparked enormous controversy not only within the medical profession but among the public as well. Almost without exception, only the mother who gives birth to or adopts the child may currently be the legal parent, even in cases where a couple plan a family together and raise their child in a stable family unit. The academy has taken the view that children in this situation deserve the security of two legally recognized parents in order to promote psychological wellbeing and to enable the child's relationship with the co-mother to continue should the other mother die, become incapacitated, or the couple separate. This position is based on evidence derived from the research literature on this issue.[2] The *Washington Times* described the stance of the academy as "an unfortunate surrender to political expediency" and accused the academy's Committee on Psychosociological Aspects of Child and Family Health of sacrificing scientific integrity in order to advance an activist agenda.[3] Is it the case that children born to lesbian couples "can have the same advantages and the same expectations for health, adjustment, and development as can parents who are heterosexual," as stated by the academy? Alternatively, is the academy simply pandering to a politically correct agenda?

Two main concerns have been expressed in relation to lesbian mother families: firstly, that the children would be bullied and ostracized by peers and would consequently develop psychological problems, and, secondly, that they would show atypical gender development such that boys would be less masculine in their identity and behaviour, and girls less feminine, than boys and girls from heterosexual families. Lack of knowledge about these children and their parents in the light of a growing number of child custody cases involving a lesbian mother prompted the first wave of studies in the 1970s. This early body of research focused on families where the child had been born into heterosexual family and then moved with the mother into a lesbian family after the parents' separation or divorce. Regardless of the geographical or demographic characteristics of the families studied, the findings of these early investigations were strikingly consistent. Children from lesbian mother families did not show a higher rate of psychological disorder or difficulties in peer relationships than their counterparts from heterosexual homes. With respect to gender development, there was no evidence of confusion about gender identity among these children, and no difference in sex role behaviour between children in lesbian and heterosexual families for either boys or girls.[4,5]

A limitation of the early investigations was that only school age children were studied. It was argued that sleeper effects may exist such that children raised in lesbian mother families may experience difficulties

From *The British Medical Journal*, June 15, 2002, pp. 1407-1408 with permission from the BMJ Publishing Group. Reprinted by permission.

in emotional wellbeing and in intimate relationships when they grow up. Further, they may be more likely than other children to themselves adopt a lesbian or gay sexual orientation in adulthood, an outcome that has been considered undesirable by courts of law. To address this question, a group of children raised in lesbian mother families in the United Kingdom was followed up to adulthood.[6,7] These young adults did not differ from their counterparts from heterosexual families in terms of quality of family relationships, psychological adjustment, or quality of peer relationships. With respect to their sexual orientation; the large majority of children from lesbian families identified as heterosexual in adulthood.

In recent years, attention has moved from the issue of child custody to whether lesbian women should have access to assisted reproduction procedures, particularly donor insemination, to enable them to have children without the involvement of a male partner. The findings from studies of these families, where the children grow up without a father right from the start, indicate that the children do not differ from their peers in two parent, heterosexual families in terms of either emotional wellbeing or gender development.[8-11] The only clear difference to emerge is that co-mothers in two parent lesbian families are more involved in parenting than are fathers from two parent homes.

A limitation of the existing body of research is that only a small volunteer or convenience samples have been studied, and thus mothers whose children are experiencing difficulties may be under-represented. Nevertheless, a substantial body of evidence indicated that children raised by lesbian mothers do not differ from other children in key aspects of psychological development. On the basis of this evidence it seems that the American Academy or Pediatrics acted not out of political correctness but with the intention of protecting children who are likely to benefit from the legal recognition of their sec-

ond parent. At present in the United Kingdom, lesbian women are individually eligible to adopt children, whether living with a partner or not. However, members or parliament have recently voted to allow unmarried couples, whatever their sexual orientation, to adopt children jointly.

References

1. Committee on Psychosocial Aspects of Child and Family Health. Co-parent or second-parent adoption by same-sex parents. *Pediatrics* 2002; 109:339-40.
2. Perrin EC. Technical report: co-parent or second-parent adoption by same-sex parents. *Pediatrics* 2002; 109:341-4.
3. Dobson JC. Pediatricians vs. children. *Washington Times* 2002 Feb 12.
4. Patterson CJ. Children of lesbian and gay parents. *Child Dev* 1992; 63:1025-42.
5. Golombok S. Lesbian mother families. In: Bainham A, Day Sclater S, Richards M, eds. *What is a parent? A socio-legal analysis.* Oxford: Hart Publishing, 1999.
6. Golombok S, Tasker F. Do parents influence the sexual orientation of their children? Findings from a longitudinal study of lesbian families. *Dev Psychol* 1996;32:3-11.
7. Tasker F, Golombok S. *Growing up in a lesbian family.* New York: Guilford Press, 1997.
8. Flaks DK, Ficher I, Masterpasqua F, Joseph G. Lesbian choosing motherhood: a comparative study of lesbian and heterosexual parents and their children. *Developmental Psychology* 1995;31:105-14.
9. Golombok S, Tasker F, Murray C. Children raised in fatherless families from infancy: family relationships and the socioemotional development of children of lesbian and single heterosexual mothers. *J Child Psychol Psychiatry* 1997;38:783-91.
10. Brewaeys A, Ponjaert I, Van Hall E, Golombok S. Donor insemination: child development and family functioning in lesbian mother families. *Hum Reprod* 1997;12: 1349-59.
11. Chan RW, Raboy B, Patterson CJ. Psychosocial adjustment among children conceived via donor insemination by lesbian and heterosexual mothers. *Child Dev* 1998;69:443-57.

Name: _____ Date: _____

ADOPTION BY LESBIAN COUPLES
by Susan Golombok

1. What are your top 3 reactions to this article?

2. If the issue of lesbian/gay couples having the ability to legally adopt children were to be debated in the classroom, how would you develop an effective argument? How would you develop a persuasive rebuttal? What types of power would you use to persuade the audience to agree with your viewpoint?

(Questions continued on back)

3. Imagine this issue became a heated discussion between you and a classmate, both of you with differing opinions on the subject. Describe how the discussion would go by explaining the types of conflict styles used, the types of power used, and the types of power games that would be played. Keeping in mind that you do not want this heated discussion to end the relationship, how would you go about resolving the potential conflict?

4. Other thoughts about the article?

Name: _____ Date: _____

INDIVIDUAL ACTIVITY #1
Understanding & Applying Intrapersonal Conflict

PURPOSE—

To assess the various internal or intrapersonal conflicts that you are facing, in effort to improve your communication.

PROCEDURE—

Use the chart below to examine your intrapersonal conflicts; if you need a few examples, review the beginning of this chapter.

Describe the details of the conflict	Describe where you believe the conflict stems from originally	Describe whom you need to discuss this conflict with, in order to find resolution	Describe a specific, timely, and realistic plan of action for resolving this conflict

(Questions continued on back)

From Michelle Burch, *Interpersonal Communication: Building Your Foundations for Success.* Copyright © 2005 by Kendall/Hunt Publishing Company.

Describe the details of the conflict	Describe where you believe the conflict stems from originally	Describe whom you need to discuss this conflict with, in order to find resolution	Describe a specific, timely, and realistic plan of action for resolving this conflict

Follow-Up—

1. Discuss as many of your intrapersonal conflicts as you can with people who can assist you in resolving them.

2. As a class, you can each discuss various conflicts from your list. This may help with finding resolution; there may be someone dealing with a similar conflict and the two of you can assist each other.

From Michelle Burch, *Interpersonal Communication: Building Your Foundations for Success.* Copyright © 2005 by Kendall/Hunt Publishing Company.

Name: _____ Date: _____

INDIVIDUAL ACTIVITY #2
Reflecting on How Your Perception
of Conflict Has Changed

PURPOSE—

To compare your perception of conflict before you read this chapter with how you feel after you read the chapter.

PROCEDURE—

BEFORE you read the chapter, write down everything that comes to mind when you think about conflict.

AFTER you have finished reading the chapter *and* you have completed the other activities, write down what comes to mind when you think about conflict.

(Questions continued on back)

FOLLOW-UP—

1. Are you satisfied with your change in your perception? Explain.

2. What do you wish this chapter would have helped you overcome regarding your conflict?

3. Discuss your responses with your classmates.

Note from the author: Keep in mind that if you feel like this chapter (or any other chapter) did not fulfill your expectations, please fill out the suggestion form at the back of the book. Your comments are essential to the improvements of this textbook. Thank you.

Name: _____ Date: _____

GROUP ACTIVITY #1
Understanding & Applying Interpersonal Conflict

PURPOSE—

To make sure you understand (1) how conflict is defined, (2) the various types of conflict we engage in, (3) the barriers to managing conflict, (4) how power affects conflict, and (5) how conflict should be managed.

PROCEDURE—

Divide into small groups. On a separate sheet of paper your group is to create a conflict scenario, including the following, *without identifying the specific terms:* types of conflict, the barriers to managing conflict, and the types of power. Do not provide a solution to the scenario.

Now that you have created the scenario, identify the terms in the space below and include two possible solutions.

Types of conflict:

Barriers to managing the conflicts:

Types of power used, or attempted to use:

Two possible solutions:

(Questions continued on back)

From Michelle Burch, *Interpersonal Communication: Building Your Foundations for Success.* Copyright © 2005 by Kendall/Hunt Publishing Company.

Finally, you are to swap the original scenario with another group, so that all groups have a different scenario to analyze. Once your group has a different scenario, analyze it to determine the following terms and try to determine two possible solutions to the scenario:

Types of conflict:

Barriers to managing the conflicts:

Types of power used, or attempted to use:

Two possible solutions:

FOLLOW-UP—

1. As a class, discuss the scenarios that were created.

2. Compare the terms each group identified to make sure they were used correctly and to make sure that everyone understands how the terms should be applied.

3. Discuss the solutions that the groups came up with, to determine if they are applicable and practical.

Name: _____ Date: _____

GROUP ACTIVITY #2
Becoming More Collaborative

PURPOSE—

To assess what you have learned about conflict, power, and conflict resolution techniques, by exploring conflicts between various cultures and the genders.

PROCEDURE—

The first two steps can be completed individually, with a group, or as an online discussion.

Step 1—Assume you are involved, either directly or indirectly, with the people described in the scenarios below.

Step 2—Identify the potential problems you may encounter, describe the potential problems, describe what types of power would possibly be used, indicate what you may do to head off any conflicts, and explain how you would manage conflict if it did happen.

1. A Mexican family—husband, wife, and four children between the ages of 6 and 13—move into a white middle-class suburban neighborhood in Georgia.

2. A gay male couple moves into an Irish Catholic family community in Boston.

3. An African-American, male, high school honor student tries to make friends with the neighborhood males (a mixture of races and nationalities); however, they view students who do well in school as sissies.

4. A 33-year-old Jewish woman plans to marry a 42-year-old Muslim man from Iraq. She is planning to tell her orthodox family of her intentions at dinner tonight.

(Questions continued on back)

5. Iris has just been offered a job at Gracious Publications as executive editor. She will supervise five male editors, all of whom are significantly older than she.

6. One of your friends constantly makes fun of Radha, a fellow classmate, because she often comes to class in her native African dress.

7. Craig and Louise are an interracial couple. Members of Craig's family treat him fairly but virtually ignore Louise. They never invite Craig and Louise as a couple to dinner or to partake in any of the family affairs. The couple decides that they should confront Craig's family.

8. Malcolm is a close friend and typically is a very open-minded person. However, he has the habit of referring to members of other racial and ethnic groups with the most derogatory language. You decide to tell him that you object to this way of talking.

9. Tom, a good friend of yours, wants to ask Pat out for a date. Both you and Tom know that Pat is a lesbian and will refuse the date; however, Tom says he's going to have some fun and ask her anyway—just to give her a hard time. You think this is wrong and want to tell Tom you think so.

10. Your parents persist in holding stereotypes about other religious, racial, and ethnic groups. These stereotypes come up in all sorts of conversations. You are really embarrassed by these attitudes and feel you must tell your parents how uncomfortable you are when you have friends over.

FOLLOW-UP—

As a class, discuss your various approaches to the scenarios. Look at the potential problems you created, how you felt you would manage any conflict that did happen, and what types of power were used in the scenarios.

From Michelle Burch, *Interpersonal Communication: Building Your Foundations for Success.* Copyright © 2005 by Kendall/Hunt Publishing Company.

CROSSWORD PUZZLE
Reviewing the Terms

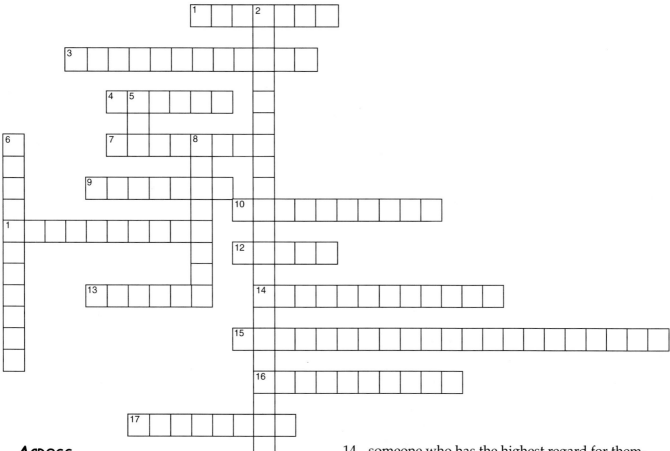

ACROSS

1. someone who chooses to avoid conflict at all costs
3. someone who is a people pleaser
4. a type of power where you can control or create something that is valuable to the other person
7. a type of power that one has because they have the ability to administer punishment
9. a type of power that one has over someone because s/he looks up to you, identifies with you, or wants to be like you
10. someone who will ask hostile questions to provoke the other person or will deny any responsibility to the conflict
11. a conflict when people in a relationship disagree over what they want, need, or expect from each other
12. a conflict that happens when at least two people disagree about what they see as valuable
13. a type of power that one has over someone else because s/he holds knowledge about something where you do not possess it

14. someone who has the highest regard for themselves and for others in a conflict
15. an expressed struggle (mental, physical, emotional, and/or spiritual) between at least two interdependent parties
16. a type of power that one has over someone else because of the justifiable position
17. a conflict that exists when there is a short or limited supply of readily available resources

DOWN

2. an internal struggle over unresolved issues or differing issues
5. a conflict to protect your pride
6. someone who appears to be fair to both parties and will provide a moderate amount of cooperativeness
8. a mental, physical, emotional, and/or spiritual struggle between people

Name: _____ Date: _____

CHAPTER QUIZ
Reviewing the Chapter

_____ 1. If you call your physician because you are ill and you want s/he to provide you a diagnosis and a prescription, what type(s) of power are you giving him/her? (a) expert (b) reward (c) legitimate (d) all of the above (e) none of them

_____ 2. Which of the following is NOT TRUE of reward power? (a) it comes from possessing something of value (b) it may come from some intangible (c) it comes from a superior-subordinate relationship (d) washing someone's car might be an example of reward power (e) all of these responses are true of reward power

_____ 3. Coercive power is UNLIKELY to be effective when: (a) there is some dependency in the relationship (b) the punishment threatened is severe (c) the punishment is likely to be administered (d) there is no history of following through (e) all of these responses enhance the use of coercive power

_____ 4. Someone who goes along in order to keep peace in the relationship is an: (a) avoider (b) aggressor (c) accommodator (d) compromiser (e) competitor

_____ 5. Power has the potential to influence others. (a) true (b) false

_____ 6. Power is a part of relationships. (a) true (b) false

_____ 7. Referent power suggests that the power holder is admired by the other person. (a) true (b) false

_____ 8. An example of legitimate power would be the power a parent has in a relationship with his/her child. (a) true (b) false

_____ 9. The fact that we are in a relationship implies that there is usually some kind of reward power. (a) true (b) false

_____ 10. Power is not based on one's perception. (a) true (b) false

_____ 11. Conflict is inevitable. (a) true (b) false

_____ 12. You have time to see one movie with your best friend; however, the two of you can't agree on what movie to go see. What type of conflict is this? (a) pseudo (b) ego (c) relational (d) value (e) resource

_____ 13. You and your parent are disagreeing over what time you need to be home from your date. They feel like you need to be in by 11 p.m., but you feel like 1 a.m. is a reasonable time. What type of conflict is this?
(a) pseudo (b) ego (c) relational (d) value (e) resource

_____ 14. You want to show your classmate that you are a better test-taker that she is. What type of conflict is this?
(a) pseudo (b) ego (c) relational (d) value (e) resource

_____ 15. A collaborator is similar to a competent communicator.
(a) true (b) false

APPENDICES

A P P E N D I X   A

SERVICE LEARNING PROJECT

Purpose: To involve yourself in the community during the learning process. Interpersonal communication happens everywhere; this project gives you an opportunity to move your learning experience outside of the classroom and into the real world.

Service learning is becoming a very popular way of experiencing the communication process and all aspects of interpersonal communication. Therefore, I have heard many people discuss their service learning projects. I am sure that I could give credit to many professors for the various components of this project; however, I would not know where to begin. To that end, I hope this project provides you with a unique experience. Please do not feel limited to following this project exactly. Make adaptations that are appropriate for your community and your situation.

Procedure:

Step 1—You need to first make a couple of decisions (though your instructor may have some of these decisions already):

1. Will this be a group project?
2. If so, what will be the size of the groups (partners, small groups, etc.)?
3. How long will you spend on this project (an entire term, half a term, etc.)?
4. How many hours will you be required per week to spend on this project?

Step 2—You need to decide what you want to learn from this project, and write your learning goal. Some learning goal examples are:

- I want to learn how homeless people perceive our community; therefore, I will work in a homeless shelter.
- I want to learn how a non-profit organization communicates its needs to our community; therefore, I will work at Big Brothers/Big Sisters.
- I want to create a video biography of the life history of an elderly person; therefore, I will work at the Sugar Hills Retirement Home.
- I want to help my local high school out by volunteering in the cafeteria, where I can watch the relationships between children.
- I want to experience how a non-profit organization handles conflict; therefore, I will work at the Youth Center.
- I want to sponsor a coat drive for the United Way.
- I want to build a Habitat for Humanity house.
- I want to cook meals for families staying at a Ronald McDonald House.
- I want to assist in putting together a Walk-a-Thon for Muscular Dystrophy.

You notice that some of the learning goals are specific and some are vague; however, all of them relate to working on a project in the community. Some students begin this project and know exactly what they want to learn more about; some students do not have a clue. Either case is fine. The idea is to just get started—*Pick a place to go and write the best learning goal that you can.*

Step 3—Work with your instructor and the placement to make sure that what you want to do meets the needs of the organization and fulfills the requirements of this project. Be sure the service learning contract is signed and in your instructor's hands prior to you working at your placement—this is essential. See your instructor for the service learning contract.

Step 4—You need to keep a journal throughout this project. This journal will be essential for what you submit at the end of the project. At the end of every visit to the site, answer as many of the following questions as you can for your journal:

1. Summarize what you did at your placement.
2. What skills have you learned at your placement?
3. What has been the most difficult part of this project?
4. What has been the most rewarding part of this project?
5. How is this project relevant to your classroom experiences?
6. What have you learned about your community that you did not already know?
7. Reviewing the chapters that we have studied, what do you understand now about communication that you did not know before this project?
8. What theories have we learned in class that you can apply to this project?
9. What have you learned about yourself because of this project?
10. Is there anything you have learned about race, gender, or culture because of this project?
11. Is this project meeting or exceeding your expectations? If so, how? If not, what can you do to make some changes or resolve some issues?
12. Are you different because of this project? If so, how?

Step 5—This step does not happen until you are nearing the end of your project. It is now time to consult with your instructor regarding what you will submit for grading. Some options your instructor may choose:

- Turn the questions from your journal into a complete paper where you examine the relationship between the concepts of the textbook and what you learned during your service project.
- Create a narrated videotape of your experiences, including answers to the questions from your journal.
- Give an oral presentation summarizing your experiences, including the answers to the questions from your journal.
- Create a portfolio, including photographs, news articles, etc. from the placement, and a written narration of what you learned.
- Use this experience as research for a debate (see service learning debate ideas under miscellaneous ideas in appendix D).

APPENDIX B

INTRAPERSONAL PORTFOLIO PROJECT

Purpose: To provide you with an opportunity to explore who you are, what your place is in the world, and what you want out of your life. This assignment can be challenging, as self-discovery usually is; therefore, this assignment will require you to be open, honest, and willing to explore. Not all parts of the portfolio will make you feel good, learning sometimes happens that way. The hope is that whatever feelings you experience will result in healthy self-growth. Interpersonal communication can only be successful if you are able to *intrapersonally* communicate.

   Portfolio Confidentiality: Everything in this portfolio is developed for the purpose of allowing you to intrapersonally communicate. The portfolio will be reviewed and graded to make sure that you are following the objectives and completing the sections. However, everything in this portfolio is completely confidential. Nothing will be discussed outside of the comments between you (the author of the portfolio) and the instructor, only when and if that is needed.

   Grading the Portfolio: Your instructor will not be grading your feelings, as that is extremely subjective. Rather, your instructor will be looking at the thoroughness of your descriptions, your achievement of the goals of the sections, and the quality of the content. See your instructor for more details and explanations.

Summary of the Sections in the Portfolio:

Sections 1–3 lay the foundation for the portfolio. Section 1 begins by having you imagine the person you want to become. In section 2 you examine how you feel about your true self, or the person you are without your roles, and you explore how your self-concept has developed. In section 3 you examine your limitations, or your fears and weaknesses, and develop a plan to overcome them.

Sections 4–6 build on your foundation and review areas of your past. In section 4 you review things in your past that you feel guilty about or are ashamed of, or that you regret; then you look at how you feel about the list and consider how you can move forward. In section 5 you explore troubled relationships through writing letters. In section 6 you examine what makes you feel good, and create ways to spend more time doing the things that make you feel good.

Sections 7–9 move you closer to your success. In section 7 you set goals for your future, this part relates back to section 2, where you examined the areas of your self-concept. In section 8 you create a mission statement that reflects the person you are striving to be. Finally, in section 9, you are to reflect and analyze how creating this portfolio has helped you communicate more effectively.

Explanation of Sections:

Section 1:   Create a picture collage of your *ideal self*, using magazine cutouts or pictures and words. Do not use real photographs, as this is a visual representation of your ideal self. Consider the following: The way you want to look, your ideal job, family, things and people that you love, things that are important, etc. This is not to say that you are not satisfied with who you are today; rather this section is to explore ways that you are willing to stretch yourself, challenge yourself, and grow.

Section 2:   *Part 1:* Describe your self-concept. You are looking at how you currently feel about yourself. Do NOT examine how others feel about you, only how you feel about yourself!

Write a description for each of the following categories:

1. Physical make-up: Examine how you feel about your physical make-up. For example, do you like the shape of your body? Do you like your height? hair? skin? eyes? etc. I am not looking for how tall you are or how much you weigh; rather, I am looking for how you feel about your physical self.
2. Relationships: Reflect on how you feel about relationships—professional, friendship, romantic, etc. Consider your values, beliefs, behaviors, and attitudes.
3. Social skills: Discuss how you are today and how you feel about your social skills. Consider—Are you outgoing? withdrawn? talkative? Do you love people all of the time, sometimes? etc. How do you feel about this?
4. Talents: Discuss what you like to do and/or what you do well. For example, music, mechanics, cooking, art, speaking, math, writing, etc. Consider how you feel about your talents.
5. Beliefs: Discuss how you feel about your beliefs. Subjects to consider: Political issues, religion, marriage, raising children, etc.

Part 2:—Discuss how your self-concept has developed. Remember that the self-concept begins developing the first year of life. Consider specific people who played a role (either positively or negatively) in developing your self-concept, how you want to change your self-concept, and the barriers you have in order to make the changes. *This section, both parts, will take several pages.*

Section 3:   Describe your fears and weaknesses in detail and then create a plan on how you want to conquer them. Create 2 columns: (1) Describe your fear/weaknesses; (2) describe a plan to conquer. Be specific. Creating this section doesn't mean that you have to go out and conquer fears or overcome your weaknesses; however, you want to acknowledge that you can make these changes if you wanted to and that you have control over your fears and weaknesses.

Section 4:   (1) Create a list of things that you feel guilty about or are ashamed of, or regret. (2) Then discuss how this list makes you feel, and what is stopping you from making amends or putting closure on the items in your list. *This list can be very challenging and very private, and may take some time.* Remember that everything you discuss in this portfolio is completely confidential.

Section 5: Write three letters to three different people in your life, currently, past, or future. The letters should go to relationships that you want to close, change, or improve. In each letter you will (1) describe your concerns or the issues, (2) describe why you feel the way that you do, and (3) describe what you want to do to create closure or resolution to your issues.

As you write the letters, remember to use "I" statements. For example, "When _____ happened, I felt _____." The letters are not about blaming the other person; the letters are for you and your closure. Consider discussing your boundaries or how you anticipate preventing a specific incident from happening again. Be realistic in your expectations.

Whom could you write your letters to? It could be your boss, a colleague, parent, friend, child, spouse, partner, relative, etc. You could write a letter to yourself, a future spouse, or a child whom you want to have in the future. The person you are writing to can be someone who has passed on or is not yet in your life. *You do not have to mail these letters, unless you choose to do so.*

Section 6: Create a list of what makes you feel good; consider the following:
1. What do you do to relax?
2. What do you do in your spare time?
3. What do you like to do with your friends?
4. What do you like to do when you are alone?

Once you have created this list, discuss how often you take the time to participate in activities that make you feel good. Finally, discuss what you could do to make more time to make yourself feel good. Create a specific plan for the future!

Section 7: Create goals for 1 year, 5 years, 10 years, and 25 years in each of the following categories. You will have a minimum of one goal per category, for each of the years listed above. Your goals should be specific, measurable, and realistic. The categories are as follows:

1. Personal/recreational
2. Friends
3. Family (current and future)
4. Professional
5. Community (volunteer, political, etc.)
6. Educational (consider not only school but talents you may want to learn)

Section 8: Create a mission statement for your life. A mission statement should be 2–4 sentences in length. A mission statement is something that reflects the person you are trying to be or your ideal self. You do not necessarily have to be that person; however, it should be the person that you are striving to be. Refer back to section one, the collage of your ideal self, for assistance in creating your mission statement.

Section 9: In the final section of your portfolio you are to write 1 1/2 to 2 pages analyzing how creating this portfolio has influenced you, what benefit(s) you received from creating the portfolio, and what you want to do with yourself and your relationships because of what you have learned.

APPENDIX C

TEAM RESEARCH PROJECT

Purpose: To apply communication theories/principles in an actual amateur research study, conducted by a team.

Procedure: This project has four parts to it. In summary, your team will (1) research a topic from your interpersonal communication studies, (2) make the research more realistic by watching interactions of people or surveying people, (3) once you have completed observations or surveys, you will then analyze them, (4) finally, you are to draw conclusions about what you have learned. In the end your group will give an oral presentation, where you will explain your experiences during the project.

Grading the Project: You need to see your instructor for specific details regarding how this project will be graded. Your instructor may have you submit written summaries of each of the 4 parts of the project, or your instructor may simply grade the end result in the final presentation.

Part 1—The Research:

- *First,* your team will pick a topic to study (perception, nonverbal communication, listening, emotions, etc.).
- *Second,* each member of the team will go out and research this topic. Find as much as you can about your subject—outside of the textbook. Use books, articles, and internet resources. *Note*—each person must have at least 3 sources per person *(excluding the textbook)*. See instructor for more detailed information/requirements about your references. Remember to save your information for a bibliography.
- *Third,* as your team is deciding how to research, you may find it useful to break your subject down into subtopics to minimize overlapping in your research. Wait until you have begun the research process to break the topic into subtopics, so you have a good understanding of the topic.
- *Fourth,* as you are completing the research, consider the relationship between your subject and a couple of demographics (examples: gender, race, religion, occupation, social status, etc.). You will use the demographics in part 2 of this project.
- *Finally,* using all the research that you have collected, it is now time to develop a research question. This will serve as your hypothesis for parts 2 through 4 in this project. The question should be one that you intend to prove. Examples of research questions are:

  - Is nonverbal communication more important than verbal communication?
  - Does culture play a role in our decision making?
  - Is perception really an expression of one's reality?

- In the American culture, do people of different ethnic groups perceive the same situation differently?
- Do men listen more effectively than women?

Part 2—The Observations or Survey:

- *First,* now that the research is completed and your team has a hypothesis, you need to decide how you will prove your hypothesis. You need to choose either to observe or survey people.
  - Topics that are good for surveys—perception, values, listening, relationships, conflict, culture.
  - Topics that are good for observations—listening, nonverbal, emotions, verbal, decision making, gender, conflict.
- *Second,* prior to conducting your observations/survey you must get the instructor's approval for what you plan to do.
- *Third,* you need to create your data sheet. This will be a multiple-choice questionnaire that everyone in the group will use for the surveys/observations.
  - Create about 6-8 questions; each question should have multiple-choice answers. See your instructor for examples.
  - Use a minimum of two demographics to compare your results in the analysis. For example, if you want to use age, have people circle a category: "Are you 0–10, 11–20, 21–30, 31–40, etc." If you want to know financial status, use ranges: "Circle your income level—under 20,000, 21,000–35,000, 36,000–50,000 or over 51,000."
  - Your instructor has examples for you to look at, as you get started.
- *Fourth,* it is time to conduct your surveys/observations.
  - How many should you do? Observations—minimum of 60; surveys—minimum of 90, unless your instructor has suggested otherwise.
  - Consider the size of your group; the more you have in the group, the easier it is to collect more data. See your instructor for more specific details.
  - It will be extremely important that you have equal numbers of your demographics for your analysis. For example, if you are comparing men and women in a survey, be sure to have 45 surveys from men and 45 surveys from women. If you do not have equal numbers, it will alter your results.
- *Finally,* once all of the data has been collected, you need to tally your results.

Part 3—The Analysis:

- *First,* your team should discuss what happened.
- *Second,* you need to identify the relationship between the initial research and what you learned from the observations, interviews, or survey.
- *Third,* you need to make a list about all the things you can see from your research data. As you are analyzing the results, here are some questions to consider:
  - What does the data that you collected tell you about your initial research from the books, journals, and websites? Did your survey/observation results come out like the research said it would?
  - What information makes more sense now that you have completed your observation/survey?
  - What did you learn from the demographics?

- What is wrong with the research you reviewed?
- What is right with the research you reviewed?
- What else does your survey/observation tell you?

Part 4—Drawing Conclusions:

Finally, you want to draw conclusions about the entire experience. Some questions to consider are:

- What would you change about the research or observations/survey?
- What did the analysis prove?
- What did you learn from your analysis?
- If you had to do this project all over again, what would you do differently?

End Result—The Team Presentation:

- Your presentation should contain the following components, in this order.
  - Your team will teach the class about your topic, using your research. You are not to teach us about what is in the textbook. Be creative, and interactive as you teach us something about your topic that we may not know.
  - Explain your hypothesis (your research question).
  - Explain the results of the observations/surveys.
  - Explain the analysis, or your interpretation, of the results.
  - Finally, explain the conclusions that your group drew.
- You will have 25 to 30 minutes, as a team, for your presentation, and you may lose points if your presentation is short on time.
- Each member of the team must equally and orally participate in the presentation.
- You may have note cards with you while you present.
- A visual aid is required. Examples: Power Point, overhead transparencies, poster board, samples, objects, etc.
- You are expected to work together during the presentation. In other words, the presentation is expected to be interactive, and you will be graded on your presentation style.

CREATE A TIMELINE FOR THE PROJECT

Your team should create a timeline at the beginning of the project. It will assist all the members of the group, and hold each person accountable, for knowing when each step of the project is due and who is responsible for specific duties. Use the syllabus/course schedule to assist you in creating the timeline.

1. The research is due _____

2. The observations, surveys, interviews are due _____

3. The results will be tallied by _____

4. The analysis is due _____

5. The conclusions are due _____

6. We will practice our presentation on _____

A P P E N D I X   D

DEBATE PROJECT

Purpose: There are many learning opportunities when participating in a debate.

1. In a communication course it is essential that you practice your communication skills, a debate is an ideal venue for that purpose.
2. During a student's academic career it is essential that one question the theories that are being presented, a debate is an ideal venue for that purpose as well.
3. Finally, social issues are relevant to our everyday communication, as they come up in conversations at home, school, work, and in the media; a debate provides us with a broader, hopefully more educated, perspective of the social issues we discuss outside of the classroom.

Forming Debate Teams:

1. Your instructor will explain how the debate teams will be formed, as it depends on class time, number of students, etc.
2. A debate typically consists of an ***affirmative team*** (a team arguing in support of the debate question) and a ***negative team*** (a team arguing against the debate question).
3. A third team is possible. This team could serve as ***judges.*** The judges would be responsible for researching both sides of the arguments, listening to the teams present, collaborate to determine a winner, and finally, give a presentation supporting their decision for the winner.

Debate Topic Ideas

This is only a list of ideas; see your instructor for specific details regarding the assignment.

Specific interpersonal communication content questions:

1. Is conflict essential for a healthy relationship?
2. Do you need to understand yourself to communicate effectively?
3. Is change necessary for maintaining a healthy relationship?
4. Is conflict communicated mostly through nonverbal means?
5. Is a balance of power essential for a healthy relationship?
6. Is nonverbal communication more important than verbal communication?
7. Should a working knowledge of Maslow's Hierarchy of Needs be required of all employees?

Scenarios that could be developed into debate topics:

1. A friend told me about a great job he's applying for; however, I don't think he'll get it. It is a job that is perfect for me. Should I apply? And if I do, should I tell him?
2. My friend's boyfriend hit on me (there was no question of his intentions). She's dated him for several years and wants to marry him. It's clear to me he'd cheat on her in a second. I think he's a dog and I don't want to see her get hurt. Do I tell her what happened?
3. It's a poorly kept secret in my office that a manager is having an affair with a staff member. He approves of her work in a heartbeat, but she doesn't do the best job. Is it wrong for me to give her my projects to make my job easier?
4. My mother questions me about my brothers, who don't share personal information with her. If I don't answer her, she is offended. However, when I do answer her, my brothers get mad at me. Should I continue to tell my mother about my brothers' personal stuff?
5. My friend just got a job at my office. For referring her, I received $2,000. She says we should split the fee because her qualifications got her the job. Should I split the cash?

Social issues:

1. Does music communicate messages that influence our decisions?
2. Should someone be disqualified for a job because they have body piercings?
3. Should gay marriages be legalized?
4. Is it ethical to exaggerate to aid in getting a job?
5. Do children (anyone under the age of 18) have the right to privacy?

Miscellaneous issues*:

1. Service learning should be a required part of the high school and college education.
2. An internship in the private sector provides more benefit than community service, to promoting professional growth.
3. Communication skills are better learned through community involvement than through classroom studies.
4. Service devoted to causes of social justice, the environment, or public health is worthier than service devoted to the arts.
5. Service learning should not include volunteer work for religious organizations.
6. Financial compensation for students engaged in service learning diminishes the spirit of service.
7. Performing community outreach for a private corporation is not consistent with the principles of service learning.

In order to have a debate you need to know what makes an effective argument and an effective rebuttal. See below for descriptions.

What makes an effective argument?

1. The purpose is to present your point and supporting information.
2. *Be sure to cite the source(s) of your information,* i.e., "according to *Time* magazine in an article entitled, 'Conflict and Your Emotions' I found that conflict is essential for a healthy relationship because. . . ."

---

*The miscellaneous issue ideas were taken from *Service Learning in Communication Studies* by Isaacson, Dorries, and Brown

3. Remember to define your terms in the early arguments.
4. Don't expect that the audience members will define or interpret the terminology the same way you do.
5. It is essential that you show the relationship between the issue you are arguing and how it relates to effective communication.
6. You may refer to something that the opposing team has brought up in an earlier argument or rebuttal; however, it is essential that you stay focused on presenting your argument.
7. Your team must work together.

What makes an effective rebuttal?

1. The purpose is to refute, or oppose, the information presented in the affirmative argument with supporting information.
2. Anyone can speak up in a rebuttal, unless your instructor expects a more formal approach to the rebuttals.
3. Everyone in the team must speak up throughout the debate.
4. Example of a rebuttal: If the affirmative team presents the case that conflict is healthy in a relationship because of various types of power, then you might refute that argument by discussing the relationship between power and perception, and how (based on perception) some types of power are unhealthy.
5. Make sure that what you say reinforces the argument that your teammate just presented.
6. *Be sure to cite the source(s) of your information during a rebuttal, just like in an argument.*

What you should know about citing sources:

1. You need to cite your sources during your arguments and rebuttals. Example, "According to . . ." or "In a book by . . ."
2. See your instructor for more specific information about how many sources you need to use, what sources are appropriate/inappropriate, etc.
3. Make sure your sources are credible, and clearly relate to your topic.
4. You may be asked to submit a bibliography.

ANSWER KEY FOR CHAPTER QUIZZES

Note to the reader: The words to find in the word search and the crossword puzzles are the terms listed in the "key terms" section at the beginning of each chapter.

Chapter 1

(1) T (2) F (3) F (4) T (5) T (6) F (7) F (8) T (9) F (10) F (11) T (12) F (13) T (14) F (15) T

Chapter 2

(1) F (2) F (3) T (4) T (5) T (6) F (7) T (8) F (9) T (10) F (11) F (12) T (13) T (14) T (15) T (16) T (17) T (18) F

Chapter 3

(1) C (2) B (3) A (4) B (5) E (6) E (7) A (8) A (9) E (10) D (11) D (12) A (13) A (14) A (15) C (16) B

Chapter 4

(1) D (2) E (3) E (4) D (5) D (6) B (7) D (8) A (9) E (10) C (11) B (12) A (13) A (14) A (15) B (16) A

Chapter 5

(1) F (2) T (3) F (4) T (5) F (6) T (7) F (8) F (9) T (10) T (11) T (12) T (13) T (14) T (15) T

Chapter 6

(1) T (2) F (3) F (4) T (5) F (6) T (7) T (8) T (9) F (10) T (11) T (12) F (13) T (14) T (15) F

Chapter 7

(1) E (2) E (3) B (4) A (5) A (6) B (7) B (8) F (9) A (10) D (11) A (12) A (13) C

Chapter 8

(1) B (2) D (3) B (4) C (5) A (6) B (7) C (8) E (9) A (10) B (11) C (12) D (13) A (14) B (15) D (16) B (17) B (18) C

Chapter 9

(1) D (2) E (3) D (4) C (5) A (6) A (7) A (8) A (9) A (10) B (11) A (12) E (13) D (14) B (15) A

REFERENCES & SUGGESTED READINGS

Alder, Ronald B., Rosenfeld, Lawrence B., and Proctor, Russell F. II. (2004). *Interplay: The process of interpersonal communication (9th edition)*. New York: Oxford Press.

Alderman, Ellen and Kennedy, Caroline (1995). *The right to privacy*. New York: Knopf.

Allen, Mike, Preiss, Raymond W., Gayle, Barbara Mae, and Burrell, Nancy (Eds.) (2002). *Interpersonal communication research: Advances through meta-analysis*. NJ: Lawrence Erlbaum Associates, Publishers.

Andersen, Peter A. (1999). *Nonverbal communication: Forms and functions*. Palto Alto, CA: Mayfield.

Beebe, Steven A., Beebe, Susan J., and Redmond, Mark V. (1996). *Interpersonal communication: Relating to others*. Boston: Allyn and Bacon.

Bolles, Edmund Blair (1991). *A Second way of knowing: The riddle of human perception*. New York: Prentice Hall.

Booth-Butterfield, Melanie (2002). *Interpersonal essentials*. Boston: Allyn and Bacon.

Branden, Nathaniel Dr. (2003). "Answering misconceptions about self-esteem." *National Association for Self-Esteem*. Dec 9 2003 *www.self-esteem-nase.org*.

Bruner, Jerome (1986). *Actual minds, possible words*. Cambridge, MA: Harvard University Press.

Burley-Allen, Madelyn (1982). *Listening—the forgotten skill*. New York: John Wiley & Sons.

Campbell, Anne (1993). *Men, women, and aggression*. New York: Basic Books.

Canary, Daniel J., Cody Michael J., and Manusov, Valerie L. (2003). *Interpersonal communication (3rd edition)*. Boston: Bedford/St. Martin's Press.

Canary, Daniel J. and Dainton, Marianne (Eds.) (2003). *Maintaining relationships through communication*. NJ: Lawrence Erlbaum.

Communication Research Associates (1998). *Communicate! A workbook for interpersonal communication (6th edition)*. Dubuque, IA: Kendall/Hunt.

Covey, Stephen R. (1997). *The 7 habits of highly effective families*. New York: Golden Books.

Crum, Thomas F. (1987). *The magic of conflict*. New York: Simon & Schuster.

Day, Laura (1996). *Practical intuition*. New York: Villard.

Devito, Joseph A. (2004). *The interpersonal communication book (10th edition)*. Boston: Pearson.

Elgin, Suzette Haden (1993). *Genderspeak*. New York: John Wiley & Sons.

Fletcher, Jack M. (1985). Nonverbal learning disabilities and suicide: Classification leads to prevention. *Journal of Learning Disabilities*. Vol. 22.

Funderburg, Lise (1994). *Black, white, other*. New York: Quill.

Fussell, Susan R. (2002). *The verbal communication of emotions*. NJ: Lawrence Erlbaum.

Gallois, Cynthia and Callan, Victor J. (1997). *Communication and culture.* New York: John Wiley & Sons.

Gamble, Teri Kwal and Gamble, Michael W. (1998). *Contacts communicating interpersonally.* Boston: Allyn and Bacon.

Gilman, Susan Jane (2001). *Kiss my tiara: How to rule the world as a smartmouth goddess.* New York: Warner Books.

Goleman, Daniel (1995). *Emotional intelligence.* New York: Bantam Books.

Goodwin, Robin and Cramer, Duncan (Eds.) (2002). *Inappropriate relationships.* NJ: Lawrence Erlbaum.

Grabhorn, Lynn (2000). *Excuse me, your life is waiting.* Charlottesville, VA: Hampton Roads.

Gudykunst, William B. and Kim, Young Yun (1992). *Communicating with strangers: An approach to intercultural communication (2nd edition).* New York: McGraw-Hill.

Hall, Edward T. and Mildred R. (1990). *Understanding cultural differences: Keys to success in West Germany, France, and the United States.* Maine: Intercultural Press.

Hargrave, Jan (1995). *Let me see your body talk.* Dubuque, IA: Kendall-Hunt.

Heart, Rosalie Deer and Strickland, Alison (1999). *Harvesting your journals.* San Cristobal, NM: Heart Link.

Hecht, Michael L., Jackson, Ronald L., and Ribeau, Sidney A. (2003). *African American communication (2nd edition).* NJ: Lawrence Erlbaum.

Hecklinger, Fred J. and Black, Bernadette (1997). *Training for life.* Dubuque, IA: Kendall/Hunt.

Helmstetter, Shad (1982). *What to say when you talk to your self.* New York: Pocket Books.

Hickson, Mark III, Stacks, Don W., and Moore, Nina-Jo (2004). *Nonverbal communication.* Los Angeles: Roxbury Publishing.

Hill, Napoleon (1983). *PMA science of success.* Northbrook, IL: The Napoleon Hill Foundation.

Hurley, Jennfier A. (Ed.) (2000). *Opposing viewpoints—American values.* San Diego: Greenhaven Press, Inc.

Isaacson, Rick, Dorries, Bruce, and Brown, Kevin (2001). *Service learning in communication studies.* Belmont, CA: Wadsworth.

Johansen, Jergen Dines and Larsen, Svend Erik (2002). *Signs in use: An introduction to semiotics.* New York: Routledge.

Katz, Dr. Stan J. and Liu, Aimee E. (1990). *Success trap.* New York: Ticknor & Fields.

Knapp, Mark L. and Hall, Judith A. (2002). *Nonverbal communication in human interaction (5th edition).* Belmont, CA: Wadsworth.

Knapp, Mark L. and Vangelista, Anita L. (2000). *Interpersonal communication and relationships (4th edition).* Boston: Allyn and Bacon.

LaRoche, Loretta (1998). *Relax—You may only have a few minutes left.* New York: Random House.

Leary, Mark R. and Kawalski, Robin M. (1995). *Social anxiety.* New York: The Guilford Press.

Lerner, Harriet G., Ph.D. (1985). *The dance of anger.* New York: Harper & Row.

Little, Sara S. (1993). Nonverbal learning disabilities and socioemotional functioning: A review of recent literature. *Journal of Learning Disabilities.* Vol 26.

Lowry, Richard J. (Ed.) (1973). *Dominance, self-esteem, self-actualization: Germinal papers of A. H. Maslow.* Belmont, CA: Wadsworth.

Manheim, Camryn (1999). *Wake up, I'm fat!* New York: Broadway Books.

Maslow, A. H. (1971). *The farther reaches of human nature.* New York: Penguin Books.

McKay, Gary D. Ph.D. and Dinkmeyer, Don Ph.D. (1994). *How you feel is up to you.* San Luis Obispo, CA: Impact Publishers.

McKay, Matthew and Fanning, Patrick (1991). *Prisoners of belief.* Oakland, CA: New Harbinger.

McKay, Matthew and Fanning, Patrick (2000). *Self-esteem.* New York: MJF Books.

Monsour, Michael (2002). *Women and men as friends.* NJ: Lawrence Erlbaum.

Myers, Jim (2000). *Afraid of the dark.* Chicago: Lawrence Hill Books.

Nolan, Riall W. (1999). *Communicating and adapting across cultures.* Westport, CT: Bergin & Garvey.

Olson, Margot and Forrest, Mary (2002). *Shared Meaning (6th edition).* Dubuque, IA: Kendall/Hunt.

Palladino, Connie (1994). *Developing self-esteem.* Menlo Park, CA: Crisp.

Plutchik, Robert (1991). *The emotions (Revised edition).* New York: University Press.

Reasoner, Robert (2003). "The true meaning of self-esteem." *National Association for Self-Esteem.* Dec 9 2003 <www.self-esteem-nase.org>.

Roach, Carol A. and Wyatt, Nancy J. (1988) *Successful listening.* New York: Harper Collins.

Rokeach, Milton (1968). *Beliefs, attitudes, and values.* San Francisco: Jossey-Bass, Inc.

Rokeach, Milton (1973). *The nature of human values.* New York: The Free Press.

Rosenburg, Marshall B. (1999). *Nonviolent communication: A language of compassion.* Del Mar, CA: PuddleDancer Press.

Ross, Ruth (1995). *Prospering woman.* San Rafael, CA: New World Library.

Rourke, Bryon P. and Tsatsanis, Katherine D. (2000). Nonverbal learning disabilities and asperger syndrome. In Ami Klin, Fred R. Volkmar, and Sara S. Sparrow (Eds.). *Asperger syndrome.* New York: Guilford Press.

Ryan, M. J. (1999). *Attitudes of gratitude.* New York: Conari Press.

Samovar, L. and Porter, R. (2000). *Intercultural communication: A reader.* Belmont, CA: Wadsworth.

Shafir, Rebecca Z. (2000). *The Zen of listening.* Wheaton, IL: Quest Books.

Sheehan, Elaine (1995). *Self-hypnosis: Effective techniques for everyday problems.* Rockport, MA: Element.

Socha, Thomas J. and Diggs, Rhunette C. (1999). *Communication, race, and family.* NJ: Lawrence Erlbaum.

Smith, Tracey L. and Tague-Busler, Mary (2000). *The key to survival: Interpersonal communication.* Prospect Heights, IL: Waveland Press.

Tannen, Deborah (1986). *That's not what I meant! How conversation style makes or breaks relationships.* New York: Ballantine Books.

Trenholm, Sarah and Jensen, Arthur (2004). *Interpersonal communication (5th edition).* New York: Oxford Press.

Ursiny, Tim, Ph.D. (2003). *The coward's guide to conflict.* Naperville, IL: Sourcebooks, Inc.

Verderber, Kathleen S. and Verderber, Rudolph F. (2004). *Inter-act (10th edition).* New York: Oxford Press.

Wardle, Francis, Ph.D. (1999). *Tomorrow's Children.* Denver: Center for the Study of Biracial Children.

Walker, Velma and Brokaw, Lynn (2001). *Becoming aware (8th edition).* Dubuque, IA: Kendall/Hunt Publishing.

Waterhouse, Debra (2001). *Outsmarting female fatigue.* New York: Hyperion.

Weaver, Richard L. (1996). *Understanding interpersonal communication (7th edition).* New York: Harper Collins.

Welch, David A. (2002). *Decisions, decisions: The art of effective decision making.* Amherst: New York: Prometheus Books.

Westra, Matthew (1996). *Active communication.* Pacific Grove, CA: Brook/Cole Publishing.

Wilmot, William W., Ph.D. and Hocker, Joyce L., Ph.D. (2001) *Interpersonal conflict (6th edition).* New York: McGraw-Hill.

Wilson, Gerald L. (2000). *Let's talk it over: Interpersonal communication in relationships (5th edition).* Boston: Pearson.

Wood, Julia T. (2001). *Gendered lives (4th edition).* Stamford, CT: Wadsworth/Thomson Learning.

INDEX

A

accommodators, conflict, 329, 331
Active Communication (Westra), 49
active listening, 49
    characteristics of, 52
    definition of, 51
    examples of, 53
Actual Minds, Possible Worlds
    (Bruner), 88, 131
adaptor gestures, 137
Adler, Ronald B., 287, 290
advisory listening, 49
    examples of, 53
    hints for, 51
affect display gestures, 137
Albert Einstein College of
    Medicine, 104
Alder, Ronald, 211
Alderman, Ellen, 9
Amazon, 28, 29
American Academy of Pediatrics,
    343
Andersen, Peter, 90
Anderson, Kare, 147, 149
"The Andy Griffith Show," 23
Annual Review of Sociology, 261
Antonissen, Heather, 69, 71
anxiety. *See* social anxiety
Asperger Syndrome, 138
Asperger Syndrome
    (Rourke/Tsatsanis), 138
Attitudes of Gratitude (Ryan), 100
attribution theory, 93
Austen, Jane, 103
avoiders, conflict, 329, 330–331

B

Backlund, P., 151–152
Bacon, Francis, 131
Barber Shop, 311
Becoming Aware (Walker/Brokaw),
    288
Beebe, Steven A., 327
Beebe, Susan J., 327
behavior
    inconsistency of, 100

    learned, 47–48
    self-actualization, 175–176
    values and, 251
beliefs, 250–251
Beliefs, Attitudes, and Values
    (Rokeach), 247
Bend it Like Beckham, 311
Bescoe, Jacqueline, 319
body language. *See also* touch
    discussion article on, 147–150
    gender differences in, 151–152
    mood expression through,
        136–137
    persona creation through,
        135–136
    touching as, 135
Boggs, Raymond, 208
Boy Scouts, 246
Brokaw, Lynn, 288
Brotherson, Sean, 339, 341
Brown, Chris, 205
Brown, Tina, 17
Bruner, Jerome, 88, 131
Buller, D. B., 151–152
Bureau of Labor Statistics,
    299
Burgoon, J. K., 151–152

C

Campbell, Anne, 328
Carnivore program, 27
Case for Marriage
    (Waite/Gallagher), 261
Cast Away, 5, 311
Ceniceros, Roberto, 25
Chamberlain, Jared, 331
channels
    auditory, 13
    communication, 12
    gustatory, 13
    olfactory, 13
    tactile, 13
    visual, 13
Chung Li Wu, 86
Clark, Bryan, 210, 319
Clark State Community College,
    246

Clinton, Bill, 139
closure, 93
coercive power, 324
collaboration
    conflict resolution through,
        332–333, 335–336
    goal of, 336
    guidelines for, 336
    terms of, 332t
collaborators, conflict, 329, 331
Committee on Psychosociological
    Aspects of Child and Family
    Health, 343
Communicate! (Communication
    Research Associates), 98
communication. *See also specific*
    types
    extrapersonal, 6–7, 128–139,
        147–152, 165–166, 320
    interpersonal, 4–6, 8–9, 17–32,
        339–342
    intrapersonal, 6
    meta-, 7, 333
    nonverbal, 6–7, 129, 134–137,
        139, 147–154, 165–166, 320
    verbal, 6–7, 128–133, 139,
        165–166, 320
communication environment. *See*
    environment,
    communication
communication process, 10f
    channels in, 12, 13
    decoding in, 12–13
    definition summary of, 11–12t
    encoding in, 10–12
    feedback in, 11
    fidelity in, 12, 14
    messages in, 11, 13
    noise in, 11, 13–14
    receivers in, 11, 12
    sources in, 10–11
communication process activities
    group, 35–39
    individual, 33
    quiz and, 43
    word search, 41–42
Communication Research
    Associates, 98

communicators, competent
    collaboration and, 332–333
    definition of, 14
    qualities of, 14–15
competitors, conflict, 329, 331
compromisers, conflict, 329, 331
conflict
    checkpoints for, 335–336
    collaboration and, 335–338
    cultural, 353–354
    definition of, 320
    examples of, 321
    expression of, 320
    extrapersonal, 323
    fallacies of, 327–328
    game playing and, 325–327
    gender and, 328, 353–354
    interpersonal, 322–324, 351–352
    intrapersonal, 321–322, 347–348
    levels of, 320–323
    power's relation to, 324–327
    relationships and, 319, 322–323,
        324–333
    resolution of, 332–333
    styles of, 328–331, 329t, 330t
    system error, 335–336
conflict activities
    crossword puzzle, 355
    group, 351–354
    individual, 347–350
    quiz and, 357–358
Contacts: Communicating
    Interpersonally (Gamble,
    T./Gamble, M.), 50
The Coward's Guide to Conflict
    (Ursiny), 332
critical listening, 52
    examples of, 54
Crocker, Jennifer, 185
Crum, Thomas, 331, 333
Cultural Revolution (China),
    223–224
culture
    conflict styles influenced by,
        328
    perception influenced by, 97

D

da Vinci, Leonardo, 224
day care
    aggressive behaviors and, 181
    quality of, 181–182

The De-Voicing of Society: Why We
    Don't Talk to Each Other
    Anymore (Locke), 17–19
decision making activities
    group, 271–272
    individual, 269–270
    quiz and, 277
    word search, 275
decision making process
    consciousness of, 254
    steps of, 254–256
Decisions, Decisions (Welch), 254
decoding, 12–13
defensive listening, 52
    examples of, 54
dependency, 287
    co-, 287–288
    inter-, 288
Devito, Joseph, 135, 292
discussion article
    body signals, 147–150
    children in day care, 181–184
    cohabitation and values,
        261–264
    conflict to collaboration,
        335–338
    family communication, 339–342
    friendship disappointments,
        217–222
    gender and communication,
        151–154
    law enforcement and
        communication, 23–26
    lesbians and adoption, 343–346
    listening to your body, 65–68
    living through pain, 223–228
    marriage and race, 299–304
    money perception, 107–112
    nursing home life, 257–260
    privacy, 27–33
    remarriage relationships,
        295–298
    self-esteem, 185–188
    silence's value, 103–106
    technology and conversation,
        17–22
    touch communication, 141–146
Drexel University, 218

E

Edwards, Audrey, 299, 303
ego conflict, 322

emails
    effectiveness of, 17
    encoding, 12
    pluses and minuses of, 17–18
emblem gestures, 137
emotion activities
    crossword puzzle, 239
    group, 235–238
    individual, 229–233
    quiz and, 241
Emotional Intelligence (Goleman),
    212
emotions. See also expression,
    emotional; intelligence,
    emotional
    components of, 203
    conflict communication and,
        320
    definition of, 203
    evaluation of, 209
    expectation and, 209
    exploration of, 231–233
    expression of, 211–212, 235–236
    facilitative v. debilitative, 208
    friendship and, 217–222
    humor and, 215
    intelligence of, 212–213
    language of, 213–214
    liberation of, 214, 237–238
    management of, 205
    nonverbal reactions to, 203–204
    observation of, 209
    pain, 223–228
    primary, 205–207, 207f
    quiz on, 241
    relationships and role of, 204
    responsibility and, 209–210
    understanding, 205
    value of expressing, 203
    vocabulary of, 205, 206t
Empire State Building, New York,
    223
EN. See external noise
encoding, 10–12
environment, communication, 57f
    definition of, 14, 56
    noise in, 56, 58
Erin Brockovich, 311
evaluative listening, 51
    examples of, 53
Excuse Me, Your Life is Waiting
    (Grabhorn), 176, 205
expert power, 324

expression, emotional
   fallacies of, 211–212
   increasing, 211
external noise (EN), 13–14
   transformations to, 56, 58
extrapersonal communication. *See also specific types*
   nonverbal, 6–7, 129, 134–137, 139, 147–154, 165–166, 320
   verbal, 6–7, 128–133, 139, 165–166, 320
eye contact, 137

F

facial expressions, 136–137
fallacies
   conflict, 327–328
   emotional expression, 211–212
families
   communication in, 339–342
   culture and, 291
   relationships in, 290–291
   types of, 290
Fann, Michael G., 23
Fanning, Patrick, 253
The Farther Reaches of Human Nature (Maslow), 175
feedback, 11
fidelity, 12
   definition of, 14
Forrest, Mary, 129
frame of reference, 90, 93
French, Bertran, 324
Frost, Ty, 322

G

Gamble, Michael W., 50, 291
Gamble, Teri Kwal, 50, 291
games
   conflict escalation through, 325–326
   example of, 326–327
Gates, Enjoli, 291
Geisen, Greg, 335, 337–338
gender
   conflict styles and, 328
   ego conflicts and, 322
   friendship bonds and, 217–222
   nonverbal communication and, 151–154
   touch receptors and, 135

gestures, 137
Gibbs, Nancy, 181, 183
Gilman, Susan Jane, 179
Goleman, Daniel, 212
Golombok, Susan, 343, 345
Grabhorn, Lynn, 176, 205
Gramsci, Antonio, 225
Grant, Gwendolyn Goldsby, 300
Gregory, Deborah, 217, 221
Griffin, M. A., 151, 153
Griffith, Terry, 319
Grubbs, Lindsey, 318

H

Hadnot, Ira J., 21
Hall, Edward T., 135
Hall, Judith, 129
halo effect, 99
Hanks, Tom, 5
Hanna, M. S., 151
Harris, Cathy, 8, 59
Harvard Research Group, 35
Harvey, Tiffany, 251, 284
Hay, Louise, 62
Healing Yourself (Rossman), 66
hearing. *See also* listening
   listening v., 46–48
Hines, Stacey, 49
horn effect, 99
Howard, Myra, 62, 87
Howard University, 300

I

identity, 134
illustrator gestures, 137
impersonal listening, 49
   definition of, 50–51
IN. *See* internal noise
information/persuasive power, 324
Ingham, Harrington, 280
instrumental values, 248–249, 248t
intelligence, emotional, 212
   components of, 213
   teaching, 213
interaction constructs, 93
interdependence, 288
internal noise (IN), 13
   examples of, 56
   transformations of, 58
International Male, 28

Internet
   communication activity for, 157–158
   communication debate and, 17–18
   emotions on, 229–230
   relationships via, 291–292
interpersonal communication. *See also* metacommunication
   factors influencing, 8
   facts about, 5
   family, 339–342
   finality in, 5
   frequency of, 5
   implications in, 5
   law enforcement article on, 23–26
   learning, 5
   privacy in, 9, 27–32
   relationships and, 5
   self-disclosure in, 6
   technology's effect on, 17–22
   training for, 5
   trust in, 9
   types of, 4–5
   unique aspects of, 5
   vitality of, 5
Interpersonal Communication and Human Relationships (Knapp), 284
Interpersonal Communication (Trenholm/Jensen), 171, 291
interpersonal conflicts
   definition of, 322
   examples of, 323
   forms of, 322–323
interpersonal listening, 49, 77
   definition of, 50
The Interpersonal Communication Book (Devito), 135, 292
Interplay (Adler/Rosenfeld/Proctor), 211, 287
interpretation
   attribution theory and, 93
   closure in, 93
   evaluation in, 93
"The Interpretive Moment" (Pine), 104
intimacy
   emotional, 286
   growth of, 285–286
   intellectual, 285
   physical, 286
   self's relation to, 286

intimate zone, 135–136
intrapersonal communication, 6
intrapersonal conflict, 322
    definition of, 321
    examples of, 321
intrapersonal listening, 49–50, 73
Ivy, D. K., 151–152

J

Jackson, Felicia, 52, 87, 172
James Mintz Group, 27
Jefferson, Thomas, 175
Jensen, Arthur, 171, 291
Johari Window, 280–282, 281f
    creation of, 307–308
Jones, Steve, 17–19
Journal of Anxiety Disorders,
    210
Journal of Social Issues, 185
Jurassic Park, 295

K

Kakareka, Mary, 182
Kass, Amy, 262
Kass, Leon, 262
Katz, Stan J., 172–173
Kennedy, Caroline, 9
Khmer Rouge (Cambodia), 224
Kilmann, Ralph, 328, 330
Kiss My Tiara (Gilman), 179
Knapp, Mark, 129, 282, 284–285,
    288–289
Kolp, Ashley, 87, 95, 169
Kowalski, Robin, 210–211
Kramer, Peter D., 103, 105

L

LaRoche, Loretta, 87
law enforcement
    communication in, 23–26
    hiring policies in, 24
Leary, Mark, 210–211
Leffel, Megan, 325
legitimate power, 324
lesbians, 343–344
Let's Talk It Over (Wilson), 90, 250
Lewis, Andrea, 319
LexisNexis, 28
Lincoln, Abraham, 175

listening. *See also* environment,
    communication
    active, 49, 51–52, 53
    advisory, 49, 51, 53
    challenges to, 60–61
    critical, 52, 54
    defensive, 52, 54
    discussion articles on, 65–72
    effects of, 60–61
    environments for, 56–58, 57f
    evaluative, 51, 53
    hearing v ., 46–48
    illness and, 65–66
    impersonal, 49, 50–51
    interpersonal, 49–50, 77
    intrapersonal, 49–50, 73
    learned behaviors of, 47–48
    passive, 52, 53
    patterns of, 51–55, 53–54t
    process of, 57f, 58–59, 75
    pseudo-, 52, 54
    quiz on, 83
    silence benefits and, 50
    statistics on, 58–59
    steps for effective, 61–62
    yoga and, 69–70
listening activities
    crossword, 81
    group, 77–80
    individual, 73, 75
    quiz and, 83
listening process, 57f, 58–59
    steps of, 59
Liu, Aimee E., 172–173
Locke, John L., 17
*Love and Survival: The Scientific
    Basis for the Healing Power of
    Intimacy* (Ornish), 148
Luft, Joseph, 280
Lynam, Andonia, 287

M

The Magic of Conflict (Crum), 331
Manheim, Camryn, 174
Manning, Maxwell, C., 300
Marano, Lou, 185, 187
Markle Foundation, 28
Markova, Dawna, 100
Marriott, Bill, Sr., 95
Maslow, Abraham, 173, 175, 285
Maslow and Self-Actualization
    (video), 175

Maslow's Hierarchy of Needs,
    173f, 208, 292–293
    essentials of, 173
    physiological needs in, 172
    safety needs in, 172–174
    self-actualization in, 175–176
    self-esteem needs in, 174–175
    social needs in, 174
McGahee, D., 151, 153
McKay, Matthew, 174, 253
Means, Randy, 23–24
memory, 59
Men, Women, and Aggression
    (Campbell), 328
messages
    definition of, 11, 13
    nonverbal, 11, 13
    verbal, 13
metacommunication, 333
    definition of, 7
    facts about, 7
Mississippi Masala, 311
moods, 136–137

N

National Association for Self-
    Esteem, 178
National City Mortgage Co., 27
The Nature of Human Values
    (Rokeach), 247
negativity, 176–177
The New Yorker, 17
NLD. *See* nonverbal learning
    disability
Nock, Steven L., 262
noise
    communication and, 11
    external, 13–14, 56, 58
    internal, 13, 56, 58
nonverbal communication, 6–7.
    See also nonverbal
    communication activity(ies)
    categories of, 134–137
    conflict expression through,
    320
    definition of, 129
    discussion article on, 147–150
    gender differences in, 151–154
    identity and, 134
    moods and, 136–137
    persona and, 135–136
    personality and, 134–135

quiz for, 165–166
tips for, 139
Nonverbal Communication: Forms and Functions (Andersen), 90
nonverbal communication activities
    crossword puzzle, 163
    group, 159–160
    individual, 155–156
    quiz and, 165–166
Nonverbal Communication in Human Interaction (Knapp/Hall), 129
nonverbal learning disability (NLD), 137
    web sites for, 138
Nonviolent Communication: A Language of Compassion (Rosenberg), 205, 333
North Dakota State University, 339

O

Ogden, C. K., 129–130
Olson, Margot, 129
organization
    frame of reference and, 93
    interaction constructs in, 93
    physical constructs in, 90
    psychological constructs in, 90
    role constructs in, 93
Ornish, Dean, 148

P

paralanguage, 136
passive listening, 52
    examples of, 53
Penthouse, 29
perception, 14
    assumptions in, 99
    awareness of, 97–100
    behavioral inconsistency and, 100
    checking, 95, 96f
    complacency's effect on, 98
    cultural influences on, 97
    defining, 87–88
    demographics and, 99
    detail ignorance in, 99
    expectations in, 99
    familiarity's effect on, 98

halo effect in, 99
hindrances to, 98–99
horn effect in, 99
money, 107–112
physiology's influence on, 97
process of, 88–93, 89f
psychology's influence on, 97
quiz on, 123–124
shared, 93, 94f
silence and, 103–106
singularity's effect on, 98
social influences on, 98
perception activities
    group, 117–120
    individual, 113–116
    quiz and, 123–124
    word search, 121–122
perception process, 89f. *See also specific steps*
    examples of, 91f, 92f
    interpretation step of, 93
    organization step of, 90–93
    selection step of, 88–90
persona
    creation of, 135
    proximity zones and, 135–136
personal zone, 136
personality, 134–135
physiology
    hierarchy of needs and, 172
    listening and, 60, 65–66
    perception and, 97
    physical constructs and, 90
Pine, Fred, 104
Plotz, David, 27, 31
Plutchik, Robert, 205–207
Plutchik's emotion wheel, 205–207, 207f
PMA Science of Success (course), 177
Popenoe, David, 261–262
power
    conflict's relation to, 324–327
    example uses of, 325
    facts about, 324
    game playing and, 325–327
    social, 324–325
Prisoners of Belief (McKay/Fanning), 253
Pritchard, Sarah, 204, 253
privacy
    discussion article on, 27–33
    facts about, 9
    medical, 29
    relationships and, 9

process, communication. *See* communication process
Proctor, Russell F., II, 211, 287, 290
Prospering Woman (Ross), 97, 209
pseudo-listening, 52
    examples of, 54
psychology
    organization and, 90
    perception influenced by, 97
Public Risk Management Association, 23
public zone, 136

R

Raborn, Gail, 65, 67
race
    friendships and, 217–222
    marriage and, 299–304
Raven, John, 324
Reasoner, Robert, 178
receivers, 11, 12
Redmond, Mark V., 327
referent power, 324
regulator gestures, 137
relational conflict, 322–323
Relational Maintenance model, 282, 283t, 291
relationship activities
    group, 309–312
    individual, 305–308
    quiz and, 315–316
    word search, 313–314
relationships
    attraction in, 284–285
    avoidance stage of, 289
    bonding stage of, 287
    circumscribing stage of, 288–289
    conflict's role in, 319, 322–323, 324–333
    dependency in, 287–288
    differentiation stage of, 287
    emotion's role in, 204
    ending, 288–290
    experimenting stage of, 283, 284
    family, 290–291, 339–342
    friend, 217–222, 291
    improvement of, 5
    initiation stage of, 283, 284
    integration stage of, 283, 285–286
    intensifying stage of, 283, 285–286

intimacy growth in, 285–286
maintenance of, 287–288
marriage, 295–304
metacommunication in, 7
movie, 311–312
online, 291–292
professional, 292
qualities of healthy, 292–294
quiz on, 315–316
rules in, 293
self-disclosure in, 280–282
stages of, 282–290, 283t
stagnation stage of, 288–289
termination stage of, 289–290
types of, 290–293
Relax - You May Only Have a Few Minutes Left (LaRoche), 87
Remember the Titans, 311
resource conflict, 322
The Responsive Community, 261
reward power, 324
Richards, I. A., 129–130
Righter, Nichol, 289
The Right to Privacy (Alderman/Kennedy), 9
Ripple Effect values model, 249f
attitudes in, 251
behaviors in, 251
beliefs in, 250–251
core values in, 250
Rockwell, Vickie, 14, 87, 175
Rokeach, Milton, 247
role constructs, 93
roles
general, 171
identity and, 171
learned, 171
multiple, 171
true self and, 169, 170f
The Rookie, 311
Roosevelt, Eleanor, 175
Rosen, Margery D., 107, 111
Rosenberg, Marshall, 205, 214, 237, 333
Rosenfeld, Lawrence B., 211, 287, 290
Rosin, Hanna, 27
Ross, Ruth, 97, 209
Rossman, Martin, 66
Rourke, Byron, 138
Rutgers University's National Marriage Project, 261
Ryan, M. J., 100

S

Schutz, William, 292
Seaver, Anna Mae Halgrim, 257–259
selection, 88–89
frame of reference in, 90, 93
selective attention in, 90
selective exposure in, 90
self
blind, 282
day care and, 181–184
hidden, 282
hierarchy of needs for, 191–192
intimacy and, 286
open, 282
questions for finding, 169
quiz on, 199
true, 170f
unknown, 282
self activities
group, 193–196
individual, 189–192
quiz and, 199
word search, 197
self-actualization
behavioral areas of, 175–176
definition of, 175
ways of practicing, 175
self-concept
definition of, 177
self-esteem's relation to, 177, 178f
social-comparison theory and, 178
self-disclosure, 6, 195–196
relationships and, 280–282
self-esteem, 174–175
basis for, 185–186
discussion article on, 185–188
effects of low, 178, 185–186
self-concept's relation to, 177, 178f
Self Esteem (McKay), 174
self-fulfilling prophecies, 176–177
September 11, 2001, 223–228
Shafir, Rebecca, 49, 51, 59, 61
Shared Meaning (Olson/Forrest), 129
Shaver, Marty, 319
Shery, Lori, 138
Shirk, Diana, 56, 86, 131
Sholin Karate Club, 246
silence
benefits of, 50
mood expression through, 136
Simon, Sidney B., 141, 145
singularity, 98
Slate, J., 151, 153
Slayden, David, 19
Smock, Pamela J., 261–262
social anxiety
domains for, 210
reasonable v. unreasonable, 211
"Social Anxiety" (Leary/Kowalski), 210
social-comparison theory, 178–179
social power, 324–325
social zone, 136
Solomon, Andrew, 223, 227
Sound Bite Culture: The Death of Discourse in a Wired World (Whillock/Slayden), 18, 19
sources, communication, 10–11
Southern Methodist University, 18
Stanton, James Stephano, 319
Stevenson, Adlai, 175
Stream, Samantha, 58, 87, 99, 132
Success Trap (Katz/Liu), 172
Swallow, Wendy, 295, 297

T

Tannen, Deborah, 289
technology, 17–22
Tennessee Municipal League Risk Management Pool (TML), 23
terminal values, 247, 248t
That's Not What I Meant! (Tannen), 289
"Theory of Human Motivation" (Maslow), 173
Thomas, Kenneth, 328, 330
Thomas & Means L.L.P., 23
Thoreau, Henry David, 175
TML. *See* Tennessee Municipal League Risk Management Pool
Today, 46
Tolson, Jay, 261, 263
Tolstoy, Leo, 224
Total Information Awareness office, 28, 29

touch
    discussion article on, 141–146
    gender differences in, 151–152
    personality and, 135
Travis, Armatine, 318
Trenholm, Sarah, 171, 291
Triangle of Meaning, 129, 130f
"The True Meaning of Self-
        Esteem" (Reasoner), 178
trust
    facts about, 9
    relationships and, 9
Tsatsanis, Katherine, 138

U

*Understanding Interpersonal
    Communication* (Weaver),
    132, 177
United States Census Bureau, 299
United States Pledge of
    Allegiance, 247
University of Cambridge, 18
University of Chicago, 261, 262
University of Colorado, 19
University of Illinois, 17
University of Michigan, 185, 261
University of Pennsylvania, 136
University of Virginia, 262
Ursiny, Tim, 332

V

value conflict, 322
values
    assessing, 265–267
    attitudes and, 251
    behavioral expression of, 251
    beliefs v., 250–251
    changing of, 253
    cohabitation and, 261–264
    core, 250
    creation of, 247
    decision making and, 253–255
    model of, 249f, 250–251
    nursing home and, 257–260
    source of, 252–253
    testing of, 253
    types of, 247–249, 248t
values activities
    group, 273–274
    individual, 265–267
    quiz and, 277
    word search, 275
Vanity Fair, 17
verbal communication, 6–7. *See
        also* words
    conflict expression through, 320
    definition of, 128
    internal limitations on, 133
    quiz for, 165–166
    tips for, 139
    words as, 129–132
verbal communication activities
    crossword puzzle, 163
    group, 159–162
    individual, 157–158
    quiz and, 165–166
Victoria's Secret, 28
Vygotsky, Lev, 131

W

Wade, Brenda, 220
Wade, Kyle, 318
Waite, Linda J., 261
Wake Up, I'm Fat (Manheim), 174
Walker, Velma, 288
Warfe, Christina, 318

Washington Times, 343
Watson, Marlene F., 218–220
Weaver, Richard, 132, 177
Welch, David A., 254
Westra, Matthew, 49
Whillock, Rita Kirk, 18–19
Whitehead, Barbara Dafoe,
        261–262
Williams, Jerriline, 319
Williams, Valerie, 301
Wilson, Gerald L., 90, 93, 151, 250
*Wing to Wing, Oar to Oar: Readings
        on Courting and Marrying*
        (Kass, A./Kass, L.), 262
The Wizard of Oz, 19
Woodall, W. G., 151–152
word meanings, 129–132
    connotative, 131
    denotation, 131
    intentional v. unintentional, 131
    Triangle of Meaning and, 129,
        130f
words
    definition of, 129
    internal limitations and, 133
    meaning's relation to, 129–130
    powerless, 132

Y

yoga, 69–70
Young, Hollie, 293
You've Got Mail, 311

Z

The Zen of Listening (Shafir), 49
zones, proximity, 135–136

AUTHOR BIOGRAPHY

Newspaper headlines have said:

"Rebel Becomes Woman with a Goal!"
"Michelle Burch's Big Comeback"
"Quad-Citian' to Watch in 1995"
"Woman Leaders of Black Hawk College"
"[Michelle Burch] Invited to Meet Clinton"

Students have said:

"Very dedicated"
"Amazing passion"
"Communicates effectively"
"Willing to learn with us"

Colleagues have said:

"Creative & imaginative"
"Challenges current ways of doing and thinking"
"She knows what she's talking about"

From a small town living down the way from her grandparents' dairy farm, to a larger city where she found the negative side of life, Michelle Burch has experienced it all. In her early twenties she began living in low-income housing projects, which in turn, was better than the homelessness she experienced while she was pregnant a short time earlier.

Fortunately, Michelle has found the positive side of life. Early in her academic career, she spent some time working in the Public Relations Office at the US Army Corps of Engineers. When she began her Master's degree, Michelle also began her own motivational/consulting business, *Foundations for Success*. While becoming a nationally-recognized speaker, she completed her master's degree from the University of Illinois.

Michelle found her love for teaching while working on her degrees. She began her teaching career in Springfield, Illinois at Lincoln Land Community College, adjuncting in public speaking. Michelle currently lives in Ohio, where she is an Assistant Professor at Clark State Community College.

Fortunately, Michelle's journey continues to stay positive because she has learned, and tries to teach others that, "in life there are no victims, only survivors learning how to be thrivers." Michelle's experiences truly are an integral part of everything she does. Though the challenges may seem easier today, Michelle is keenly aware that her son, Calvin, is beginning his teenage years.

You will find that in everything Michelle does, she wants to reach you and challenge you to communicate more effectively in all of your relationships. You have the ability, now she will be your guide. Enjoy the journey.

SUGGESTION FORM FOR FUTURE EDITIONS

1. Overall, did you have a positive or negative experience with this textbook?
   _____

2. On a scale of 1 – 10, how would you rate this textbook (1 – would not ever suggest anyone using this textbook; 10 – this is the best textbook I have ever used)? _____

3. What did you enjoy **most** about the textbook? (Use the back of this form for additional space for any question.)

4. What did you enjoy the **least** about the textbook?

5. What additional **chapters** would you like to see in a future edition?

6. What **changes** would you suggest making in a future edition?

7. Do you have an individual or group **activity** that you like to see added in a future edition? If so, please attach it to this form. Please include any information that would help us obtain permission from the author of the activity. If you have an idea for an activity, please write down your ideas. (Use the back of this form for additional space.)

8. What was the course name and number where this textbook was used?
   _____

9. What was the name of the college/university where this textbook was used?
   _____

10. Are you a student or an instructor? _____

Please mail this form to: Kendall/Hunt Publishing Company
4050 Westmark Drive
PO Box 1840
Dubuque, IA 52004-1840
Attn: A. Willenbring